Best Bike Rides
Minneapolis and St. Paul

Best Bike Rides
Minneapolis and St. Paul

Second Edition

Great Recreational Rides
in the Twin Cities Area

STEVE JOHNSON

FALCONGUIDES

GUILFORD, CONNECTICUT
HELENA, MONTANA

FALCONGUIDES®

An imprint of The Rowman & Littlefield Publishing Group, Inc.
4501 Forbes Blvd., Ste. 200
Lanham, MD 20706
www.rowman.com
Falcon and FalconGuides are registered trademarks and Make Adventure Your Story is a
trademark of The Rowman & Littlefield Publishing Group, Inc.

Distributed by NATIONAL BOOK NETWORK

Copyright © 2019 The Rowman & Littlefield Publishing Group, Inc.

Interior photos by the author unless otherwise indicated
Cover photo by Perrine Dailey
Maps by Melissa Baker

British Library Cataloguing-in-Publication Information available

Library of Congress Cataloging-in-Publication Data available

ISBN 978-1-4930-4068-1 (paperback)
ISBN 978-1-4930-4069-8 (e-book)

∞™ The paper used in this publication meets the minimum requirements of American
National Standard for Information Sciences—Permanence of Paper for Printed Library
Materials, ANSI/NISO Z39.48-1992.

Printed in the United States of America

**The authors and The Rowman & Littlefield Publishing Group, Inc. assume
no liability for accidents happening to, or injuries sustained by, readers who
engage in the activities described in this book.**

Contents

Roads   Mountain Bike Trails   Paths

Overview

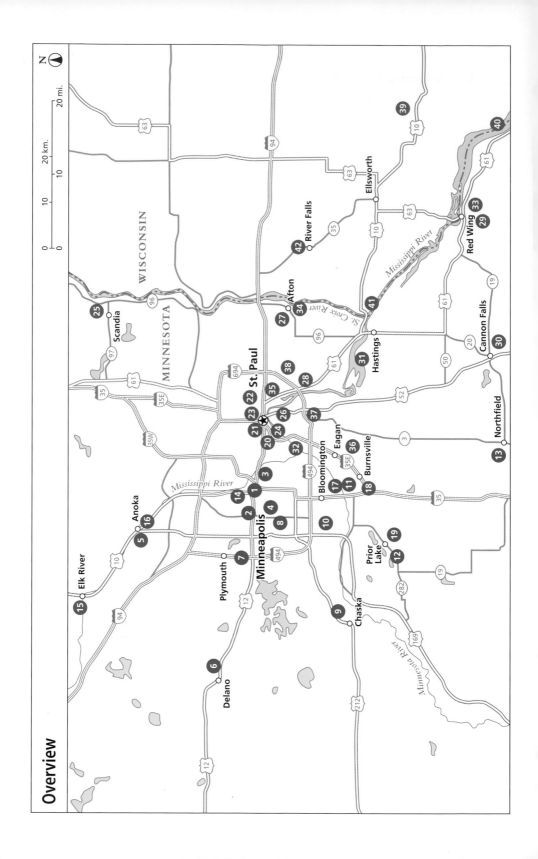

Sweet singletrack into the trees at Murphy-Hanrehan Park in Savage
NICK PETTIS

Preface

A good life is when you smile often, dream big, laugh a lot,
and realize how blessed you are for what you have.

—Anonymous

A keen observation, and my bet is it was uttered by someone on a bike.

I was about 10, smiling and about to realize a dream, when Dad helped me build a little BMX/cruiser Frankenstein bike, cobbled together with cast-off (or pilfered) parts from by brother's bike, rusty nuts and washers, and anything else within reach. Rolling down our cracked and sun-faded driveway for the first time on my new rig, with a black paint job that looked just like the grizzled pavement, I couldn't muster an elegant quote like Anonymous did, but my hoots and hollers of delight felt just as poignant.

Like most squirrely, outdoor-loving kids, I saw summer, and every other season, from the seat of my bike, noodling along the gravel roads and deer trails and field paths around my country neighborhood and small hometown. Those two wheels were an outlet for pent-up energy and a vehicle for adventure. Could we make it all the way to town for a candy bar? How far down the hill can we skid the rear tire?

With longer legs and a 10-speed in the summer before high school, Dad lashed a beat-up tent and ragged sleeping bags to our bikes and we rode in cut-offs and T-shirts, way over our fitness levels, on a two-day odyssey to our Wisconsin cabin (Okay, two days doesn't quite qualify as an odyssey but it felt like it at the time.). Years later in southern California, my buddy Doug, winning races without ever training, sparked a competitive streak and a couple of decades of on-and-off racing. So, a progression of just riding around to touring to hitting the afterburners has me back where I started, savoring the journey and getting out there.

One thing I do have in common with Anonymous is being blessed with what I have, and after the important stuff—roof over my head, great kids, food on the table—I live in a killer place to ride a bike. The Twin Cities are overlaid with a spaghetti tangle of cycling routes, following velvet-smooth pathways along intimate creeks, vibrant city neighborhoods, wide boulevards, and quiet country roads. You can spin a leisurely loop overlooking the Mississippi River, with a patio lunch stop, or hammer 80 hilly, quad-crushing miles. All the action is supported by a hyper-dedicated and enthusiastic core of pedal power fans running the gamut from tykes on trikes to hipster and spit-polished bike shops, pro racers, high-profile government brass and grassroots coalitions, and easygoing cruisers. Heading to the office by bike has become so popular, every Minneapolis office building is required to have bicycle storage, and every city bus and train is equipped to carry bikes. Winters of late have not stemmed the tide, either. There has always been a diehard faction of riders who never tire of layering up wide as the Michelin Man to keep pedaling, but the draw now is stronger than ever. The mild (embarrassing, really, for natives) winters surely have stoked this fire, but there is an almost palpable feel out there that people are amped to be on their bikes all year, even when the city is frozen. Join the fun and ride with like-minded friends in a local bike club. The metro area is packed with great clubs, from recreational to full-on racing. Check out groups like the Twin Cities Bicycling Club, the largest in town with a year-round calendar of spectacular rides all over the place for all abilities. It's always more fun to log some miles with a buddy.

Where to ride might be as easy as rolling out the back door for some, but even hometown residents don't know every mile in every neighborhood, and a new twist on old favorites is good for the soul. This book's features forty-two rides in and around the Twin Cities, selected to present an array of choices for the many moods and desires and skill levels of area riders. I've ridden here all my life, and chose routes I deemed worthy of our state's two-wheeled fanatics, including many of my personal go-to rides. I'm continually amazed at the quality and variety of miles available to us here, and how it just keeps getting better. There are bike lanes appearing on more roadways, new bike paths being constructed or old ones repaved, and there always seems to be a new mountain bike trail built or extended or beefed up. Minnesota is now on par with places like Moab for destination mountain biking (I think it's even better.). Best thing is, there are more people riding than I've ever seen. The other day I spotted a family of five merrily riding along a path and they crossed the road in front of me, strung across an intersection like a gaggle of ducklings following their parents. Dad in front, mom pulling a toddler in a bike trailer, and two adorable girls behind on bikes with streamers on their handlebars. Hope, and an unforgettable day with the kids, springs eternal from the seat of a bike.

There is not nearly enough space in this, or any, book to include all of the great ride destinations in the Cities, and it is a tall order to write a best-of book that appeases everyone. Calling theses rides the "best" is, of course, a matter of opinion. I get to do it by having my name on the cover, but your best ride might not be here, your local bike shop probably has a route they love, and some of you might think a few of these just don't warrant a "best" title. It's a select group, to be sure, so I gathered intel on a sampling of what I believe shows off our towns' finest riding locales, and hope you will enjoy the picks. Caveat: I did my best on these pages to present the ride details along with entertaining, or at least informative, text. To accomplish that I had to be more than just a writer. I also wore the hat of cartographer, historian, investigator, photographer, and ambassador. Please forgive any flubs, and toast the successes.

My sincere gratitude to all of the bike shop managers I pestered, Gary Sjoquist from Quality Bicycle Products for his otherworldly dedication to our sport; Ryan Lieske and all of the volunteers with MORC; Rich Omdahl and Sue Seeger for the inspirational Hillside trails; Loren Stiles for making me stronger; Nick Pettis, Chris Nelson, and Wayne Hoklas for generous assistance in the field; Rachael Wood; Kimberly Streich; and my editors at Falcon for the opportunity to write about what I love and their patience to see the results.

I hope you will enjoy reading and using this book as much as I had writing it. It's an honor and a pleasure to share my experiences and favorite routes with you. Grab your bike and go for a ride. Hope to see you out there!

A fall colors pathway
SHUTTERSTOCK.COM

Introduction

The best in the country.

Always finishing with the front-runners, Minneapolis gained two-wheeled supremacy in 2010 as the nation's #1 bike city in *Bicycling* magazine's annual ranking, nudging aside Portland, longtime ruler of this throne. A cyclist from, say, Boulder, might also smugly wonder how our short-seasoned, terminally cold town earned such lofty laurels. Ask any rider on our hometown streets and he or she will say, "Yeah, of course this is the best city" and "What took so long?" We don't have skyscraping mountains, or crashing ocean surf, or palm-lined boulevards, but we have lakes, 15,000 of them, and thousands of miles of rivers, like nowhere else, near which we recreate

Aspens along the Gateway Trail.

with verve all year long. Our metro area celebrates water with pathways and pavilions and open space filled with trails and teeming with wildlife, and we gravitate to them like little kids to a sledding hill. Minnesota's outdoor heritage is rich with explorers and historical sports firsts, like intrepid voyageurs paddling untold miles of wilderness, the invention of water skiing, and early ski jumping champions. Self-propelled fans carry that tradition proudly today, packing our parks and trails, roads and waterways to get out there in this special place, or to push themselves to new competitive limits. Industry followed to meet our demands for the best gear, particularly in the bicycle world, with titans like Park Tool, HED Cycling, and Quality Bicycle Products all based right here, innovating, promoting, and supplying the world with all the right stuff. Minneapolis's former mayor R.T. Rybak is a big cycling fan, often spinning across town to meetings on his bike, and remains a strong proponent for consistently improving bicycling infrastructure. One of Rybak's big wins is Nice Ride Minnesota, a nonprofit bike share program launched in 2010 through the Twin Cities Bike Share Project initiative and the City of Lakes Nordic Ski Foundation. (More details in the Area Clubs and Advocacy Groups section on page 271.) Surrounding suburbs are also staying vigilant of their residents' two-wheeled wishes, with comprehensive cycling programs and blankets of bike routes over their streets, all working to keep the Twin Cities at the top of the best-of list.

And at the top we will stay, because on any given day, there is a kid on a bike with a gleam in his eye, pedaling behind his dad on a Saturday morning to the bakery next to the neighborhood bike shop, where a group of elite racers roll out for a training ride, passing a grinning man in his 80s, spinning slowly on an old Schwinn to fetch the morning paper and a cup of coffee. Yeah, it really is about the bike, and here in the Twin Cities, the bike is life.

About the Twin Cities

Minneapolis and St. Paul are indeed twins in that they are geographically side by side, and they share a common bond in the Mississippi River, but they have distinctly different personalities. Minneapolis has been likened to a West Coast city, with its urban artsy chic, action-packed nightlife, and glimmering office towers. The city's park system is legendary, and a very visible and key cog in its character, as seen most every summer day in the healthy and active vibe around Lakes Calhoun and Harriet. St. Paul is more relaxed, cradled by bluffs and elegant, European-inspired historic districts, with an oft-quieter mood. Stately boulevards give way to miles of forested river frontage blending into a picturesque river harbor. In cycling-speak, Minneapolis is kind of like

Vibrant summer foliage flanks a hidden trail.

Summertime lake view along the Gateway Trail.

a track bike, full speed with no brakes, while St. Paul is a balloon-tire cruiser. Both cities do, however, combine their characters to make this an award-winning place to call home. Each downtown boasts a vibrant arts scene, with renowned theaters and museums and a stacked schedule of headliner performances. An array of Fortune 500 corporations base their operations here, and amateur and pro sports teams perform on grand stages like Target Field and the Xcel Energy Center. Both have qualities of the other, being such close siblings and all, like miles and miles of book-worthy riding, a yearlong calendar of lively, two-wheeled events, and a cycling community forged from the very essence of the sport.

On the ground, the Twin Cities reflect the same glacially influenced origin as the rest of the state, highlighted by lakes and rivers and gently rolling topography. You won't find Alps-like climbing here, but there are enough short, steep hills to test your legs, especially in and around the river bluffs, and the mix of flat, riverside cruising in town and undulating countryside in surrounding communities rounds out a palette of made-to-order riding terrain.

The latitude line on the globe makes the Twin Cities the coldest major metro area in the United States. Bah. Think a little snow and cold slows us down? Sure, climate-controlled skyways were inspired here so people could move about the cities with a normal body temperature. Some days are so frigid that being outside too long could be deadly, or at least freeze off a finger, and we have seen wind chills approaching -70 to -100 degrees, but that's what we're made of and what makes us proud. Just put on another layer and get out there. Take a look around next winter. The bike paths and streets are still full of bikes, pedaled by riders bulbous with gear to ward off the chill. Big, burly steeds with names like Pugsley plow furrows through new snow leading to the office or coffee shop or bike shop. You just know there's a smile behind that icicle-fringed balaclava. The flip side of our winters is, well, the other six months of the year. Warm-weather riding that can be short-lived, but what a glorious time it is. Spring can be finicky with unpredictable days of cold, wet, and wind, but it is an easygoing transition time, in step with emerging flowers and leaves and a rising thermometer. Summer days are typically perfect, with temps around 80, but watch out for bouts of stifling humidity when it feels like you can grab handfuls of air and you sweat buckets just reaching down to tie a shoe. With red-orange-yellow proclamations, the sauna-like conditions are cleansed by crisp fall air settling over apple festivals and corn on the cob and family picnics. More than a few of your brethren will declare this the best riding season of them all, and it's hard to argue when you coast down a sinuous ribbon of tarmac unrolling through a deep crease in a bluff, smoldering in fiery autumn dress.

Oh ya, you betcha, doncha know. Grab a buddy, corral the kids, hop on your bikes, and go for a ride in America's best bike city. There's never been a better time.

How to Use This Book

The rides in this book were chosen by their best qualities to represent some of the best places for Twin Cities cycling. I included downtown and suburban routes, open rides in the country, and a few magical getaways in neighboring Wisconsin. All rides are within roughly an hour's drive of the metro. Each route is introduced with the traditional guidebook fare of location, distance, highlights, GPS coordinates, and other vital information, followed by a narrative of the ride including what to expect, local history, area bike shops and restaurants, and sidebars with bonus nuggets. All of this will help you choose which rides are best before heading out:

Start: Starting location of the ride

Distance: Miles from start to finish

Approximate riding time: Strong, skilled riders may be able to do a given ride in less than the estimated time, while other riders may take considerably longer. Also bear in mind that severe weather, changes in trail conditions, or mechanical problems may prolong a ride.

Best bike: Best gear for the terrain—road, mountain, hybrid, or cyclo-cross bike

Terrain and surface type: A look at what to expect for ups and downs, and on what kind of surface (smooth road, choppy road, dirt singletrack, etc.)

Highlights: Special features or qualities that make the ride worth doing (as if we needed an excuse!); cool things to see along the way, historical notes, neighboring attractions

Hazards: Anything with the potential to disrupt your ride, like traffic, a huge pothole, busy train crossing, too many ice cream shops

Other considerations: Anything extra specific to the ride, like debris on the trail after a heavy rain

Maps: USGS maps are noted for each ride, along with any other worthy maps. (Note: The maps in the book are for general navigation only. Always be prepared with an updated map or accurate directions before heading out.)

Getting there: How to reach the trailhead from a major nearby location, including GPS coordinates

Note that riding time is just that—the time your bike is actually moving. Allow more time for rest or scenic stops, and of course for speed. Slower riders will naturally spend more time on the road than go-fast racers. Some riders stop for lunch, while others hammer start to finish, hardly coming up for air. GPS coordinates are included for all trailheads and some key photo locations of superlative viewing sites or other notable route landmarks.

Elevation profiles are also provided to at least get a rough idea of what's in your uphill future. What appears on paper is at times difficult to match to the road; profiles might look easier or much tougher than what you see from your handlebars. Turn-by-turn Miles and Directions allow for efficient route planning, but your own variations (detours, rest stops, side trips) along with terrain, riding technique, and even tire pressure can affect odometer readings and skew the whole works, so consider mileages listed as a solid, but not bulletproof, reference.

Remember, the real world is always in flux, and road conditions and trail routes might look completely different, or be gone altogether, in the time it took this book to make it into your hands. Mountain bike trails, especially, are in an almost constant state of rebuilding or rerouting or other modifications. I know of two trails in the south metro alone that had changed their tune before I even finished the first round of edits. Always plan ahead and refer to detailed maps before hitting the road or trail.

After the ride specs comes a few paragraphs of description that focuses on highlights you can expect to encounter along the ride. This is followed by the Miles and Directions, which is a detailed mile-by-mile description of the ride.

Key to icons used in this edition:

Roads   Mountain Bike Trails   Paths

Safety

In some areas of the Twin Cities, the terrain can change drastically from one mile to the next. Even on "easy" and flat routes, it is important to be ready before you ride. Flying out the door in March for a century ride will shock your off-season, leaden legs into an abrupt and painful revolt. Put in plenty of base miles for a solid fitness level ahead of time, and know your limits. Clean rims, brakes, handlebars, seat, shifters, derailleurs, and chain to make sure they survived the last trip and are functioning properly. Get into this habit after your ride, as well.

A helmet is essential for cycling. It can save your life and prevent serious injuries. Don't ride without one. My face landed on a log one day on a mountain bike ride, and thanks to my helmet I left the scene with only a big knot on my head. Cycling gloves are another indispensable piece of safety equipment that can save hands from cuts and bruises from falls, encroaching branches, and rocks. They also improve your grip and comfort on the handlebars.

Always pack or carry at least one full water bottle. On longer rides, don't leave the house without two (or even three) bottles, or plan your ride so it passes someplace where potable water is available. (Most every ride in this book passes relatively close to a convenience store or other oasis.) A snack or energy bar will keep your quads cranking for extra hours and prevent the dreaded "bonk"—the sudden loss of energy when your body runs out fuel. Dress for the weather, and if it looks suspect, pack a jacket that repels both wind and water to prevent a truly horrible and potentially dangerous ride. Don't forget sunglasses, sunscreen, lip balm, and insect repellant for the fat tire rides, which is especially critical in early to midsummer riding in Minnesota.

A basic tool kit can save you from a long walk home or further damage to your bike. A tire pump or CO_2 cartridge and tube patch kit are vital, and a few other tools can make the difference between disaster and a 5-minute pit stop. Carry an all-in-one tool for tightening or adjusting seat post, handlebars, chainrings, pedals, brake posts, and other components. While I generally carry just a minimum, some folks aren't comfortable unless they bring a whole shop's worth of tools. They're weighted down and wrenches rattle with every bump in the trail, but they are rarely stranded by mechanical failures.

Ride Finder

Ride No.	Ride Name	River Cruises	Rail-Trail Rambles	Out in the Country	City Tours	Suburban Explorers	Hills!	Park Reserves	Fat Tire Light (easygoing mountain bike trails)	Fat with Extra Dirt (challenging mountain bike trails)
1	Downtown Sampler	●								
2	City and Lakes Loop				●					
3	Grand Rounds				●					
4	Dakota Rail Regional Trail—Lake Minnetonka Loop					●				
5	Elm Creek Park Reserve							●		
6	Long Lake—Delano Loop			●						
7	Luce Line State Trail		●							
8	LRT Loop		●							
9	Chaska Loop			●						
10	Hyland Park Trails							●		
11	Minnesota River Greenway									
12	Farms and Forests Ride			●						
13	Northfield Loop			●						
14	Theodore Wirth Park								●	
15	Hillside Park									●
16	Elm Creek Fat Tire Trails								●	
17	Minnesota River Trail—Bloomington Segment									●
18	Terrace Oaks Park								●	
19	Murphy-Hanrehan Park Reserve									●

Map Legend

Transportation

Interstate/Divided Highway	94
Featured US Highway	61
US Highway	61
Featured State, County, or Local Road	CR 610
Alternate route	CR 610
State Highway	58
County/Local Road	CR 610
Featured Bike Route	····················
Bike Route	■■■■■■■■■■■■■■■■■

Hydrology

Lake/Reservoir/ Major River	
River	

Land Use

State Park	
State Line	— · — · — · —

Symbols

Trailhead (Start)	10
Mileage Marker	17.1 ◆—
Small Park	♠
Visitor Center	❓
Ski Area	🎿
Point of Interest/ Structure	■
Museum	🏛
Capitol	✹
Town	○
Bridge	‿
Picnic Area	🛆
University/College	🎓
Direction Arrow	→

Minneapolis Road and Pathways

The City of Lakes does its riding residents proud with nearly 200 combined miles (and counting) of on- and off-street bike lanes and trails. Much of this mileage is centered along water, around which Minneapolis was born and prospered, be it lakes, rivers, or streams. Sinuous pathways trace the banks of the mighty Mississippi River, from the historical downtown mill ruins south through forested limestone bluffs. Cyclists can linger all day long in the city, rolling along the Greenway through one of the hottest restaurant and arts

Stone Arch Bridge looking east to St. Anthony Falls
WAYNE HOKLAS

scenes in the country, ride with the lively college vibe at the U of M campus, take in vibrant neighborhood festivals, or kick back on an overlook high above the river. A popular summertime destination is the chain of lakes, just south of downtown, with well-traveled pathways circling a foursome of tree-lined lakes, highlighted by Lakes Calhoun and Harriet, with sailing races, kite festivals, live music at the bandshell, and good old-fashioned days of fun in the sun.

A wooded corridor spurs off the south end of Lake Harriet like a long tail of a letter Q, and riders can follow the curves and twists and meanders of Minnehaha Creek all the way to its namesake park and falls at the eastern edge of the city. Other trails mirror the spokes of your wheels, radiating to neighboring towns on routes like the Cedar Lake and LRT Trails, passing homegrown coffee and ice cream shops along the way. Enjoy watching wildlife? Wander through Elm Creek and Hyland Parks to spot dozens of species of flora and fauna, many of them native to Minnesota. And miles of open country roads await in suburbs surrounding the city, for easy spins or all-day epics.

Downtown Sampler

A short spin around the city might be just what you need to put some spring in your step. This approximately 8-mile sampler tour rolls right through the heart of downtown and loops past the U of M to cross the Mississippi for a perfect start to the day or weekend cruise.

Start: North end of Loring Park

Distance: 7.6-mile loop

Approximate riding time: 45 minutes

Best bike: Road or hybrid

Terrain and surface type: Flat, paved city streets and pathways

Highlights: Nicollet Mall, Hennepin Avenue Bridge, old Main Street, U of M action, Mississippi River

Hazards: Use caution at all road crossings; stay alert for damage to pathways (potholes, washouts, big cracks)

Other considerations: Pathways can get crowded on summer weekends. Watch for errant riders.

Maps: *USGS Minneapolis South*

Getting there: From I-94, take the Hennepin/Lyndale Avenues exit, follow Hennepin Avenue north to Maple Street, and turn right to Loring Park. GPS: N 44 58.235 W 93 16.988

Washington Avenue Bridge and East River Boulevard and trail
WAYNE HOKLAS

Bike Shop

For over three decades, legions of Twin Cities cyclists have made **Freewheel Bike Shop** their go-to shop. Passionate staff at their flagship West Bank, Midtown Bike Center (on the Greenway), and Eden Prairie locations bring their love of the sport to customers and to the road. Midtown is a popular commuter hub close to everything, with storage, rentals, public repair shop, and cafe. Main store at 1812 S. 6th St., Minneapolis; (612) 339-2219; freewheelbike.com.

THE RIDE

Progeny of glacial Lake Itasca in northern Minnesota, the Mississippi River is the state's iconic waterway, steeped in timeless history and inspiration to American Indians; industrial pioneers; and nature-loving, adventurous spirits. Minneapolis and St. Paul are closely tied siblings with very distinct and proud personalities, and while the river marks a fluid boundary between the two, its dynamic spoils also hold them together. This ride starts in Loring Park and follows car-free Nicollet Mall to Ol' Miss and the Stone Arch Bridge, within sight of the city's birthplace. Only a few short years ago, bicycles were not allowed on Nicollet Mall, but with the city's ever-progressing, bike-friendly ways, we have the okay to ride here. It's a fun trip, too, cruising among the shops and patio restaurants, and is especially cool at night, all lit up in a glow of lights.

At the northern end of the Mall, jog over to Hennepin Avenue and cross the landmark bridge with the huge GRAIN BELT BEER sign off to your left. Hang a right on Main Street and hug the riverbank past St. Anthony Falls and Hennepin Island Park to surface streets leading underneath I-35 west and up to University Avenue. Cruise to the outskirts of the U of M's East Bank at 13th Avenue SE, and dart onto the bike path leading to East River Road and across the river on the old No. 9 railroad bridge, with drop-dead views upstream and down. A quick spin past the U's West Bank leads to the Hiawatha Bike Trail, ducking under I-35W and past US Bank Stadium back into downtown. Ride along 3rd Street to reconnect with Nicollet Mall for the return cruise to Loring Park.

Ol' Miss

Minnesota's most prodigious export, the **Mississippi River** watershed, the second largest in the world, extends from the Allegheny Mountains to the Rockies, draining 31 states from its tranquil origin at Lake Itasca to the wide delta exit into the Gulf of Mexico. The river's 2,350 miles are home to dozens of water-dependent wildlife and its basin is a critical migratory flyway for hundreds of bird species. Minnesota claims the Mississippi's narrowest point, at the 25-foot-wide headwaters, and naturally occurring widest, over the 2-mile span of Lake Pepin. On this trail ride along the river's urban wilderness stretch through the Twin Cities, look to the trees and skyward for myriad songbirds, bald eagles, and red-tailed hawks. Spot statue-still great blue herons stalking lunch along the river's shoreline, otters drifting with the current, and white tails of deer bouncing through Bluffside Park.

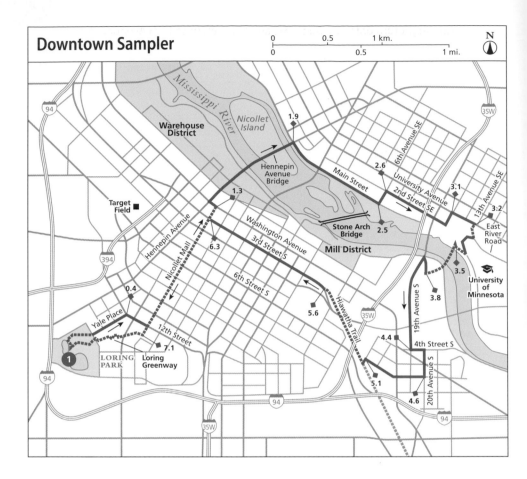

MILES AND DIRECTIONS

0.0 Loring Park. Start at north end of the gourd-shaped pond and ride out of the park to Yale Place.

0.4 Right turn onto 12th Street.

0.5 Left turn onto Nicollet Mall.

1.3 Turn left onto Washington Avenue and quick right onto Hennepin Avenue.

1.9 Turn right onto Main Street.

2.5 Turn left onto 6th Avenue SE.

2.6 Right turn onto 2nd Street SE, and then left onto 11th Avenue.

3.1 Right turn onto University Avenue.

3.2 Ride onto the bike path at 13th Avenue.

3.3 Turn right onto East River Road.

3.4 Hang a right along the northern spur of East River Parkway to the head of an old railroad bridge.

3.5 Left turn to cross the river.

3.8 Turn right onto 20th Avenue S.

3.9 Turn left onto 10th Avenue S, blending into 19th Avenue S.

4.4 Turn left onto 4th Street S.

4.5 Turn right onto 20th Avenue S.

4.6 Right turn onto 6th Street S.

5.1 Left turn onto 15th Avenue S and right onto the Hiawatha Bike Trail.

5.6 Merge onto 3rd Street S.

6.3 Turn left at Nicollet Mall.

7.1 Turn right onto the Loring Greenway bike path and follow back to Loring Park.

7.6 Arrive back at Loring Park trailhead.

RIDE INFORMATION

Restaurants

Jump-start with java and a huge muffin at **Dunn Bros. Coffee,** 329 W. 15th St.; (612) 872-4410; dunbros.com.

Overindulge after the ride with Italian decadence at **Buca di Beppo,** 1204 Harmon Place; (612) 288-0138; bucadibeppo.com.

2

City and Lakes Loop

The City and Lakes Loop shows off a highlight reel of historic and new attractions in Minneapolis and points west, following some of the city's most popular bike trails. Cruise the lakes area, the Midtown Greenway, and downtown's riverfront. Plan your ride right and catch a Twins game at Target Field on your way by.

Start: Start in downtown Minneapolis or Hopkins. This trailhead option is at the Depot Coffee House in Hopkins, 9451 Excelsior Blvd.

Distance: 22.7-mile loop, with shorter options

Approximate riding time: 1.5–2 hours

Best bike: Road or hybrid

Terrain and surface type: Flat to gently rolling bike path and roadways

Highlights: Mid-ride goodies at Birchwood Cafe, great downtown skyline views, superb metro trail system loop, Lake Calhoun attractions, Mississippi River views, downtown Mill and Warehouse Districts, Target Field

Hazards: Traffic at road crossings, crowded pathways on summer weekends

Other considerations: Potential for extra traffic on game days at Target Field; Greenway and Cedar Lake trails attract diverse group of riders (blazing fast to slow and squirrely) and other trail users.

Maps: *USGS Hopkins*

Getting there: From US 169, exit Excelsior Boulevard. Depot Coffee House is 0.1 mile east of US 169. GPS: N 44 55.434 W 93 23.962

Hennepin Avenue Bridge and GRAIN BELT BEER sign
WAYNE HOKLAS

THE RIDE

As you fuel up with organic, locally roasted coffee and a sandwich at the Depot, take a minute to reflect on this neighborhood landmark. A busy rail hub on the Minneapolis and St. Louis Railway line for nearly one hundred years, the 1902 depot continues its service today as a unique community project. Ambitious student volunteers from the Hopkins School District planned the renovation and staff it seven days a week, providing a place to learn and hang out in a positive environment. A bonus for young kids and train buffs: There is a Canadian Pacific switching yard just west of the depot, where big locomotives prepare for a hard day's work.

Start the ride heading north from the depot and connect with the Cedar Lake Trail on the north side of Excelsior Boulevard, warming up with an arrow-straight 3 miles through nondescript urban scenery. Use caution at street crossings of Blake Road, Wooddale Avenue, and Beltline Boulevard. A bend finally appears in the path as it nears Lake Calhoun, and at about 4 miles, the route reaches the junction with the Kenilworth Trail and an optional mileage variation. The Kenilworth Trail leads north between Lake of the Isles and Cedar Lake, and past the elegant, historic homes of the Kenwood neighborhood to the northern spur of the Cedar Lake Trail. This effectively cuts the loop in half for shorter rides on either side of the lakes area.

The Kenilworth junction also marks the transition to the Midtown Greenway, the wildly popular, 5.5-mile corridor trail stretching from Uptown to the Mississippi River. Also a former railroad line, the Greenway is a major transportation throughway for the self-propelled, supported by the active Midtown Greenway coalition, which helps maintain the trail and sponsors all sorts of cool events year-round, like the Greenway Glow (see Area Events below). The trail is even plowed in winter to accommodate the city's stalwart cyclists.

Less than 0.5 mile east of the lakes, the trail passes the vibrant Uptown area, packed with all manner of shops and restaurants, in easy reach via city streets. Two blocks east of Chicago Avenue is Freewheel Bike's Midtown Bike Center, an oasis and launch pad for trail users. Continue eastbound and cross Hiawatha Avenue over the stunning Martin Olav Sabo Bridge. At 30th Avenue, take a detour from the Greenway and ride up to 25th Street to get to Birchwood Cafe for a mid-ride rest stop. Thirty-sixth Avenue leads to West River Parkway and the start of a scenic section of parks and river views, on the bike path following the ridge above the river. Watch for towboats guiding barges

Bike Shops

A respected name in the bike business and feared in the regional peloton since the mid-70s, the Flanders brothers, Scott and Jim, remain a successful duo and their store a Minneapolis mainstay, as well as sponsor of the Minneapolis Bicycle Racing Club. Lightning-fast group rides and easygoing gentlemen's rides every week. **Flanders Bros. Cycle,** 2707 Lyndale Ave. S; (612) 872-6994; flandersbros.com.

Rest, repair a flat, glean sage wisdom at **Freewheel Bike's Midtown Bike Center.** On the Greenway, 2 blocks east of Chicago Avenue. (612) 238-4447; freewheelbike.com.

The Alt has been part of the Minneapolis community since 1974, when it started life as a small bike repair shop. Ahead of their time, the shop added skateboards and snowboards to its product line in the late '70s, and the local favorite remains proudly run by Minneapolis natives and father-son duo Jay and Joel Erickson. 3013 Lyndale Ave. S.; (612) 374-3635; thealtbikeboard.com.

up and down the river, and resident wildlife darting around in the woods. The trail soon slides beneath the Washington Avenue Bridge, with access to the lively 7 Corners and Stadium Village areas at the University of Minnesota campus.

Reaching I-35W, the trail passes the 35W Bridge Memorial, a stone marker remembering lives lost in the August 2007 bridge collapse, and naturally a somber point in the ride. Riding into downtown, the trail enters the historic Mill Ruins district, passing the Guthrie Theater, Mill City Museum, and the Stone Arch Bridge (details on this area follow on the Grand Rounds ride). Ride past the Hennepin Avenue Bridge and look for the junction with the Cedar Lake Trail. A quick curve takes the path close to Minneapolis's warehouse district, and within a block of a rest stop at Dunn Bros. Coffee on 3rd Avenue. Just past 4th Street, the trail passes the Target Field baseball stadium, goes under I-94, and leaves the city along I-394.

Behind you are great views of the city and, if you time it right, a look at the Northstar Commuter train departing to points northwest. Westbound from Minneapolis, riders follow the "bike freeway" portion of the Cedar Lake Regional Trail, the first of its kind in the nation. A triple ribbon of pathways, one for each direction of bicycle travel, and one for running and walking, runs from downtown to MN 100 in St. Louis Park, turning to its southwesterly track at the junction with the Kenilworth Trail. After passing through some light industrial sections, roll through Dakota Park, a couple of green space areas, and Aquila Park before reaching Excelsior Boulevard and the Depot trailhead.

Hometown Brew

From stone-walled production rooms and recessed antechambers, the **Minneapolis Brewing Company** introduced Golden Grain Belt beer in 1893. The brewery's massive, castle-like facility on the banks of the Mississippi River in Northeast Minneapolis crafted the popular brew with locally grown Minnesota grains and clear waters to make Grain Belt their best-selling brand. Tavern-goers across the Midwest savored the elixir's origin, drawn from wooden kegs and delivered to their favorite watering hole by horse-drawn wagon. The huge Grain Belt billboard on Nicollet Island, overlooking the Hennepin Avenue bridge, was built in 1940; the iconic landmark with the giant bottle cap lit up the riverfront through the mid-1970s. Recent efforts to preserve the sign and light it once again succeeded and the sign shines again.

City and Lakes Loop

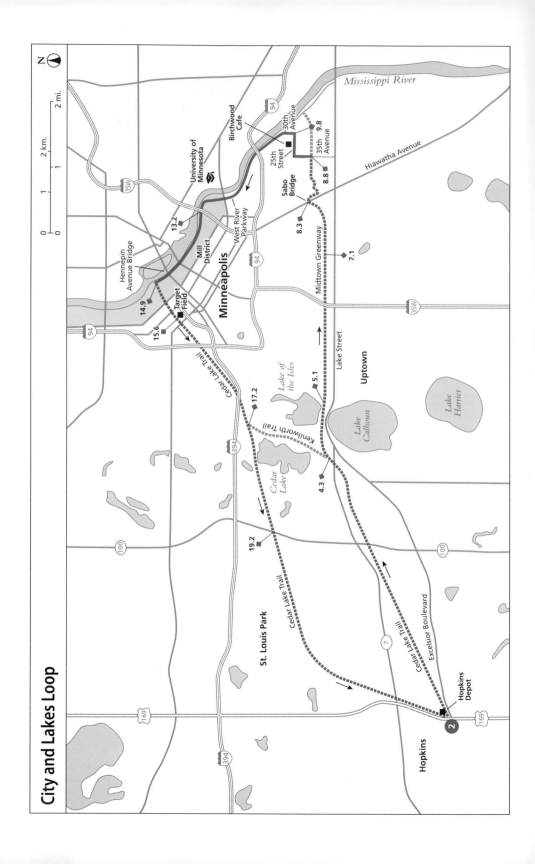

MILES AND DIRECTIONS

0.0 Start at the trailhead. Follow the Cedar Lake Trail north past Excelsior Boulevard, then turn east, heading toward downtown.

4.3 Junction with Kenilworth Trail. Continue straight ahead onto the Midtown Greenway.

5.1 Pass Lake of the Isles and Uptown.

7.1 Midtown Bike Center.

8.3 Sabo bridge crossing at Hiawatha Avenue.

8.8 Left turn onto 30th Avenue.

9.6 Right turn onto East 25th Street.

9.8 Rest stop at Birchwood Cafe.

9.9 Left turn onto 35th Avenue.

10.0 Turn right onto 24th Avenue, and left again onto West River Parkway.

13.2 Pass under I-35, and the 35W Bridge Memorial.

13.3 Ride through Mill Ruins Park and downtown riverfront.

13.4 Pass Stone Arch Bridge.

14.7 Ride under Hennepin Avenue bridge.

14.9 Left turn onto Cedar Lake Trail.

15.6 Pass Target Field.

17.2 Pass Kenilworth Trail.

19.2 Pass under MN 100.

22.7 Arrive back at the trailhead.

RIDE INFORMATION

Restaurants

Organic produce, free range eggs, and fair trade coffee highlight **Birchwood Cafe's** homegrown approach to a good meal. The former dairy and neighborhood grocery also sponsors a bike racing team and a bi-yearly cleanup day on the Green way. 3311 E. 25th St.; (612) 722-4474; birchwoodcafe.com.

Perennial best-in-Minnesota award winner **Pizza Luce** makes unforgettable handmade, gourmet pies, with a convenient location right off the Cedar Lake Trail for post-ride indulgence. 210 N. Blake Rd., Hopkins; (952) 767-0804; pizzaluce.com.

Treat yourself to stellar lake views and a plate of smoked mac and cheese or grilled seafood on the patio at **Lola's Café** at the Lake Calhoun Pavilion. Northeast corner of the lake, near East Calhoun Parkway and Lake Street; (612) 823-5840; thetinfish.net.

Area events

Fund-raising was never so much fun. The **Northern Spark** is part art show, part rolling party to celebrate bikes and raise moola for the Midtown Greenway Coalition. Light up your bike and ride the Greenway at night. Second week in June; midtowngreenway.org.

Grand Rounds

The Grand Rounds Scenic Byway explores the best of Minneapolis's copious scenery, culture, and history on a collection of manicured parkways, bike paths, and quiet streets through the city's seven byway districts. This squiggly, 33-mile loop (or choose a shorter route) follows the country's longest continuous system of urban parkways, past mirrored glass skyscrapers, showcase flower gardens, a vibrant chain of lakes, and the iconic Mississippi River. Take most of a day and roll this route like a wide-eyed kid on a balloon-tired cruiser—stop often, soak in the city's vibe, take a wrong turn on purpose. Ain't it grand?

Start: Minnehaha Park, at 4801 Minnehaha Park Dr.

Distance: 50 miles total included in the Grand Rounds. This loop follows the main, 33-mile parkway route. Many shorter options available.

Approximate riding time: 1 hour to all day

Best bike: Road or hybrid

Terrain and surface type: Flat and gently rolling paved pathways and roads

Highlights: Downtown riverfront, Mississippi River bluffs, city lakes scene, wildflower gardens, military memorials

Hazards: Use caution at all road crossings; watch for traffic on city streets

Other considerations: Plan on extra time to see the sights; pack extra food and water, and bring a camera.

Maps: *USGS Saint Paul West*

Getting there: From downtown Minneapolis, follow MN 55 (Hiawatha Avenue) south to the park. From MN 62 (Crosstown Highway), near MSP International Airport, follow MN 55 north to the park. GPS: N 44 55.026 W 93 12.692

THE RIDE

Much of America's richest natural and cultural rewards survive today thanks to farsighted visionaries from the past. Horace Cleveland, a landscape gardener for the city of Minneapolis park system in the late 1800s, urged city officials to look forward and preserve the area's ample outdoor attractions. His inspiration sparked what is now the country's premier national scenic byway and a veritable playground for cyclists. Informational kiosks and signed routes lead riders past a dozen lakes and a couple of waterfalls, through parks and wildflower gardens, big city bustle and quiet neighborhoods. Over fifty interpretive sites also dot the loop, showing off our city's best in exhibits and historical sites, like the Longfellow House, historic Main Street, and Mill Ruins Park. You can throw a dart anywhere at a map of the Grand Rounds to start this highlight reel ride. With so many options to satisfy your every two-wheeled desire, this route description tours each byway district on a counterclockwise loop starting at Minnehaha Falls.

Mississippi River District

Roll away from Minnehaha Park along Godfrey Road to the start of the pathway above the river, just upstream from the Ford Dam (Lock and Dam #1). The smooth path winds past big trees with, naturally, superb views of the Mississippi River Gorge all the while. This is a don't-miss stretch with fall colors lighting up the day and reflecting in the river's lazy current. As you pass Lake Street and stately homes bordering West River Parkway, the University of Minnesota appears on the near horizon, its sprawling campus occupying real estate on both sides of the river. Riverside green spaces open up beneath the I-94 bridge, and soon the path rounds a curve and through the shadow of the I-35W bridge toward downtown Minneapolis.

Downtown Riverfront District

West of I-35W, the path enters Mill Ruins Park and the historic Mill District of Minneapolis, first passing the renowned Guthrie Theater, then the Mill City Museum. Built into the ruins of the old Washburn A Mill, once the world's largest flour mill, the museum is a must-stop for a fascinating look at the city's history in the flour milling industry. Adjacent to the museum is the Stone Arch Bridge, an iconic Minneapolis landmark and another statement to the city's rich memoirs. Built by railroad baron James J. Hill with native granite and limestone, with twenty-three crescent arches spanning the Mississippi, the bridge was used to transport goods and other commercial uses through 1965, and it remains one of the most visited destinations in the state. From here, riders have a choice of directions to continue the Grand Rounds. Stay on

Beautiful Minnehaha Falls
JIM HOFFMAN

the parkway to the Hennepin Avenue Bridge and follow surface streets, cross the Hennepin bridge and cruise back down old Main Street, or cross right here over the Stone Arch Bridge. As this is the most direct and traffic-friendly route, take the Stone Arch across and follow surface streets to the city's northeast neighborhoods.

Northeast District

Ride north to Stinson Boulevard and Ridgeway Parkway and the proud northeast area of Minneapolis, steeped with influence from European immigrants. Follow the quiet Ridgeway Parkway past Hillside Cemetery to St. Anthony Boulevard. Head northwest for a few challenging hills (the route becomes St. Anthony Parkway) and plan for a photo stop in the Deming Heights area, with a stellar view of the downtown skyline. Stay on the parkway and cross the river again at the 42nd Avenue bridge. A quick right onto Lyndale Avenue North leads to Webber Parkway and the next byway district.

Victory Memorial District

Webber Pond and the surrounding sights of its namesake park and Shingle Creek greet riders along Webber Parkway. This is a fine setting for a rest stop and to note that this section of the nearby Mississippi River is the point at which barge navigation begins (one of those little nuggets of river lore to tell your non-Minnesota friends). Just past the park the route moves on to Victory Memorial Drive, a 3-mile section of parkway honoring Hennepin County soldiers who lost their lives in WWI. The stately boulevard is a fitting tribute, with granite and marble monuments and memorials and a series of American flags in a central plaza. Ride south on the parkway to the start of the historic Wirth Park section of the trip.

Theodore Wirth District

Cruise into Minneapolis's largest regional park on its curvy namesake parkway along Bassett's Creek and the golf course. (Check out the elegant stonework of the 1920s golf chalet on the way by.) The parkway S-turns past the ski and mountain bike trails and the MN 55 junction to Wirth Lake. A short spin east on Glenwood Avenue, past Wirth Lake's southern shore, leads to the park's spacious picnic areas (and historic pavilion), a 4H garden, and access to the Luce Line and Cedar Lake trails. South of this intersection is the don't-miss Eloise Butler Wildflower Garden (see sidebar and spend some time there) and the park's quaking bog, two big reasons why Wirth is the city's perennial best-of for nature lovers.

Chain of Lakes District

South of I-394, the Grand Rounds enters the city's iconic Chain of Lakes area, inspiration for our City of Lakes nickname and veritable playground for cycling. The shores of Lakes Harriet, Calhoun, Cedar, and Lake of the Isles are bordered by scenic parkways and bike paths, with enough mileage and accompanying

Bike Shops

Zombie Interval Training. That's the pre-season vibe at **The Hub,** the Cities' only bike shop co-op. Their twisted spin class pits riders with the undead: Watch a zombie movie and sprint like mad whenever a creepy gives chase to innocent townsfolk. Dedicated staff bring that enthusiasm to their customers, and donate 5 percent of profits to the People and the Planet Fund. Check with the shop for the latest information. Stores at 301 Cedar Ave., 3020 Minnehaha Ave., and the U of M Bike Center, Minneapolis; (612) 238-3593; thehubbikecoop.org.

A senses-teasing aroma of freshly brewed coffee and chain lube greets customers at **Angry Catfish Bicycle Shop + Coffee Bar** in south Minneapolis. Mix in the presence of Lynskey, Foundry, and Rapha bikes and gear, and you've walked into owner Josh Klauck's childhood dream. His circa 2010 store is one of the city's most popular bike and brew shops, with a palpable stay-a-while vibe. 4208 28th Ave. S; (612) 722-1538; angrycatfishbicycle.com.

sister activities to fill up an entire summertime afternoon. Ride south on Cedar Lake Parkway along the lake's northern end, which kind of looks like Snoopy's head, skirt past the big bay in the middle, and curve around to Dean Parkway at the southern shore. Stay eastbound to Lake of the Isles for a loop around the squiggly border of this picturesque lake, engineered by the city in the late 1800s to "improve" its shoreline and create a more formal park setting. Much of the lake's original wetlands have disappeared, but the lake still retains some of its wild feel. Don't miss the elegant homes in the historic Kenwood neighborhood at the lake's northern panhandle. Meander back down Dean Parkway, past the Calhoun Beach Club, a post-WWII social club-turned luxury apartments and commercial complex, to Lake Calhoun. The largest lake in Minneapolis, this is a popular place for the water- and land-based active lifestyle the city is so well-known for. When the wind is favorable, look for sailboats and wind surfers on the waves, and the trails around the lake are always lively with bikers, skaters, walkers, and runners.

Eloise Butler Wildflower Garden

At the south end of Theodore Wirth Park, just a few miles from downtown Minneapolis, is a 15-acre oasis of native wildflowers, wetland, tamarack forest, and upland prairie, spared from the city's earliest development scourge by the inspiration of Eloise Butler. A Minneapolis botanist and teacher, Butler's dedication and keen mind for conservation were the impetus to set aside this small, unique natural area for future generations, and in 1907 the city park board established her namesake garden.

The oldest public wildflower garden in the country, the **Eloise Butler Wildflower Garden and Bird Sanctuary** bursts with more than 500 plant and 130 bird species growing and living in habitats from wetland bog to open prairie. Wood chip pathways wind a gently hilly course through fern glens, mature forest, and prairie, with interpretive signs for self-guided tours. On the garden's west edge is a rare (practically nonexistent today) tamarack bog, with sphagnum moss slowly pulsing with life and providing living quarters for the likes of trout lilies and broadleaf arrowhead, frogs, and songbirds, and is best viewed up close from the floating poly-boardwalk. A must-visit destination in all seasons, the spring and summer flower extravaganza is especially spectacular. Stop in and, like the gate at the main entrance says, "Let nature be your teacher." Open Apr–Oct. Theodore Wirth Parkway and Glenwood Avenue; (612) 370-4903; minneapolisparks.org or friendsofeloisebutler.org.

William Berry Parkway links Calhoun to its slightly smaller neighbor, Lake Harriet. The parkway passes the western edge of the sprawling Lakewood Cemetery, a fixture here since 1872. The Lake Harriet Bandshell anchors the lake's northwest corner, as well as the Linden Hills Station and streetcar museum, two must-see attractions on your lakeside ride. Riding either direction around the lake is great fun, but the counterclockwise option brings a bonus with the stunning Lyndale Park Gardens, an amazing display of various rose varieties, a peace garden, and bird sanctuary. Plan on extra time to enjoy this postcard-perfect landmark. Continue around the lake to the southeast corner, and exit onto Minnehaha Parkway for the next segment.

Minnehaha Park District

Minnehaha Creek begins its 22-mile journey from Grays Bay in Lake Minnetonka, and it saves its best for the sinuous stretch from Lake Harriet to the Mississippi River, the finale of this version of the Grand Rounds loop. Never leaving sight of the clear and gently flowing stream, the recreation paths and parkway wind past idyllic picnic areas, stately homes, and vibrant neighborhoods on the way to Lake Nokomis, host to summer weekend sailboat races, canoeing, swimming, and cruising the parkways. Ride past the lake and follow Minnehaha Parkway to its namesake park and relax with a treat from the ice cream truck and a view of 50-foot Minnehaha Falls. The Grand Rounds Information Center is also close by, adjacent to the falls at the historic Longfellow House.

Minnehaha Falls in winter
JIM HOFFMAN

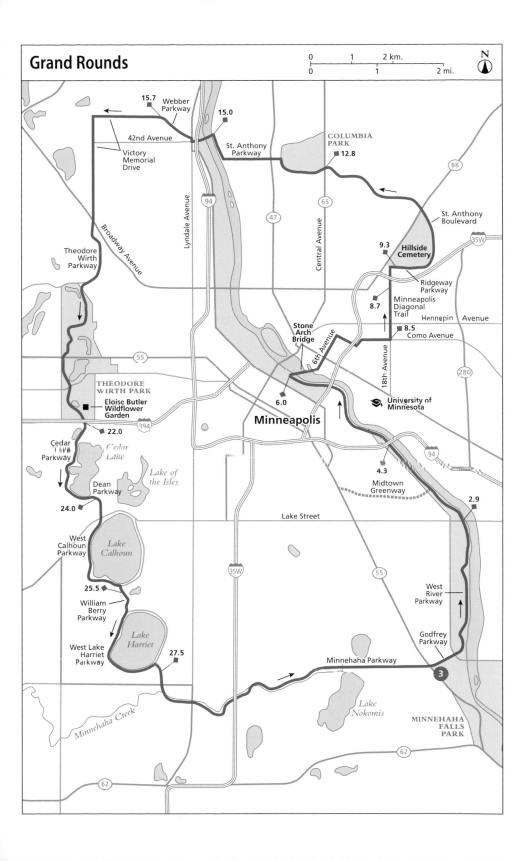

Grand Rounds

0   1   2 km.
0   1   2 mi.

N

15.7 Webber Parkway
15.0
42nd Avenue
St. Anthony Parkway
Victory Memorial Drive

COLUMBIA PARK
12.8

88

Lyndale Avenue
94
47
65
Central Avenue

St. Anthony Boulevard
35W

9.3 Hillside Cemetery

Theodore Wirth Parkway
Broadway Avenue

Ridgeway Parkway
8.7 Minneapolis Diagonal Trail
Hennepin Avenue

55

Stone Arch Bridge
8.5 Como Avenue

6th Avenue
18th Avenue

280

THEODORE WIRTH PARK
Eloise Butler Wildflower Garden

6.0

Minneapolis

University of Minnesota

394
22.0

Cedar Lake Parkway
Cedar Lake

4.3 Midtown Greenway

94

Dean Parkway
Lake of the Isles

2.9

24.0

Lake Street
35W
55

West Calhoun Parkway
Lake Calhoun

25.5
William Berry Parkway

West River Parkway

West Lake Harriet Parkway
Lake Harriet
27.5

Godfrey Parkway

Minnehaha Parkway
3

Minnehaha Creek

Lake Nokomis

MINNEHAHA FALLS PARK

62

62

3

MILES AND DIRECTIONS

0.0 Start at the trailhead at Minnehaha Falls Park pavilion. Head east along Godfrey Road and north on the bike path following West River Parkway.

1.8 Pass horseshoe bend at Mississippi Park.

2.9 Pass underneath Lake Street.

3.3 Junction with Midtown Greenway Trail. Continue straight ahead.

4.3 Pass beneath the I-94 bridge. Great views of the U of M campus.

5.2 U of M West Bank to your left and the Bohemian Flats area. Trail curves northwest to pass beneath I-35 west.

6.0 Arrive at Mill Ruins Park and Mill District. Continue on the path.

6.4 Junction with Portland Avenue. Turn right to cross the Stone Arch Bridge. Cross the river and ride northeast on 6th Avenue.

Alternate routes:
Continue along West River Parkway, past Broadway Avenue, to 22nd Avenue N. Turn left onto 2nd Street N, and ride north all the way to the junction with 42nd Avenue N. Or cross the river at Broadway Avenue, turn left onto Marshall Street, and ride along the east side of the river to 42nd Street.

7.4 Turn right onto 8th Street SE, cross I-35 west, and continue to 11th Street.

7.8 Left turn onto 10th Avenue.

7.9 Right turn onto Como Avenue.

8.3 Turn left onto 18th Avenue SE.

8.5 Junction with Hennepin Avenue. Continue straight ahead on the Minneapolis Diagonal Trail.

9.5 Turn right onto Ridgeway Parkway, riding along Hillside Cemetery.

10.2 Left turn onto St. Anthony Boulevard. Follow a winding, northwest track to great downtown skyline views at Deming Heights.

12.8 Junction with Central Avenue. Continue straight ahead, passing Columbia Park and golf course.

15.0 Junction with 37th Avenue NE. Turn left and cross the river (route continues on 42nd Avenue North.

15.2 Right turn onto Lyndale Avenue North, and immediate left onto Webber Parkway, paralleling Webber Park.

15.7 Junction with Victory Memorial Parkway. Continue straight ahead. Follow the parkway west, then south, passing Broadway Avenue at mile 18 and blending into Theodore Wirth Parkway just south of 29th Avenue North. (No turns; one parkway turns into another.)

20.0 Enter Theodore Wirth Park. Continue riding south through the park.

21.4 Junction with Glenwood Avenue. Eloise Butler Wildflower Garden is at the southeast corner. Continue riding straight ahead on the parkway.

22.0 Cross I-394 into the Chain of Lakes district, on Cedar Lake Parkway.

22.5 Lean left on the Cedar Lake Regional Trail, along the west shore of Cedar Lake.

> The Lyndale Park Rose Garden is the second oldest of its kind in the country. Don't miss the rainbow colors of blooms from mid-June to early October. Also on the grounds is the Roberts Bird Sanctuary, home to migratory and nesting birds like warblers and great horned owls. Located at the northeast corner of Lake Harriet.

24.0 Junction with Dean Parkway. Take an optional loop around Lake of the Isles, or turn right to continue main route.

24.1 Junction with Lake Street and Lake Calhoun. Continue straight ahead, now on West Calhoun Parkway.

25.5 Turn right onto William Berry Parkway at south end of Lake Calhoun.

26.0 Turn right onto West Lake Harriet Parkway. Pass the bandshell and ride south, along the west shore of Lake Harriet.

27.5 Right turn at Minnehaha Parkway.

32.0 Pass northern shore of Lake Nokomis.

33.0 Arrive back at the Minnehaha Falls Park trailhead.

Riding along the parkway
WAYNE HOKLAS

RIDE INFORMATION

Restaurants

Got a sudden urge for seafood? Skip the Clifbar and try oysters on the half shell or crab chowder from **Sea Salt Eatery.** Top it off with a scoop of hometown favorite Sebastian Joe's ice cream to make this a perfect day. Open Apr–Oct. 4801 Minnehaha Ave. S; (612) 721-8990; seasalteatery.wordpress.com.

Eat fresh and local at **Urban Eatery,** a block from the route in the Calhoun Beach Club. Try the white pizza or beer-battered cheese curds. 2730 W. Lake St.; (612) 920-5000; myurbaneatery.com.

Area events

There's always something to do around Minneapolis, but a few favorites:

The **Minneapolis Aquatennial Festival** celebrates seventy-three years in 2013, delighting visitors with the festively competitive milk carton boat races and the Torchlight Parade. Mid-July in downtown; aquatennial.com.

2019 marks the nineteenth year of great live music at the Cities 97 **Basilica Block Party** in downtown Minneapolis. Three stages host two dozen bands belting out the tunes on hot summer evenings at the annual, two-day bash; basilicablockparty.org.

Tote the family to the downtown riverfront for the annual **Stone Arch Bridge Festival,** a free event with 250 artists, live music, a car show, and great food; stonearchbridgefestival.com.

Best Bike Rides Minneapolis and St. Paul

Dakota Rail Regional Trail—Lake Minnetonka Loop

To the delight of cycling fans, the Minnetonka-area trail system added the Dakota Rail Trail in 2009, treating riders to a flat cruise between Wayzata and St. Bonifacius. This 22-mile route combines the rail-trail with a squiggly, scenic tour of the neighborhoods around Lake Minnetonka. Don't-miss stops include the Minnetonka Drive-In, Noerenberg Gardens, historic Wayzata Train Depot, and boat watching on the lake.

Start: Wayzata swimming beach park at 175 Grove Lane in Wayzata

Distance: 22.5-mile loop

Approximate riding time: 2–2.5 hours

Best bike: Road or hybrid

Terrain and surface type: Flat to rolling on paved path and city streets

Highlights: Noerenberg Gardens, train depot, great lake views, Minnetonka Drive-In

Hazards: Light traffic on neighborhood streets (busier on weekends); use caution at road crossings

Other considerations: Trail will be busy on weekends, especially from Wayzata to Mound

Maps: *USGS Excelsior*

Getting there: Follow I-394 west of I-494 to MN 101. Head south to Lake Street and west to Grove Lane into beach parking lot. GPS: N 44 58.154 W 93 31.153

Bridge over headwaters of Minnehaha Creek
CHRIS NELSON

THE RIDE

Legions of lake lovers descend upon Wayzata Beach to soak up the sun, build a sand castle, or launch into the water to start a triathlon or other uber-endurance event like the 9-mile Open Water Championship. Swimming to some distant point too far away to see land sounds, well, far. Let's stick to two wheels and follow the short access street westbound from the beach, across Shoreline Drive, and onto the Dakota Rail Trail. The silky smooth path parallels Shoreline Drive for the entire first stretch of this ride, first passing a couple of quiet neighborhoods, then along scenic marshes and bays near Browns Bay and Tanager Lake. Right around 3 miles is the junction with North Shore Drive, which leads away from the lake to Noerenberg Memorial Gardens on the shores of Crystal and Maxwell Bays. This is the former estate of Grain Belt Brewery founder Frederick Noerenberg. His 1890 Queen Anne–style home was one of the first permanent homes on Lake Minnetonka, and the family established an elegantly manicured landscape that today is favored as one of the finest formal gardens in Minnesota. The Noerenbergs' generosity shone bright through generations, culminating in the early 1970s when the estate was bequeathed to the park district (now managed by Three Rivers Park District) and renovated to a public garden and park. The roughly 2-mile ride to the gardens follows the busier North Shore Drive, but the road has an ample traffic buffer in a wide shoulder.

The trail continues to a skinny spit of land between Browns and Crystal Bays, crossing the narrows over a short bridge and rounding a curve to the tony Lafayette Country Club. Unless you carried your clubs with you, keep riding into the sleepy village of Navarre, one of Lake Minnetonka's original towns. Keep right on heading west past Shadywood Road, and for the sole reason of making a beeline to the Minnetonka Drive-in for an early break. Resistance is futile when this legendary, 50-year-old landmark tempts you with a made-on-site root beer float. After spoiling your riding form, turn back east on the trail to Shadywood Road (at around 9 miles) and turn right, riding past skinny peninsula fingers, boat clubs, and marinas along exclusive lakeshore property. The road becomes Manitou Road about halfway down, and soon enters the Tonka Bay neighborhood. At the junction with the Lake Minnetonka LRT Regional Trail (take a deep breath to say that trail name) turn left. This is a packed, crushed limestone path that, while maybe not ideal for high zoot bikes with pencil-thin tires, is typically in great condition, and best of all, traffic-free. The path rolls into the feel-good town of Excelsior, a mid-1850s village with a solid hold on its historical roots, including a bike and pedestrian-friendly main street and the *Minnehaha Steamboat,* an invaluable passenger travel boat on Lake Minnetonka near the turn of the century. The skiff was scuttled in 1926 with declining ridership, left to its watery fate at the lake bottom off Brackett's Point, raised to the surface in 1990 by determined preservationists, restored, and again carries passengers on tours from the Excelsior port.

Continue riding across the narrows between St. Albans and Excelsior Bays, paralleling Minnetonka Boulevard through Greenwood, home of the historic Old Log Theater, to the junction with Tonkawood Road at mile 18. Turn left and follow a wide shoulder on this tree-lined stretch to the northern branch of Minnetonka Boulevard and turn left again onto Fairchild Avenue, a twisty road with great lake views and a fun descent to Libbs Lake. Fairchild meets Grays Bay Boulevard at mile 19 and takes on that name, and traces past old-money lake cabins and immense, modern mansions near Grays Bay to a dead end at a city water management station. Follow the path out of the back side of the dead end and head for the skinny bridge crossing the headwaters of Minnehaha Creek. It's rare to see the virgin headwaters of a stream or river,

Bike Shop

In and around the bike business since high school, Steve Phyle's **Tonka Cycle & Ski** shop has been a family favorite for over fifty years, and a local, year-round go-to for bikes, skis, and snowboards. 16 Shady Oak Rd., Hopkins; (952) 938-8336; tonkacycleandski.com.

> ## Tonka Toys
>
> All respectable kids worth their weight in slingshots and squirt guns always had a big ol' Tonka Toy in their backyard sandbox. These were rough-and-tough toys and they built roads and pits and mountains, and plowed ditches that carried temporary rivers poured from pails. Dozers, loaders, cranes, and the burly dump truck—the crew boss. Fat black tires dirty with mud. Faded yellow paint streaked with scars of rust. A dent or two in its cavernous box made of real metal. All the while lugging payloads of sand, rocks, logs, or lesser toys with no business being in the work zone.
>
> Generations of kids nurtured that heavy equipment creativity thanks to three farsighted tinkerers from Mound Metalcraft, who decided sturdy children's toys would make a good sideline to their company's other products. Taking inspiration from the Dakota-Sioux word tonka (meaning "great"), the Mound-based company, housed in a small schoolhouse basement, introduced a steam shovel and crane design to the toy market in 1947. The brawny toys were a huge hit, selling out the entire inventory in a few months, and ushering in a 65-year tradition of construction-based fun. The company changed its name to **Tonka Toys** Incorporated in 1955, and continued to develop new designs, like forklifts, rescue vehicles, and a preschool line. The iconic Tonka factory closed its doors in 1991 after joining toy giant Hasbro, and with nearly 300 million of the venerable metal toys in the hands of kids all over the world, Tonka is still king of the sandbox.

and it's pretty cool that this is the birthplace of one of the state's most famous waterways. Across the creek, Crosby Road leads north to McGinty Road, a busier corridor, but a wide shoulder allows for comfy riding. Minnetonka and Wayzata meet two of their corners at a busy intersection at McGinty Road and MN 101, with less-than-reliable crossing signals. Use caution and continue westbound on Shady Lane to Lake Street and back to the trailhead, where a well-deserved cool-down swim awaits.

MILES AND DIRECTIONS

0.0 Wayzata swimming beach trailhead. Follow Dakota Rail Trail westbound.

1.0 Pass northern shore of Browns Bay, followed by Smith Bay.

Dakota Rail Regional Trail—Lake Minnetonka Loop

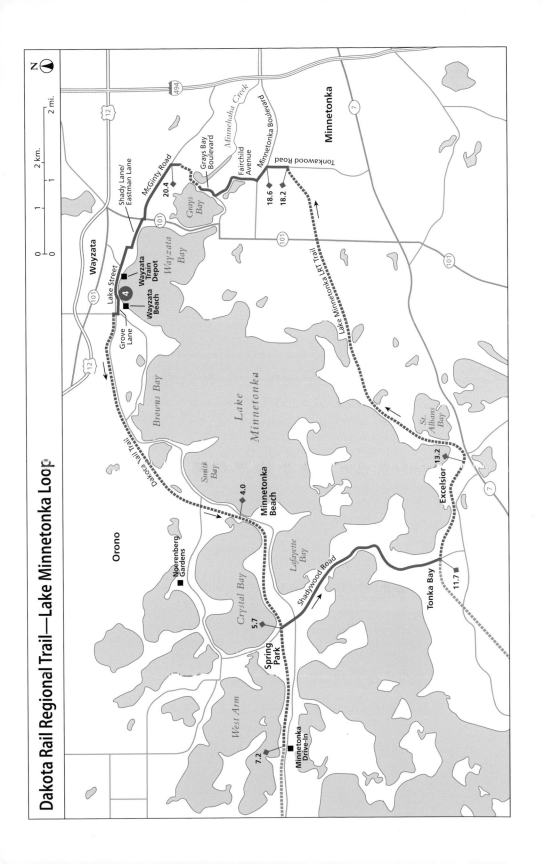

4.0 Cross narrows at Crystal Bay and ride past the ritzy Minnetonka Beach neighborhood.

5.7 Pass junction with Shadywood Road.

7.2 Root beer rest stop at Minnetonka Drive-In. Return on trail eastbound to Shadywood Road.

8.8 Junction with Shadywood Road. Turn right, passing bay of Lake Minnetonka to village of Tonka Bay.

11.7 Junction with Lake Minnetonka LRT Regional Trail. Turn left.

13.2 Trail curves north, between Excelsior and Saint Albans Bays, then turns east along Minnetonka Boulevard.

18.2 Left turn onto Tonkawood Road.

18.5 Left turn onto Minnetonka Boulevard.

18.6 Right turn onto Fairchild Avenue.

19.4 Fairchild Avenue blends into Grays Bay Boulevard, continuing the route northbound.

19.8 At the back side of the cul-de-sac, follow the bike path bridge across the headwaters of Minnehaha Creek.

20.1 Ride north on Crosby Road to McGinty Road.

20.4 Turn left onto McGinty Road.

21.2 Junction with MN 101. Continue west on Shady Lane and Eastman Lane to East Lake Street.

21.7 Left turn onto East Lake Street.

22.5 Left turn onto Grove Lane; arrive back at the trailhead.

> The prolific boogie-woogie harmony trio The Andrews Sisters grew up in Mound, and retained close ties with their hometown throughout their career. The city honored the girls with The Andrews Sisters Trail, a brick and paved pathway along Lost Lake. andrewssisterstrail.com.

RIDE INFORMATION

Restaurants

Family-owned for fifty years and counting, the **Minnetonka Drive-In** still serves up mouthwatering burgers and made-on-site root beer. Don't miss Hot Rod and Classic Car nights on summer Thursday evenings. 4658 Shoreline Dr., Spring Park; (952) 471-9383.

Locals know it as "The Muni," Wayzata's first municipal liquor store and bar-turned-area favorite **Wayzata Bar & Grill,** only 0.5 mile from the trailhead. Refuel with a Muni Melt and frosty mug. 747 Mill St., Wayzata; (952) 473-5286; wayzatabarandgrill.com.

Stay westbound on the Dakota Rail Trail to St. Bonifacius and gobble a BLT on the patio at green-friendly **St. Boni Bistro.** The entire menu is locally sourced and organically inspired. 38516 Kennedy Memorial Dr.; (952) 446-9198; stbonibistro.com.

Area events

Family fun at September's **James J. Hill Days** in Wayzata, with a coaster cart derby, car show, parade, and art show; wayzatachamber.com.

Hone your farmhand skills at **Gale Woods Farm** in Minnetrista. Summer camps, gardening classes, and cow-milking lessons. Easy access from the trail. 7210 CR 110 W, Minnetrista; (763) 694-2001; threeriversparks.org.

5

Elm Creek Park Reserve

Roll on 15 miles of sinuous pathways through woods, marshland, meadows, and six lakes in the largest reserve in the Three Rivers Regional Parks system. Elm Creek's 4,900 acres host over 30 miles of trails, with connections to the Rush Creek and Medicine Lake Regional Trails. Keep an eye out for the park's resident wildlife, and don't miss Eastman Nature Center's stacked calendar of interpretive programs.

Start: Northern trailhead access at Elm Creek Road and Hayden Lake Road, adjacent to the off-leash dog park

Distance: 15-mile loop. Easy access to more miles on the Rush Creek and Medicine Lake Regional Trails.

Approximate riding time: 1–1.5 hours

Best bike: Road or hybrid

Terrain and surface type: Flat to gently rolling on wide, paved pathways

Highlights: Impeccable trails, deep woods wilderness feel, Eastman Nature Center, Pierre Bottineau House, rich variety of critters

Hazards: Stay alert for other trail users and sudden appearance of wildlife; low-traffic residential streets when connecting to Rush Creek or Medicine Lake trails

Other considerations: Trails are busy on summer weekends

Maps: *USGS Anoka*; Three Rivers Parks map

Getting there: From US 169 and I-94, head north on US 169 5 miles to MN 610 and go west 3 miles to Fernbrook Lane. Turn right and go north 1 mile to Elm Creek Road. Turn right and follow it east 3 miles to the Hayden Lake Road trailhead. GPS: N 45 10.113 W 93 25.324

THE RIDE

On the day I rode Elm Creek's trails, I saw a little girl on a squeaky trike patrolling the visitor center, and two racers decked out in their team gear speeding around a turn on a perimeter trail. There was a pack of runners looking very businesslike, training for an upcoming event, and an elderly couple next to prairie wildflowers with binoculars trained on a bluebird. This confirmed what I'd always heard: Elm Creek really does have something for everyone. Whatever your plans are for visiting this north metro park, pad some extra time. The scenery is ride-off-the-trail gorgeous; the visitor center alone is worth a stop; and with a swimming hole and on-site mountain bike trails, there is a full day of fun all over the place.

Access points to the park's trail system are dotted all around its boundary, and I chose the Hayden Lake Road location for its proximity to alternate activities (mountain biking trails and dog park). Skinny and fat tires on the same day, right? Ride north on the paved road for about 100 yards to the trail crossing and turn left. The path starts right off with a cruise through an open meadow with songbirds flitting about, then curves through a shadowy copse of woods to cross Elm Creek Road. Roll along some minor elevation changes past borders of 6-foot sumac trees, all the while surrounded by a landscape of meadow and scattered trees and pockets of wetlands on a gradual descent to a view-packed junction between Goose and Mud Lakes. Drop down past the southern horn of Goose Lake and up a small grade past a handsome stand of aspen on a southerly trajectory, moving from open land into a dense canopy of mixed hardwood forest that leads to the park entrance road. The trail serpentines its way to the visitor center, passing the championship-caliber disc golf course on your right.

Just around the curve from the visitor center is the Pierre Bottineau House, resplendent today as it surely was in the 1800s. Imagine the great adventurer Monsieur Bottineau planning his next exploration from his outpost here in the wilds of a largely unknown territory. Perhaps he might have benefited from directional signs the likes of which stand today at the trail kiosk just a short way past his front door. Explorers today can turn here to ride the 15-mile

Bike Shop

Maple Grove Cycling has been a north metro go-to shop since 1988. Owner Dan Book treats riders to a classy show floor and full-service repair shop, plus guided, weekly group rides around the Twin Cities area. 13950 Grove Dr., Maple Grove; (763) 420-8878; maplegrove cycling.com.

Medicine Lake Regional Trail to French Regional Park and connect to the Luce Line Trail in Plymouth. Today, continue across a bridge over Elm Creek and hang a right at the next split, heading back north on an initial, arrow-straight trail past 10-foot sumacs and wetlands loud with bird calls. The path heads due north at the next junction and crosses Elm Creek again, then climbs up into a wildflower-packed meadow with butterflies, bluebirds, goldfinches, and red cardinals merrily enjoying life. The laudable efforts of the park's forestry, wildlife, and water resources teams are evident throughout the ride. Eighty percent of the park is managed or retained to its natural state, and officials are constantly striving to preserve wildlife and rare plant species. It is an uplifting sight to see such a vibrant relationship thrive. After crossing Elm Creek Road, the trail introduces the northern tier of the park with a long coast down to a long, wooden bridge over the wetlands draining Powers Lake. Approach stealthily for a good chance to spot water-based critters. Past the bridge, the

French Lineage

Perched on a hill adjacent to the park's main entrance, the restored **Pierre Bottineau** house looks over the historic stomping grounds of a legendary Minnesota frontiersman.

Born of French-Canadian and half-Sioux Ojibwe blood, the swarthy Bottineau was equally capable of hand-hewing a boat, romancing ladies, or leading explorations of trackless wilderness. He was an intrepid voyageur, and his travels through the wild corridor northwest of the present-day Twin Cities opened the area to settlement and forged Minnesota into a prosperous state. The multilingual Bottineau, a "walking peace pipe," was a savvy diplomat and integral in drafting Indian treaties, planning cities, and establishing successful trade. His 1854 home at Elm Creek Park was the first built in the original Maple Grove Township.

Winding through the woods

path ricochets between huge trees and breaks free once again to open land and a quick kiss with French Lake Road at the park's far north, before angling back toward the official mountain bike trailhead, accompanied by a cornfield and meadow jammed with a Crayola palette of wildflowers.

A gentle climb leads up away from the woods to a nice view of Lemans Lake, skirts another meadow to a fringe of a Champlin commercial area, and drops back down into the woods again past a purple martin sanctuary, buzzing with comings and goings of said species. This is an Audubon Society Purple Martin Conservation Project, and has gone far in providing habitat for these threatened birds, which have seen a 78 percent decline in population around the Great Lakes in the past four decades. Cruise through the woods and meadow again on a fun and winding homestretch to the trailhead.

MILES AND DIRECTIONS

0.0   Start at the Hayden Lake Road trailhead.

1.0   Junction with Elm Creek Road. Head straight across.

1.6   Pass junction with spur trail heading east.

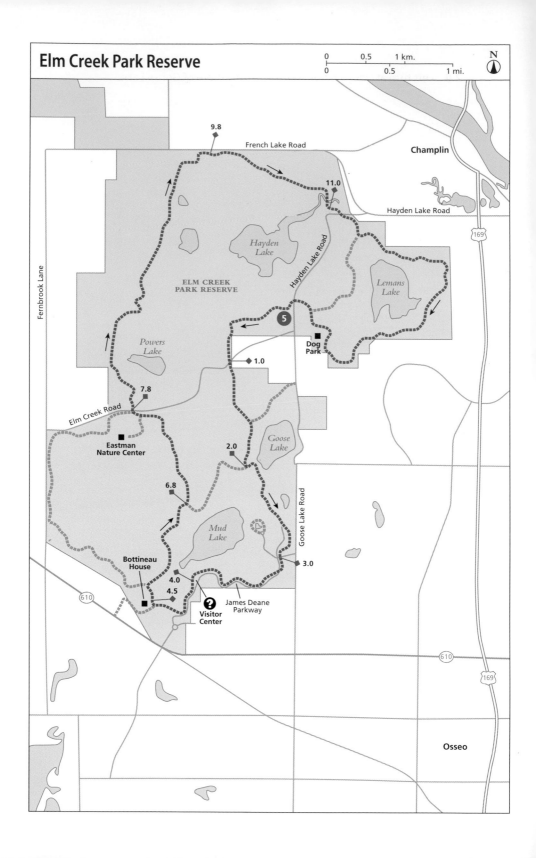

Elm Creek Park Reserve

0   0.5   1 km.
0   0.5   1 mi.

N

Champlin

9.8

French Lake Road

11.0

Hayden Lake Road

Hayden Lake Road

169

Hayden
Lake

Lemans
Lake

ELM CREEK
PARK RESERVE

5

Powers
Lake

Dog
Park

1.0

7.8

Elm Creek Road

Eastman
Nature Center

2.0

Goose
Lake

6.8

Goose Lake Road

Mud
Lake

3.0

Bottineau
House

610

4.0
4.5

Visitor
Center

James Deane
Parkway

610

169

Osseo

Fernbrook Lane

2.0 Left turn at trail junction, skirting south shore of Goose Lake.

3.0 Junction with James Deane Parkway. Ride across to continue on the bike path.

4.0 Pass the chalet/visitor center.

4.5 Roll past the Bottineau House.

4.6 Junction with the Medicine Lake Regional Trail and info-packed kiosk with maps of area trails.

6.8 Left turn at trail junction.

7.8 Cross Elm Creek Road.

9.8 Briefly parallel French Lake Road.

11.0 Ride past the northern mountain bike trailhead.

15.0 Arrive back at trailhead.

RIDE INFORMATION

Restaurants
Head to **The Lookout Bar & Grill** for homemade-good grub and a seat on Maple Grove's largest outdoor patio. Family-owned since 1958, the local favorite hosts volleyball, horseshoes, and live music. 8672 Pineview Lane, N; (763) 424-4365; lookoutbarand grill.com.

Area events
The Purple Ride raises awareness and funds for pancreatic cancer, with various loops in the Maple Grove area, including Elm Creek Park; pancan.org .purpleride/learn_about_purpleride.html.

Roll out from a beachside trailhead on this 32-miler linking two charming towns and a pair of parks, with no less than sixteen lakes along the way, ice cream at the halfway point, and great country views.

Start: Nelson Lakeside Park

Distance: 31.7-mile loop

Approximate riding time: 2.25 hours

Best bike: Road or hybrid

Terrain and surface type: Rolling, on paved roads

Highlights: Great beach at the trailhead, Baker Park, Lake Rebecca Park, old-town charm in Long Lake and Delano, open country roads

Hazards: Watch traffic on Wayzata Boulevard and crossings of US 12

Maps: *USGS Excelsior*

Getting there: From US 12, take the Long Lake exit and follow Wayzata Boulevard 1.8 miles to Nelson Lakeside Park. GPS: N 44 59.227 W 93 34.177

THE RIDE

Time your ride for an early morning departure and enjoy beauteous sunrise views across the entire length of Long Lake. Originally known as Cumberland Town in 1855, the little village was made up of the traditional makings of a town, like the general store, schoolhouse, and sawmill. A flour mill and hotel followed, and in the early 1900s the young town enjoyed a successful run producing strawberries and raspberries, filling orders from as far away as North Dakota and ramping up promotion of the red delicacies through the newly established Minnesota Fruit Growers Association.

Ride west on Wayzata Boulevard to Brown Road, following the bike path north past wooded residential neighborhoods to CR 6, shoot over to Willow Drive, and keep heading northbound, gradually leaving the "suburbs" of Long Lake for rural country of farms and woods. The 2-mile stretch along CR 24 skirts the northern edge of Baker Park Reserve, a 2,700-acre portion of Three Rivers Park District enveloping Katrina Lake and hugging the eastern shore of Lake Independence. Turn north again at CR 19, riding away from Lake Independence through scattered farm fields, and dart west just before reaching the diminutive burg of Loretto. Cruise west for about 7 flat miles to a gradual coast to County Line Road, at the far southwest corner of Lake Rebecca Park Reserve, another Three Rivers Parks gem packed with wildlife, copious wetland areas, and a Trumpeter Swan reintroduction program. The park also has around 4 miles of rolling mountain bike trails that are a blast to ride, so keep this fat tire destination in mind for another day.

Follow CR 30's descent to River Street and ride south into Delano along the Crow River. Long the home and hunting range of the Sioux and Chippewa Indians, white settlers moved in to the area in the early 1800s, and the start of a settlement here began with a trading post at Lake Pulaski, accessed via a primitive road from the Minneapolis lakes area. The first peoples to set down roots in what would become Delano likely traveled this road, living in ramshackle shanties as a village slowly developed around them. The

Bike Shop

A proud part of the Long Lake area since 1993, **Gear West Bike & Triathlon** continues its tradition as a great neighborhood shop and key player on the Midwest tri scene. Owner Kevin O'Connor, an accomplished elite-level athlete, channels his competitive fire to superb customer service and shop-sponsored events. 1786 W. Wayzata Blvd., Long Lake; (952) 473-0093; gearwestbike.com.

railroad stepped up the area's growth rate, with agriculture and industrial shops sprouting rapidly. Delano's working-class roots still run deep, with a still-strong sense of community and an inviting historic downtown near the river. Stop for a raspberry shake at the family-run Peppermint Twist Drive-in, and ride south out of town on CR 17, along the river back into rural environs with some ups and downs to the final, 3-mile westbound track toward Long Lake. Cross US 12 carefully one more time and roll down the last mile to the trailhead for a post-ride swim.

MILES AND DIRECTIONS

0.0 Start at Nelson Lakeside Park. Ride out of the park on Lake Street and west on Wayzata Boulevard to Brown Road.

0.3 Turn right onto Brown Road.

1.0 Turn left onto CR 6.

1.4 Turn right onto Willow Drive.

2.9 Turn left onto CR 24.

5.4 Turn right onto CR 19.

7.5 Turn left onto CR 11.

14.0 Junction with County Line Road. Continue straight ahead on CR 30.

14.7 Left turn onto River Street.

16.0 Cross US 12 and ride south on CR 17.

20.1 Left turn onto CR 6.

27.6 Turn left onto 6th Avenue North.

30.4 Right turn onto Willow Drive.

31.0 Left turn onto Wayzata Boulevard.

31.7 Arrive back at the Nelson Lakeside Park trailhead.

Long Lake—Delano Loop

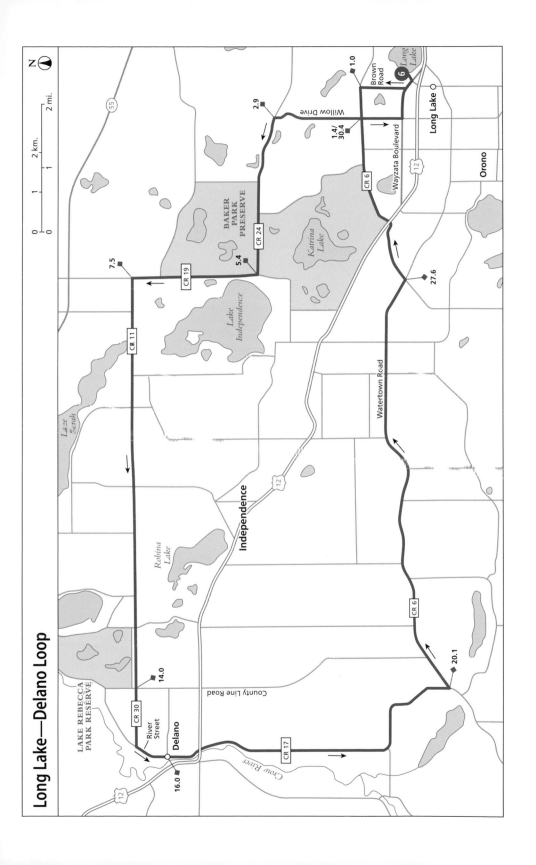

N

0   1   2 km.

0   1   2 mi.

BAKER PARK PRESERVE

Katrina Lake

Lake Independence

LAKE REBECCA PARK RESERVE

Robina Lake

Lake Sarah

Long Lake

Brown Road

Willow Drive

Wayzata Boulevard

Long Lake

Orono

CR 6

CR 24

CR 19

CR 11

CR 30

River Street

Delano

County Line Road

Crow River

CR 17

CR 6

Watertown Road

Independence

1.0

2.9

1.4/ 30.4

5.4

7.5

14.0

16.0

20.1

27.6

6

12

12

12

55

RIDE INFORMATION

Restaurants

Burgers and creamy delicious shakes at **The Peppermint Twist,** 115 Babcock Blvd. W, Delano; (763) 972-2572; thepepperminttwist.com.

Belly up to the bar or score a quiet corner table at the **Red Rooster,** a lively pub and restaurant with traditional favorites like Summer Brat Night and Taco Night. 1832 Wayzata Blvd., Long Lake; (952) 473-4089; redrooster.com.

Area events

Bring the family out for **Concerts in the Park** at Delano's Central Park Gazebo, Wednesday evenings; delano.mn.us.

Luce Line State Trail

A Minnesota rail-trail gem, the multiuse Luce Line traces a 63-mile route from cul-de-sacs to tumbleweeds, following the path of the former Electric Short Line Railroad. This 28-mile stretch passes through maple woodland and remnant tall-grass prairie with a quiet country road feel, great views, and plentiful wildlife.

Start: Vicksburg Lane and 10th Avenue North in Plymouth

Distance: 28.5 miles one way to Winsted, 56 miles out and back, with options for more or less at any point on the trail

Approximate riding time: 1 hour to all day

Best bike: Hybrid, road bike with wider tires, or cyclocross bike

Terrain and surface type: Flat ride on crushed limestone surface

Highlights: Flat, easy-going ride, Wood-Rill SNA, great open country views, lots of mileage options

Hazards: Use caution at road crossings; stay alert for random wildlife on the trail

Maps: *USGS Osseo*

Getting there: From I-494 in Plymouth, exit CR 6 and head west 1.4 miles to Vicksburg Lane and turn left. Parking and trailhead about 0.4 mile south at 10th Avenue. GPS: N 44 59.361 W 93 28.951

Bike Shop

Chad Czmowski somehow finds time to run his **Outdoor Motion** bike shop along with being active on practically every Hutchinson-area committee, board, and group around. An equally enthusiastic staff accompanies him at 141 Main St., Hutchinson; (320) 587-2453; outdoor motionbikes.com.

MILES AND DIRECTIONS

0.0 Start at Vicksburg Lane trailhead in Plymouth.

0.5 Cross a cool trestle bridge over a peninsula of Gleason Lake.

2.6 Roll past the Wood-Rill SNA.

3.8 Cross US 12.

7.1 Skirt past north side of Stubbs Bay.

16.8 Pass north shore of Oak Lake near Watertown.

19.4 Cross Crow River in Watertown.

28.5 Arrive at Winsted Lake and county park.

RIDE INFORMATION

Restaurants

The **Luce Line Lodge** is a go-to favorite, with a long list of irresistible flatbreads and pizza, and a side order of history with the Lodge's railway past decor. 305 Lewis Ave. S, Watertown; (952) 955-1305; luceline lodge.com.

Get a mid-ride chicken sandwich at the **Blue Note Bar & Ballroom,** 320 3rd St. S, Winsted; (320) 485-9698; bluenoteballroom.com.

Area events

Summertime in small-town Minnesota is alive with festivals celebrating heritage, community, and the brief and beautiful absence of snow cover. Hutchinson's **Riversong Festival** showcases the region's artistic and musical talents, like Lucy Micelle and the Velvet Lapelles and kids' tunes by the Bunny Clogs; riversongfestival.org.

In Hutchinson, cycling is not the only hobby on wheels. As a tribute to the Luce Line's past, the Luce Line Railroad Club in Hutchinson hosts model railroad shows and displays to keep Minnesota railroad history alive and moving and preserve memories of a bygone era. Cyclists passing through Hutchinson can trade one set of wheels for another and be a kid again while exploring the fascinating world of model railroads.

LRT Loop

This 30-mile loop with a tail features two of the region's premier rail-trails, linked on the western end by rolling county roads and jam-packed with postcard scenery. Dramatic, river bluff views along the southern corridor complement spacious suburban environs to the north, and multiple trailheads make it easy to custom-build a perfect day on the bike.

Start: Depot Coffee House in Hopkins, 9451 Excelsior Blvd., Hopkins

Distance: 30 miles for the full loop. Southern corridor trail covers 11 miles to Chaska. Northern corridor trail is roughly 15 miles to Victoria.

Approximate riding time: 2–3 hours for the full loop

Best bike: Road bike with wider tires, hybrid, or cyclocross bike

Terrain and surface type: Trails follow flat routes on hardpacked, crushed limestone; roads are rolling on smooth tarmac

Highlights: Birch Island Woods, Seminary Fen, National Wildlife Refuge, Carver Park Reserve, spic-and-span neighborhoods of the western suburbs

Hazards: Use caution at road crossings and along county roads between Chaska and Victoria.

Other considerations: Be aware of less-than-ideal trail conditions after heavy rains, and watch for other cyclists, runners, and walkers.

Maps: *USGS Hopkins*

Getting there: From US 169, exit Excelsior Boulevard. Depot Coffeehouse is 0.1 mile east of 169. GPS: N 44 55.434 W 93 23.962

LRT trail near Dell Road in Eden Prairie

THE RIDE

The LRT regional trails are key cogs in the southwest metro area cycling experience. Blending cityscapes, wooded parkland, and river bluff country, these trails embody the variety of a Minnesota bike ride, all within an established rail-trail system perfect for leisure riders and eco-friendly commuters alike. The two former rail corridors combine to make three popular trail segments: Cedar Lake, Minnesota River Bluffs, and Lake Minnetonka, the latter two featured on this loop.

Bike Shops

Five-time Top 100 Bicycle Retailer **Bokoo Bikes** wows customers in their Rodeo Drive worthy store with bikes and paddle gear stacked floor to sky-high ceiling. Close to the LRT trail at 550 Lake Dr. E, Chanhassen; (952) 934-6468; bokoobikes.com.

Best Bike Rides Minneapolis and St. Paul

The Rolling Stones anthem "You Can't Always Get What You Want" was allegedly inspired by the town's roving ambassador, Mr. Jimmy. According to local lore, Mick Jagger ran into Mr. Jimmy at an Excelsior drugstore after performing at a nearby venue. Mr. Jimmy ordered a cherry Coke but received a regular Coke instead, and turned to Jagger and said, "You can't always get what you want." The song's lyrics mention a drugstore, a cherry Coke, and a Mr. Jimmy, and though the Stones have never verified the legend, Excelsior's love for this special town character, who passed away in 2007, keeps the story alive and well.

The Cedar Lake Trail (featured in Ride 2) ends at the Depot Coffeehouse and from here, the two LRT branches fork to their respective western destinations. Both are surfaced with hardpacked, crushed limestone on grades of less than 5 percent. The southern branch, the Minnesota River Bluffs Trail, traverses Minnetonka and Eden Prairie on the way to Chaska, through largely well-to-do residential neighborhoods veiled from view on the trail by a buffer of mature trees. The Lake Minnetonka Trail wanders through Minnetonka and Excelsior to Victoria. Akin to many other Twin Cities bike routes, these conduits are convenient avenues of escape into the natural treasures right outside our doors.

From the Depot, roll out with an arrow-straight 1.5 miles through Minnetonka commercial areas to Shady Oak Road, the portal to a scenic corridor of lakes, wetlands, woods, and intermittent meadows. Cruise between Shady Oak and Minnetoga Lakes to Rowland Road and a side trip trail well worth a look. One fork of the spur loops east over hill and dale and past a restored prairie to Lone Lake Park for a great lakeside picnic stop, while the other side of the fork leads south about 2 miles to Bryant Lake Regional Park and more trail mileage. On the main path, ride beneath I-494 to the Baker Road crossing. Stay alert here at this busy road for traffic whizzing by. High-speed traffic and urban buzz aside, the wide swath of wetland bordering Glen Lake to the northwest is a favorite haunt of white-tailed deer and a bevy of bird life, including the likes of great blue herons and snowy egrets. The trail hops the Crosstown Highway over a short bridge and continues toward Birch Island Lake. Plan time for a side trip at the Edenvale Boulevard/Indian Chief Road junction. About 200 yards north on Indian Chief Road is the Birch Island Woods Conservation Area, a small jewel of water, woods, and wetlands preserved by the city of Eden Prairie and determined citizens. A 0.5-mile trail through the woods

Holy Land

Across Flying Cloud Drive near the end of the LRT trail is one of Minnesota's most prized natural gifts. **Seminary Fen,** named for the Catholic seminary once standing on the grounds, is a calcareous fen, the rarest type of wetland, which forms on the lower flanks of glacial moraines, such as the high limestone bluffs along the Minnesota River. Calcium-charged water rises to the surface and maintains a thick layer of peat, subsequently sustaining a habitat for equally rare plant species, like the marsh arrow-grass and white lady's slipper. There are only around 500 calcareous fens left on the planet, and nearly 200 of them are right here in Minnesota. Near constant threats from development and other human impacts haunt the fen like a spectral ghoul (driving a bulldozer), but heroic efforts by state officials have realized this area's importance and the fen is currently intact and healthy.

treats visitors to elegant hardwood forest punctuated with wild bird calls and the Picha Heritage Farm, a 100-year-old Eden Prairie homestead (don't forget a bucket to load up on fresh raspberries!). Ride past quiet neighborhoods to the bike/pedestrian bridge over Valley View Road, a modern-day replacement of the former Graffiti Bridge, made famous in the 1960s by antiwar protesters making their views known with cans of spray paint. The outdoor artwork tradition continued with another burst of legend for the bridge, when it was prominently featured in *Purple Rain,* the 1984 movie starring local music hero Prince. The bridge was demolished a year later to accommodate a growing Eden Prairie. From here the trail rolls along to pass under MN 5 and follows US 212 to Eden Prairie Road, where a detour right turn leads to a rest stop at the historic Smith Douglas More house, an 1877 vintage house restored by the city and now home to a Dunn Bros. Coffee shop. Back on track, follow a winding section over US 212, past Miller Park, and onward to the ritzy Bearpath gated community of immense homes surrounded by manicured grounds spiffy enough to make English royalty proud. Exiting Bearpath, the trail shoots through Riley Lake Park and past Eden Prairie's oldest settler homestead, the Jacques-Riley home.

Pioneer Road unofficially marks the start of bluff country above the Minnesota River Valley, with great views and long stretches of dense woods and an active wildlife scene, especially in the form of deer, fox, rabbits, and scores of bird species. The path drops in a lazy bend and crosses an earthen bridge over a deep ravine, once spanned by an 1800s wooden trestle bridge. Ogle sweeping views of the river valley from here, followed by more of the same of

Shakopee and the wider valley to the west. Watch out at the MN 101 crossing, as the trees and blind turns hide traffic barreling along the steep road. Skirt the edge of the deep V of Bluff Creek Ravine and reach Bluff Creek Drive at mile 12. The path continues a short distance to Flying Cloud Drive but dead-ends there. (In need of refreshment? One additional mile on that busy, unfriendly road takes you to Chaska, where you can hit up the Holiday convenience store or McDonald's for a quick in and out.)

To start the link to the northern corridor LRT, head north on Bluff Creek Drive, gradually climbing out of the river valley, passing beneath US 212 and winding through Pioneer Pass Park. This connector stretch through Chanhassen is a bright highlight of the ride, mixing bike path routes through scenic parks like Bluff Creek Preserve with easygoing neighborhood riding. Wind along Stone Creek to a jog west to Galpin Boulevard, a main thoroughfare through the city, but flanked with a bike path for smooth sailing northbound to Lake Lucy Road. A big hunk of open space has been miraculously left alone to the west of Lakes Lucy and Ann, and future trails are planned to circulate near the lakes. A quick ride up Yosemite Avenue past Clasen Lake leads to Mill Street, and about 0.5 mile north is the junction and crossing of MN 7 to the Lake Minnetonka LRT, the northern corridor route.

Ride northeast into the welcoming streets of Excelsior and a must-stop at Adele's Frozen Custard. If you timed your ride right, alternate gulps of custard with long gazes at sunset views over Excelsior Bay, then roll on eastward past the southern bays of Lake Minnetonka, through ritzy Deephaven neighborhoods, and past some light industrial areas. This last stretch closely follows Minnetonka Boulevard, then curves south once past Shady Oak Road, coursing through dense woods that keeps the trail in perpetual shade and cools you down on the steamiest of summer days. Follow the trail past MN 7 to Main Street in Hopkins (a great hot rod cruisin' hangout back in the day) and hang a right onto 5th Avenue, dropping south past Excelsior Boulevard to the southern corridor trail, and drift back east to the Depot.

MILES AND DIRECTIONS

0.0 Start at Depot trailhead.

1.5 Shady Oak Road underpass.

2.1 Pass Dominick Drive and spur trail to swimming beach at Shady Oak Lake.

2.7 Pass Rowland Road and optional spur to Lone Lake Park and Bryant Lake Regional Park.

Area events

Excelsior's legacy as a destination for fun in the sun on the shores of Lake Minnetonka is as strong as ever. The town embraces its reputation and finds excuses for celebration at seemingly any given moment throughout the year. No surprise here, but the brightest of them all is the **Fourth of July,** when Excelsior's town park hosts a legendary fireworks show over the lake, accompanied by a performance by the Minnesota Orchestra; ci.excelsior.mn.us.

The Hiawatha Bicycling Club hosts the annual **Tour D'Amico Bike Tour** in Eden Prairie on July 4. Choose from three different routes (31, 44, and 60 miles) with full support and rest stops at D'Amico & Sons restaurants, followed by an Italian buffet lunch; tourdamico.org.

Chaska Loop

The idyllic countryside of Carver County has long been a go-to area for local cycling clubs. This 16-mile, boot-shaped loop primer rises out of the cozy Minnesota River valley to Ireland-like hill and dale for a short tour around crop fields and horse farms on rolling terrain with oft-present, and challenging, winds.

Start: Firemen's Park in downtown Chaska (Chaska Boulevard and CR 41)

Distance: 16-mile loop

Approximate riding time: 1.5 hours

Best bike: Road

Terrain and surface type: Rolling on smooth, paved roads

Highlights: Quaint, riverside ambiance, bucolic farmsteads, great river valley views

Hazards: Moderate traffic; some roads have low to no shoulders

Other considerations: Stay alert on country roads with low shoulders

Maps: *USGS Shakopee*

Getting there: Firemen's Park is in the heart of downtown Chaska. From CR 41, go west on Chaska Boulevard 1 block to the park. GPS: N 44 47.351 W 93 36.220

9

THE RIDE

This south metro river town squashes any preconceived notions that Minnesota's terra firma is a drab, monotonous landscape. Indeed, there is a reason that local cycling clubs return to this area time after time. Starting in the heart of Chaska, a charming and tidy town nestled against the Minnesota River, this ride rapidly trades the quaint downtown for a brilliant horizon of horse farms and rolling hillsides. The route follows the same course as the bike leg of the River City Days Triathlon, climbing out of town past forests and well-manicured residential land out into the country, and looping back into Chaska.

The ride begins at Firemen's Park, inspired and built by area firefighters giving back to the city and cleaning up remains of an 1800s-era brickyard. The park sports picnic shelters, a playground, beach, and plenty of parking. Attentively maintained by the city's Parks and Recreation Department, this is also the site for fishing contests, reunions, sporting events, and musical performances throughout the year. A few blocks away, in City Square, are several Indian mounds dating to the early 1700s, evidence of the earliest residents of the area.

Head out onto Chaska Boulevard and make a swift right onto Creek Road, rapidly leaving behind the laid-back buzz of the town for the calming flow of Chaska Creek. The creek's namesake road begins a steady, winding incline straight away, serving up a 1.5-mile warm-up, with a phalanx of dense woods bordering the narrow V passage out of the cozy confines of the river valley. Unseen from the road, cul-de-sacs encroach on the bluff top, seemingly ready to spill over into the narrow valley. Cool and calm underneath the deciduous canopy, Creek Road continues to climb nearly 300 feet to emerge in a roller-coaster landscape of ribboned crop fields watched over by tidy farmsteads. Prepare for ubiquitous breezes up here that of course never seem to be in the form of a tailwind. At the crest of the hill, the road ducks beneath US 212 and curves gently past a couple of farms to Engler Boulevard, a typically low-traffic road with big ol' shoulders, and horizon-wide views of rolling farmland—open country riding at its finest. The route heads north on Guernsey

Bike Shop

The classic garage-born success story, **Paul's Bicycle Repair Shop** began as a repairs-only hobby and now takes requests from all over the world for expert restoration of classics like Schwinn Krates and Speedsters. A family-run, hometown shop, at 120 Holmes St., Shakopee; (952) 688-6820; paulsbicyclerepair.com.

> ## The Landing
>
> Just a short drive north from Chaska on US 169 is **The Landing** (still affectionately called by its former "Murphy's Landing" title by us longtime locals), a fascinating heritage park on the Minnesota River in Shakopee. The 88-acre living museum has been part of this area since 1969, and it still offers visitors an up-close look at authentic nineteenth-century buildings, interpretive tours, and a December holiday festival.

Avenue through more farm-centered landscape to the outskirts of Victoria, turning left just before reaching MN 5 and loping back west and south past a half-dozen picturesque lakes. Keep your eyes open for ducks and geese doing fly-bys near Wasserman and Pierson Lakes. Jog over to CR 43, and ride southbound through the common refrain on this ride: rolling farmland all around. CR 140 shoots back east, under US 212 and into scattered residential with good views of the river valley before gliding back into the woods on a gradual descent into Chaska.

MILES AND DIRECTIONS

0.0 Start at Firemen's Park. Ride west on Chaska Boulevard to Creek Road.

1.0 Turn right onto Creek Road (CR 10), climbing out of the river valley.

2.7 Turn left onto Engler Boulevard (CR 10).

3.1 Turn right onto Guernsey Avenue (CR 11).

6.3 Turn left at Church Lake Boulevard (CR 43).

> Stroll through downtown Chaska and it is plain to see the town literally has color —the characteristic yellow of its brick buildings. Chaska's land alongside the Minnesota River possesses rich, uniquely colored clay, which made brick manufacturing an important part of the young city's economy in the 1850s. The prized bricks and larger, construction-worthy stones were shipping to St. Paul by steamboat, and many of the state's capital city buildings also originated from Chaska clay.

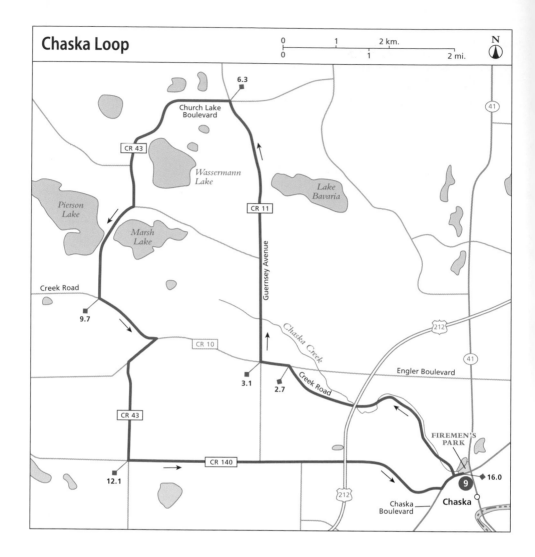

Chaska Loop

9.7 Turn left onto CR 10.

10.5 Right turn onto CR 43.

12.1 Turn left onto CR 140.

15.5 Turn left onto Chaska Boulevard.

16.0 Arrive back at Firemen's Park trailhead.

RIDE INFORMATION

Restaurants

Shamelessly replenish burned calories with a few pickin's from the menu of old-fashioned goodies at **Tommy's Malt Shop,** hometown-owned since 2005, and only 5 blocks south of the trailhead at 2 River Bend Place; (952) 227-0263; tommysmaltshop.com.

Pizza, giant sandwiches, cold brew. Perfect training food. Served up on the riverside patio at **Cuzzy's Brick House,** 2880 Chaska Blvd.; (952) 448-5594; cuzzys.com.

Area events

The largest **Renaissance Festival** in the country kicks off every year in late August, in the woods next to the Minnesota River. A tradition since 1971, the festival boasts over 250 artisan booths, live entertainment, jousting, and delicious food of all kinds, in a lively tribute to medieval times; renaissancefest .com.

the Bush Lake Ski Jump on the way in (go ahead, you know you want to try it) and access for a nice loop around Normandale Lake. There is no trail access from the ski hill side, so turn back south from the nature center, and at the junction across from Bush Lake, turn left to ride through scattered pines and into a short finger of dense woods to an easy descent into a more meadow-based environment. Keep following a clockwise direction into the park's interior, gradually descending to one more junction looping around past the overflow parking area to the north side of Hyland Lake and the visitor center.

You're just getting warmed up, so ride back on the trail you started on, but this time keep on southbound past Sumac Knoll, leaning right and into the woods. Follow this trail to the park's southern boundary and exit into the parking lot of Quality Bicycle Products (see sidebar). The rest of this southern extension is on city streets (and one riverside trail), so switch your alert level to match the increase in traffic. Ride south on Hampshire Avenue and carefully cross Old Shakopee Road into a large light industrial area. Take a quick jog over to Minnesota Bluffs Drive and cruise the wide road to Bloomington Ferry Road, the old route down the hill to cross the river. Follow Crest Avenue (a new name for the Ferry Road's descent to the river) on its steep drop to the bike/pedestrian bridge. For decades, the now-dismantled highway bridge was a vital link for commuters heading to the office from the young and growing south metro, with a parade of cars creeping slowly along the winding roadway. A big replacement river crossing was moved just a short trip upstream,

QBP—Keeping the Bike Industry Rolling

At the southern end of Hyland Park is **Quality Bicycle Products,** the largest bicycle parts distributor in the industry and supplier to over 5,000 independent dealers. Founder Steve Flagg has watched his company grow at a meteoric pace, from humble beginnings in a small St. Paul office to the current 135,000-square-foot facility in Bloomington. Winner of an armload of best-of honors, QBP's headquarters is environmentally friendly, from its waterless toilets to the natural lighting through walls of windows and directed skylights, and those efforts earned the company Gold LEED certification. Continuously active in bicycle advocacy, QBP is a regular presence at federal-level funding initiatives and a key player in the planning and creation of bike route and trail-building actions, like the nationally recognized Cuyuna Lakes Trail near Brainerd, Minnesota, and trail standard leader Lebanon Hills in Eagan. QBP's employees, of course, are big fans of commuting, collectively logging over 350,000 miles in 2008 alone. No surprise that this is a perennial winner of national and local "best places to work" awards.

Interior woods at Hyland Park

leaving this corridor to the self-propelled crowd. Cross the river and ride the trail (the old road) along the river flats to its terminus at MN 101. Imagine the spring flood of 1965, submerging this road under 20 feet of muddy water.

Backtrack across the bridge and up the hill to option B of this southern stretch. Turn east onto Auto Club Road, a fun and curvy cruise past the manicured grounds of the Minnesota Valley Country Club. This road was named for the Minneapolis Automobile Club's site located on this section of the bluff in the early 1900s. The original building burned down in 1918, was replaced soon after with a bigger and fancier one, and enjoyed great success until business could not be carried through the long winters. The buildings were eventually razed in the 1950s to accommodate homesite development. Curve past the country club to River Bluff Drive and ride through the ritzy neighborhood back to Auto Club Road and the return. Retrace your route back to QBP and the park trails to the visitor center.

MILES AND DIRECTIONS

0.0 Start at visitor center trailhead.

0.3 Turn right at first junction.

0.7 Cross the entrance road.

0.9 Stay left, paralleling Bush Lake Road.

1.8 Pass the Bush Lake Beach entrance.

2.3 Left turn at this junction across from Bush Lake.

3.6 Turn right to head to interior of the park.

4.2 Continue straight ahead at this junction.

4.4 Left turn at this junction, curving around to Hyland Lake's north shore.

5.0 Arrive back at the visitor center trailhead. Ride south for the bonus leg of this route.

For over one hundred years, daredevil athletes have soared through the air at the Bush Lake Ski Jumps in Bloomington. The Minneapolis Ski Club sponsors an active jumping club and annual tournaments, and "try it out" sessions for all ages; mscnordic.com.

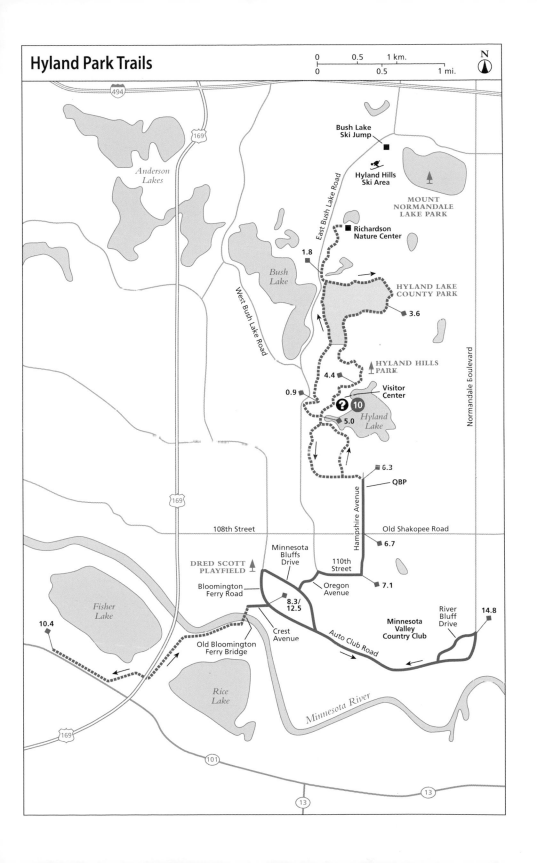

Hyland Park Trails

0   0.5   1 km.
0   0.5   1 mi.

N

494

169

Anderson Lakes

169

West Bush Lake Road

East Bush Lake Road

Bush Lake

Bush Lake Ski Jump

Hyland Hills Ski Area

MOUNT NORMANDALE LAKE PARK

Richardson Nature Center

1.8

HYLAND LAKE COUNTY PARK

3.6

HYLAND HILLS PARK

4.4

0.9

Visitor Center

? 10

Hyland Lake

5.0

Normandale Boulevard

6.3

QBP

Hampshire Avenue

108th Street

Old Shakopee Road

6.7

DRED SCOTT PLAYFIELD

Minnesota Bluffs Drive

110th Street

7.1

Bloomington Ferry Road

Oregon Avenue

Fisher Lake

10.4

8.3/ 12.5

Minnesota Valley Country Club

River Bluff Drive

14.8

Crest Avenue

Old Bloomington Ferry Bridge

Auto Club Road

Rice Lake

Minnesota River

169

101

13

13

6.3 Exit the park at the parking lot of Quality Bicycle Products, and head south on Hampshire Avenue.

6.7 Junction with West Old Shakopee Road. Watch traffic and head straight across.

7.1 Turn right at 110th Street.

7.4 Turn left at Oregon Avenue.

7.6 Turn right at Minnesota Bluffs Drive.

8.0 Turn left onto Bloomington Ferry Road.

8.3 Turn right onto Crest Avenue. This is the old route down the hill to the former Ferry Bridge river crossing.

10.4 Reach junction of MN 101. Take a break and retreat back to the river and up the hill.

12.5 Turn right onto Auto Club Road.

14.8 Left turn at River Bluff Drive.

15.2 Right turn to backtrack on Auto Club Road.

16.3 Veer right to Minnesota Bluffs Drive.

16.7 Right turn onto Oregon Avenue.

16.9 Right turn onto 110th Street.

17.2 Turn left onto Hampshire Avenue. Ride north all the way back to QBP and the park trails.

18.0 Back into the park on the bike path.

19.0 Arrive back at the trailhead.

RIDE INFORMATION

Restaurants

Get your ice cream fix at **Dairy Queen**, at France Avenue and Old Shakopee Road.

Area events

Guided snowshoe hikes through oak forests and open prairies at **Richardson Nature Center** in February. 8737 E. Bush Lake Rd., Bloomington; (763) 694-7676; threeriver sparks.org.

Minnesota River Greenway

Cruise along the meandering Minnesota River on one of the metro's newest trails. The short out and back route winds through the Minnesota Valley National Wildlife Refuge and comes complete with a bike repair station and picnic area at the trailhead.

Start: Minnesota Riverfront Park Black Dog trailhead, east of I-35W on Black Dog Road

Distance: 7.5 miles out and back

Approximate riding time: 1 hour

Best bike: Road or hybrid

Terrain and surface type: Flat paved path

Highlights: Quiet river cruise, wildlife, access to more miles at both ends of the trail

Hazards: Possible high water during traditional spring flooding

Maps: *USGS Bloomington*

Getting there: From I-35W, exit at Black Dog Road. Go east 0.2 mile to the trailhead parking area on north side of the road.
GPS: N 44 80.054 W 93 28.543

Curving along the river

THE RIDE

When completed, the Minnesota River Greenway will travel through Burnsville, Eagan, and Mendota Heights on its way to Lilydale Regional Park. Connector trails from there deliver cyclists hither and yon through St. Paul and beyond. This short out and back sampler tours along the Minnesota River on silky smooth new trail.

Minnesota River Greenway

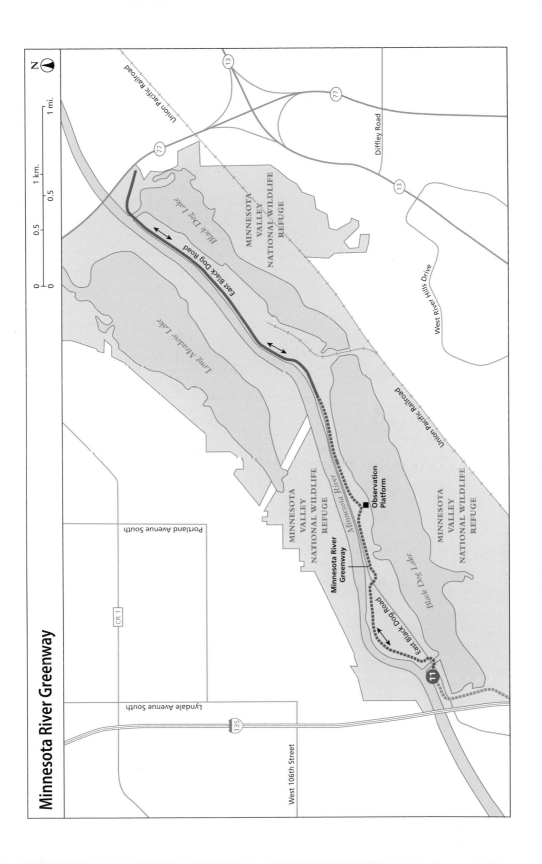

11

Black Dog Village

Around 1750, the Dakota chief Black Dog and his band of about 250 set up a village on the spit of land between the Minnesota River and Black Dog Lake, named after the chief.

From Minnesota Riverfront Park on Black Dog Road, ride eastbound paralleling the river on your left and Black Dog Lake on your right. After a couple of lazy curves, the trail reaches a spur path leading to an observation platform with beauteous views of the lake and hordes of lively wildlife. This is part of the 14,000-acre Minnesota Valley National Wildlife Refuge, a Twin Cities-area gem and one of the largest in the country. Keep an eye out for river otters, wood ducks and many other waterfowl species, and the magnificent bald eagle overhead.

From here, keep riding east, passing through the sprawling Xcel Energy plant property. Past the plant, the trail follows the roadway for the last stretch to Its eastern terminus at the Cedar Avenue Bridge.

About face for the return trip to the trailhead.

MILES AND DIRECTIONS

0.0   Minnesota Riverfront Park trailhead. Ride east along the river.

0.8   Trail crosses Black Dog Road.

1.2   Junction with path to observation deck.

1.9   Arrive at Xcel Energy plant. Follow the trail/roadway.

3.7   Turnaround point at Cedar Avenue Bridge.

7.5   Arrive at trailhead.

Farms and Forests Ride

This 30-miler starts with a rollout across the narrows linking Upper and Lower Prior Lake, and quickly heads out to wide-open countryside. Ride past a dozen lakes, a tiny farming community steeped in local history, and scenic woods on this low-traffic route in Scott County's quiet western reaches.

Start: South Lake Village Mall, at MN 13 and Duluth Avenue

Distance: 30 miles

Approximate riding time: 2 hours

Best bike: Road

Terrain and surface type: Mix of flats and rolling countryside on smooth, paved roads

Highlights: Bucolic farmsteads and scenic, rolling countryside, raptors overhead, low traffic

Hazards: Low to no shoulders on some stretches

Maps: *USGS Prior Lake*

Getting there: From I-35, follow 185th Street west 7 miles to MN 13. Turn left and head 0.7 mile to South Lake Village Mall on south side of road. GPS: N 44 42.311 W 93 26.071

THE RIDE

Like most small towns, Prior Lake grew up around a general store and post office. When the Milwaukee Railroad routed tracks through the narrows between the big lake nearby in the late 1870s, the village and lake were named in honor of Charles Prior, a railroad superintendent. A saloon, blacksmith shop, and hotel followed, and the young town grew to a popular tourist destination, luring visitors from as far away as (gasp!) Minneapolis. The lake and idyllic countryside defined the town for generations, and although the influence of suburbia has changed its personality on the surface, Prior Lake is still a small town at heart.

Carefully cross MN 13 and ride north on Duluth Avenue, coasting down to St. Michael's Church and the junction with Eagle Creek Avenue (CR 21). This is a busy, four-lane road, but bike paths conveniently parallel both sides for safe passage. Curve around to the Wagon Bridge crossing the narrows between Upper and Lower Prior Lake, where the Grainwood House opened in 1879. The grand hotel and entertainment establishment was the fledgling community's siren call, attracting the well-to-do from as far south as the Gulf states and eventually more guests from Minneapolis and St. Paul. Fire destroyed the lakeside resort twice, with the round-two, 1930 fire leaving little to salvage. Past this historical and scenic section of town, the route darts north to the junction with CR 82. Turn left (bike paths accompany this road, as well, for about 2 miles) for a gentle climb up to and past the sprawling Mystic Lake Casino and The Meadows at Mystic Lake golf club. With casino and suburban buzz receding, continue westbound on smooth tarmac past a smattering of lakes hidden now and again behind folds of hills or betwixt trunks of oak and maple trees to Marschall Road. Named for one of Shakopee's earliest homestead families in the Minnesota River Valley a few miles north, this road has long been a main corridor from the river to farming communities to the south. Turn left here and a quick right onto CR 72 to stay on a westward track past scattered subdivisions and open farmland to the miniature community of Marystown. The route turns south here on Marystown Road, traveling through cropland

Bike Shop

Enthusiasm from the staff at **Michael's Cycles** pours out their front door. Inside are top-shelf bikes and gear, skateboards, skis, and snowshoes, and the store's bike rehab program has donated over 200 rejuvenated bikes to the community. Check out weekly group rides with the Great Scott Cycling Club. 16731 MN 13 S, Prior Lake; (952) 447-BIKE; michaels cycles-mn.com.

Rolling countryside

plump with veggie bounty, skirting Geis Lake, and following a barely-there rise to MN 282, an intermittently busy road linking Prior Lake to Jordan. Ride 0.5 mile east to CR 79, a quiet county road with ample shoulders, and head south through more idyllic countryside to CR 10, a short, westbound stretch with the potential for a tad more traffic, and continue southbound on CR 15 to CR 8, both smooth and mellow cruises. After crossing MN 13, the route hugs the lazy U-shaped southern shoreline of Cynthia Lake and passes the Minnesota Horse and Hunt Club, one of the country's premier sport hunting and horse facilities, with 600 acres of rolling, upland prairie and forestland. Roll up to Doherty's Tavern at the junction with Panama Avenue, and sidle up to the bar for a cold beverage to amp up for the ride's homestretch. This crackerbox tavern has changed little over the decades and is still a friendly oasis on a hot summer day.

Just east of Doherty's is a mild climb (finally) that rises quickly above St. Catherine Lake, and the hill's top, with the lake's namesake church at your left shoulder, shows off great views of the small lake and farmland yonder. The ensuing descent lets you coast nearly all the way to the turn back north at CR 87 (Mushtown Road). As the name implies, this road used to be gravel, and many a year saw it turn nearly impassable with frost heaves that seemed to morph before your eyes, and undulating waves of ooze that could stop a burly Chevy pickup in its tracks. No troubles like that today, as the road unfurls in smooth, bituminous bliss up a short climb past McMahon Lake, then along a gradually descending 2 miles, followed by one blip of a hill in the next 2 miles, with postcard views in all directions. (A shout-out here to the author's

If You Build It, They Will Come

A lake as large and diverse as Prior Lake is prime territory for water sports, and Jim Peterson wanted a ski jump. Thwarting his dream, however, was the high cost of actually building the thing and maintaining it. The local water ski enthusiast enlisted a group of like-minded friends, built a jump in 1958, and put on a water ski show to help support their hobby. That one-off show led to the formation of the **Prior Lake Water Ski Association** (known today as Shockwaves), now over 180 strong with regular performances all over the upper Midwest by the club's show team and tournament skiers. Along with wowing the crowds, the group welcomes newbies with ski and wakeboard lessons and sponsors a fun Junior Development team for young 'uns ages 8 to 16. Join them on the water (or at least watch them hit that jump) at splwsa.org.

Quiet country road

boyhood home halfway along this stretch.) Cross CR 68 to a short, roller-coaster section, a wetland and pond busy with waterfowl, and a final series of gentle curves back to Prior Lake. Indulge post-ride at the Dairy Queen, a convenient 200 yards from the finish line.

MILES AND DIRECTIONS

0.0 Start at South Lake Village Mall at MN 13 and Duluth Avenue. Cross the highway and head north on Duluth Avenue.

0.6 Left turn at Eagle Creek Avenue (CR 21).

1.5 Left turn at CR 82.

3.5 Junction with CR 81. Continue westbound.

4.1 Junction with CR 17 (Marschall Road). Turn left.

4.8 Right turn at CR 72.

7.3 Left turn onto Marystown Road (CR 15).

Northfield Loop

This two-college town's laid-back vibe sets the stage for a rolling, 23-mile cruise through verdant farmland and forested valleys, with windy roads and one big ol' climb to keep things interesting. See the latest in wind power technology at the start of the route, and a charming, 1800s-era church mid-ride. Take some time for extra noodling around Northfield's historic downtown and trail along the Cannon River.

Start: Spring Creek soccer fields, 510 E. Jefferson Pkwy.

Distance: 23 miles (18.8 on alternate route)

Approximate riding time: 1.75 hours

Best bike: Road

Terrain and surface type: Flats and rolling hills on low-traffic, paved roads

Highlights: Close-up of Carleton College's wind turbine; scenic, rolling farmland; Valley Grove Church

Hazards: Light traffic in Northfield, lighter yet on country roads

Other considerations: Increased tractor traffic and occasional field detritus on roads during fall harvest

Maps: *USGS Northfield*

Getting there: From MN 3 in Northfield, follow Jefferson Parkway 0.5 mile east to the soccer fields. Ample parking available, and a playground for the kids. GPS: N 44 26.295 W 93 09.178

Wind power

THE RIDE

"Cows, Colleges, and Contentment" is Northfield's offbeat tagline, and a cursory glance leaves the uninitiated with the belief that this is indeed just another sleepy town surrounded by cornfields and cow pastures. Stay awhile, however, and the city's deep historical roots, vibrant spirit, and palpable community feel are evident from downtown to outlying farmsteads. A lumber- and flour-producing hotbed since its inception, Northfield also became, almost simultaneously, a college town when St. Olaf and Carleton Colleges were founded in the late 1800s. The higher education influence and

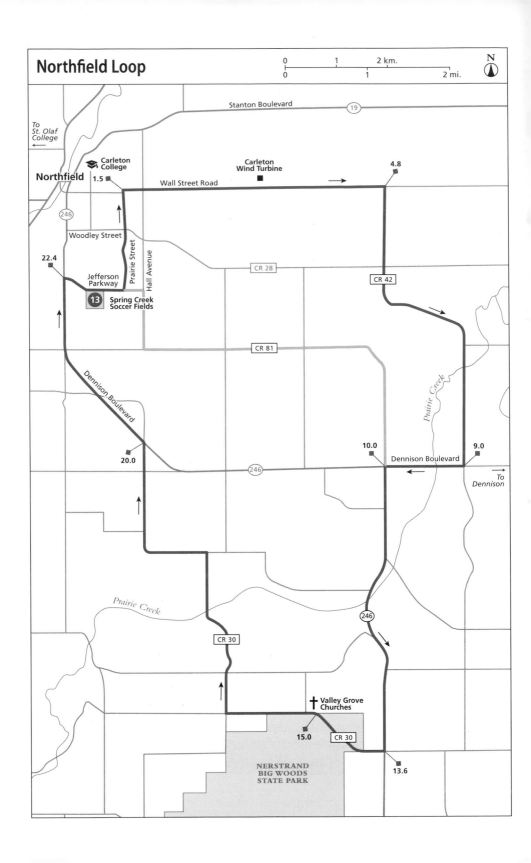

MILES AND DIRECTIONS

0.0 Start at Spring Creek Soccer Fields. Ride east 0.3 mile to Prairie Street.

0.2 Left turn onto Prairie Street.

0.8 Junction with Woodley Street. Continue straight ahead.

1.3 Junction with 7th Street. Municipal pool is 2 blocks west. Continue straight ahead.

1.5 Prairie Street ends and morphs into Wall Street (CR 79), curving eastbound.

3.2 Pass Carleton College's wind turbine.

4.8 Junction with CR 42. Turn right.

5.0 Junction with CR 20. Keep heading south.

9.0 Turn right at Dennison Boulevard.

10.0 Junction with MN 246. Left turn.

13.6 Junction with CR 30. Turn right.

15.0 Valley Grove Churches historic site.

15.8 CR 30 turns hard right, heading north.

17.0 Great valley views, with the big hill dead ahead.

18.0 Crest of the hill. Turn left.

18.6 CR 30 turns hard right, continuing northbound.

20.0 Junction with MN 246. Watch traffic and turn left.

22.4 Junction with Jefferson Parkway. Right turn.

23.0 Arrive back at trailhead.

Alternate route:

Be aware that the stretch of CR 79 and CR 42 are bumpy, teeth-rattling shells of their former selves. We're hoping to see resurfacing soon but for another option, follow this alternate route (resurfaced as of Spring 2018).

0.0 Ride east from the trailhead 0.61 mile to Hall Avenue and go right. This is a short gravel section but typically in great shape.

wilderness routes in the city, epic Iron Range trails, and venerable classics in the far north. So what gives with the turnaround from flyover land to world class? Credit is collectively due to the hardworking riders and local officials who sweated it out for years promoting, building, and maintaining trails, but we can zero in closer on one man, and one determined rider group.

Gary Sjoquist is advocacy director at Quality Bicycle Products in Bloomington, working tirelessly in the name of all that is good with our sport, with regular appearances at federal government legislation throwdowns, trade shows, and local committees. A large chunk of what you see today out on the trails can be linked in some way to Sjoquist's work and crystal ball vision, like the sustainably constructed Lebanon Hills trails in Eagan, used as a model for dozens of other paths; the nationally renowned Cuyuna State Recreation Area trails in Crosby; and his latest lead role in the Minnesota High School Cycling League, which fired the starting gun at its first competition in September 2012.

Mountain bikers should also salute Minnesota Off-Road Cyclists (MORC), a nonprofit, volunteer organization (co-founded by Sjoquist) dedicated to the future of fat tire riding in our state. MORC's handiwork on many of the metro area's premier trails is evident, and under the lead of chair Ryan Lieske, more trails are being consistently added. MORC members are enthusiastically active and put in lots of trail time with tools in hand, providing you with unforgettable off-road riding. Lieske himself is a prime example, a guy who just likes being out in the woods, learned trail-building skills at International Mountain Biking Association (IMBA) camps, and now inspires legions of other fat tire fans. Check the MORC website, morcmtb.org, for a comprehensive trail list, reviews, and updates on events and volunteer opportunities.

Think mountain biking hasn't seen a similar uptick to road riding in the winter months? One look at the packed start line at winter races or any given snow-covered road or pathway will change your tune. Trail riding on a puffy layer of new snow is damn fun, and skittering along an oval track cleared from a frozen lake, with studded tires popping at the ice like miniature firecrackers and holding you right at that adrenaline-fired edge of hitting the deck . . . well, you just have to get out there and check it out.

That said, I have included some of the gems in the Twin Cities area mountain bike trail collection. Yes, there are more out there, lots more, especially in outstate Minnesota and points to the far north. This is just a teaser of what put Minnesota on a meteoric rise to the upper ranks of the destination riding elite.

Theodore Wirth Park

Theodore Wirth Park is not only steeped in local history, it is packed corner to corner with year-round activity for all outdoor lovers, be it on the golf course (club or disc), hiking trails, swimming beach, or skis. The short but lively fat tire trip through the woods is a gem in the Minneapolis park system, with an orbit of feeder trails for express access and après-ride distractions.

Start: Parking available at the lot along Glenwood Avenue on the south side of Wirth Lake. Access also available from Hidden Lakes Parkway and the road south of the golf course clubhouse.

Distance: 4.5 miles total for both loops

Approximate riding time: 30-40 minutes to complete the loop

Best bike: Mountain

Terrain and surface type: Rolling hills on packed singletrack, with short sections of cross-country ski trails

Highlights: Said obstacles above, along with fast and flowing trails in scenic woods, switchback climbs, and jumps

Hazards: Rock gardens and other obstacles, hikers, light traffic at road crossings

Maps: *USGS Minneapolis South*; maps through minneapolisparks.org

Getting there: The official parking lot for bikers is at Glenwood Avenue on the south side of Wirth Lake. From I-394, exit at Penn Avenue and head north to Glenwood Avenue, then left (west) to the parking area at the south end of Wirth Lake. To reach the north loop, ride west on Glenwood Avenue and turn right (north) onto the paved bike trail that runs along Theodore Wirth Parkway, past the railroad tracks, to the Luce Line Trail. Follow the Luce Line to the mountain bike trail gate. N44 98.866 / W93 33.121. The south loop starts at the northwest corner of MN 55 and Theodore Wirth Parkway. GPS: N 44 58.905 W 93 19.248

THE RIDE

T-Wirth is like a Tootsie Roll Pop. Ask a Twin Cities mountain biker to describe Theodore Wirth Park and a likely answer resembles the iconic lollipop, with a shiny, enticing exterior and bonus treat in the middle. This stellar trail system is the result of a solid relationship between MORC, the Minneapolis Parks and Recreation Board, and Minneapolis Off-Road Cycling Advocates (MOCA). Initially just a city demonstration project, the T-Wirth trails show off a sustainably built, safe, and just plain fun trail that is compatible with the park's natural landscapes. The fast and flowing trail rolls around in the park's old hardwood forest on a masterfully planned route perfect for intermediate riders, and scattered obstacles like log piles and jumps challenge experienced riders. Development of more trail miles is in the works, including more challenging terrain and technical features.

Especially cool about the Wirth trails is the spider web of bike trails leading to the park from all around the city, like the Cedar Lake and Luce Line Trails. It's a great warm-up and fun to cruise post-ride to your favorite watering hole.

Start the short, under-1-mile south loop on the singletrack past the trail kiosk and veer left at the first split, climbing gradually to the twisty Enchanted Forest section. All of T-Wirth's main trails run clockwise and one-way, so just follow the path. At the top end of Enchanted Forest, you can roll onto the paved trail to reach the north loop, or continue south on Skyline back to the trailhead.

For the longer north loop, follow the paved trail north over the railroad track to the Luce Line Trail, take a left along the south side of the golf course, and head west to the mountain bike trail gate. The path starts with mostly easygoing curves on the Conundrum and Snake Trails paralleling the railroad track, with a challenging uphill rock garden, then winds deeper into the woods on Hoeg's Hill. The trail crosses the hiking/ski trail on several occasions, so stay alert for hikers. The Twister section stays true to its name and winds around in a convoluted series of bends and rollers to the west side of the oak-dotted

Bike Shops

A fixture in the Twin Cities since 1957, **Penn Cycle's** walls are heavy with best-of awards. Seven area stores with all the right two-wheeled stuff. Closest shop at 710 W. Lake St.; (612) 822-2228; penncycle.com.

One on One Bicycle Studio, a longtime hipster-vibe shop and coffee house that can hand-build a wheel and brew a mean cup of joe. 117 Washington Ave. N; (612) 371-9565; oneononebike.com.

Serpentine turn on the trail
NICK PETTIS

prairie. North of the prairie, the Pond Loop follows a hammerhead course to the North Star Trail and a spur heading into adjacent neighborhoods. Stay right here, starting your return trip southbound. Cruise the long curve of Zip, and fly along sloped turns and a winding downhill, with an optional jump near the exit.

Minnesota's First Skyscraper

Hardly considered a skyscraper by today's standards, the **Foshay Tower** nevertheless was the first one built west of the Mississippi and stood proudly as the tallest in Minneapolis until the IDS tower booted it to second fiddle in 1971. The obelisk shape was inspired by real estate tycoon Wilbur Foshay and intended as a tribute to the Washington Monument. Listed on the National Register of Historic Places, the tower is now home to the W Minneapolis Hotel, and welcomes visitors to the Foshay Museum and Observation Deck. 821 Marquette Avenue; whotels.com.

MILES AND DIRECTIONS

0.0 Start at the Glenwood Avenue trailhead.

0.4 Top of Enchanted Forest trail and access to paved bike path. Stay right to finish loop.

0.7 Back to trailhead. Follow paved trail north across railroad tracks to start the north loop.

1.1 Junction with Luce Line Trail. Turn left into the woods.

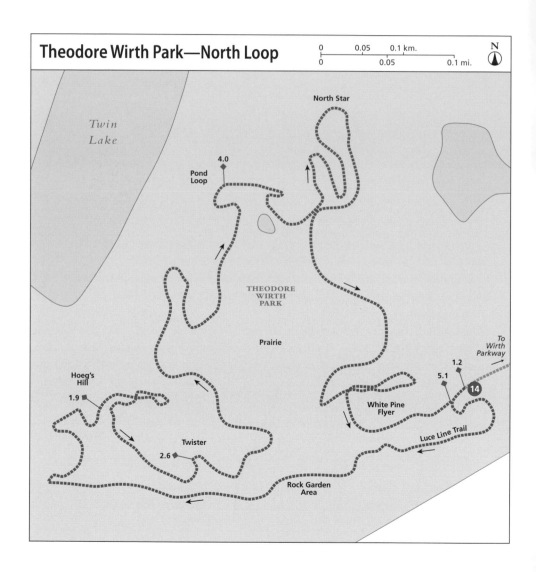

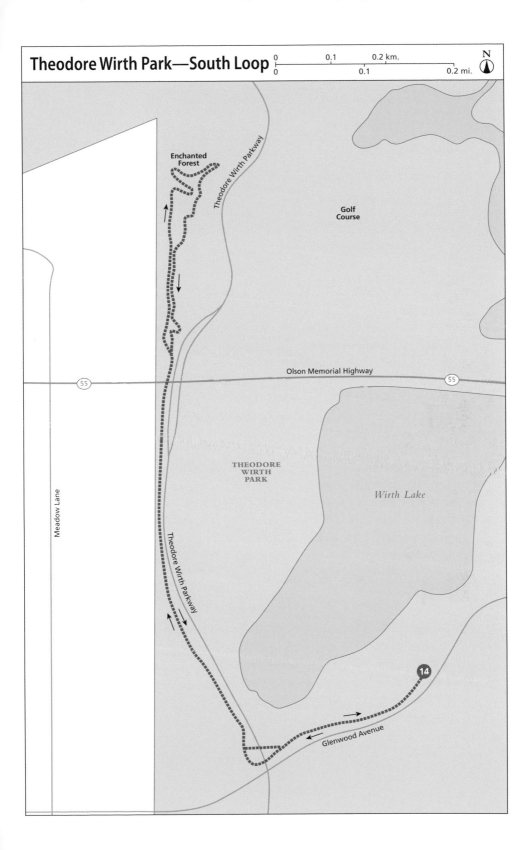

Theodore Wirth Park—South Loop

Enchanted Forest

Theodore Wirth Parkway

Golf Course

Olson Memorial Highway

55

55

Meadow Lane

THEODORE WIRTH PARK

Wirth Lake

Theodore Wirth Parkway

14

Glenwood Avenue

N

0   0.1   0.2 km.
0   0.1   0.2 mi.

1.2 Turn left off the Luce Line onto the singletrack trail into the woods.

1.4 Start climbing toward the rock garden.

1.9 Hoeg's Hill section.

2.6 Dive into the Twister stretch, and curve around to edge of the prairie.

4.1 Start the hammerhead loop around the pond.

4.3 Junction with spur trail to adjacent neighborhoods. Veer right.

4.5 Back to Luce Line Trail. Retrace this and the paved path back to the Glenwood Avenue trailhead.

RIDE INFORMATION

Restaurants

Summertime. Patio table. **Sebastian Joe's** waffle cone. Three ingredients for a perfect day. Ride over after your ride to unwind and reload. Less than 2 miles from T-Wirth on the bike trails. 1007 W. Franklin Ave.; (612) 870-0065; sebastianjoesicecream.com.

Treat yourself to a frosty brew and coal fired pizza at **Black Sheep**; 600 Washington Avenue N; (612) 342-2625; blacksheeppizza.com.

Area events

The City of Lakes Loppet cross-country skiing festival livens up winter with a host of ski races, tours, skijoring competitions, and a bike race held on a frozen course near Uptown. Early February; cityoflakesloppet.com.

South Minneapolis sets the stage for family fun and blazing-fast racing at the midsummer Big Waters Classic **Southside Sprint.** Kids races, stunt shows, great grub, and go-fast pro events. In the south side's 48th and Chicago neighborhood; bigwatersclassic.com.

The giant spoon and cherry at the Minneapolis Sculpture Garden is arguably the most recognized Twin Cities landmark. The oversize utensil and bright red fruit combine to make a unique fountain, with water misting from the cherry's stem. Walk the rest of the 11-acre grounds at 725 Vineland Place; .walkart.org.

Hillside Park

Hillside is mountain biking unplugged. Raw and wild trails flowing naturally over their host terrain, sustainably constructed with the sweat and blood of a core group of committed trail stewards and maintained by MORC. Expect plenty of elevation changes on the 7.5-mile loop with challenging obstacles, along with more mellow sections for beginner riders. And don't miss the supercharged fall and winter racing scene.

Start: Park is located at 10801 181st Ave. NW, Elk River.

Distance: 7.5 miles

Approximate riding time: 50 minutes

Best bike: Mountain

Terrain and surface type: Flat and rolling on hardpacked singletrack. Some short and steep climbs, with about 1,000 feet total elevation gain per lap.

Highlights: As noted above for advanced riders, including a seesaw, elevated log rides, and jumps. Beauteous forest packed full of aged, mixed hardwood with dense understory of ferns, wildflowers, and other shrubbery. "Real" mountain bike experience with natural changes in trail texture, roots, and other surprises.

Hazards: Twisty, technical sections with rocks, logs, roots, and a couple of steep descents. Plagues o' mosquitoes in summer.

Other considerations: Non-resident day-use fee applies. All funds go directly to keeping this one of the area's premier trails. Worth every penny.

Maps: *USGS Elk River*; Hillside Park map

Getting there: From Minneapolis, follow I-94 west to US 169, and north 21 miles to CR 12 in Elk River. Turn right and follow CR 12 1 mile to the Hillside Park entrance. GPS: N 45 17.959 W 93 32.377

THE RIDE

Who knew it would be so much fun to ride on a pile of garbage? Hillside Park is the site of the old town landfill, long ago converted to park land, and in 1999 groundbreaking commenced on a fledgling mountain bike trail. Flying just below the radar of more visible trails in the metro, Hillside has quietly become one of the area's finest trail systems, with a palpable rustic feel and natural features left in place for a more primitive riding experience. Even the remains of the dump add to the ambiance, when big rains uncover, say, a washing machine or kitchen sink. Even an old race car was discovered during trail construction and is now a trailside sculpture. The park boasts the hilliest riding for this part of the state, with hardly any flat sections, but the place is so masterfully designed that brand-new riders will enjoy it just as much as the experts. Four different trail sections roll through the dense woods of Elk River, with rock gardens, balance beams, big teeter-totters, and the Pirate Bridge complete with rope handrails. This is all thanks to Bob Mueller, the original inspiration and builder of the trail, and local resident Rich Ohmdahl, who when approached by Elk River officials to parlay his vision and event promotion experience into a mountain bike trail, ran with it and unveiled some of best riding in the state.

The park is divided into four quadrants, bisected by a skinny gravel road (the old dump road), and run in a counterclockwise direction. From the trailhead, ride into a handsome maple-poplar forest on flowy trail. A teeter-totter comes up for a quick challenge (with a bailout path), and the path loops along the side of a bowl-shaped depression before meandering up and down the side of a bluff. A big climb up the ridge leads to a split (experts left, beginners right). The expert trail goes through a cool rock garden, and the easier option follows a long, obstacle-free descent. The trails rejoin and meet at a little log drop, continuing through the woods on a winding and rolling path into the heart of the park. A second junction appears and takes experts down a jump line made from a series of rocks, embankments, and railroad ties. Beginners stay at elevation above the jump line and rejoin again to cross under the powerline to section 2.

Bike Shop

Forty-one years strong and still a metro favorite, **Erik's Bikes and Boards** does bikes right and sponsors cool events like the Tour de Cure in June, benefiting the American Diabetes Association and treating riders to superb tour routes in Minneapolis and surrounding areas. 2120 Northdale Blvd. NW; Coon Rapids; (763) 862-0091; eriksbikeshop.com.

This is the "easiest" of the four sections (sections 1 and 2 lean toward beginner status), with more beginner terrain and the least amount of obstacles, but still a blast to ride. A sandy/dirt singletrack snakes through the woods to a cool bowl where the trail drops along an S-curve into a bowl and shoots out the other side, rolling along to a tough climb with a sandy switchback and roots at the top. Ride around the top of the hill and descend down a curvy hill over some log steps. There is "seasonal" sand here and there, especially with heavy rains and in low areas. Exit section 2 on a longer descent with curves and sand, around the south side of the back parking area. There is also an optional exit here to the dirt road if you want to bail out early. Yeah, right. This is way too much fun.

Enter section 3 and take on a big descent and switchbacks, with roots and rocks, then into a flowing section ahead of twisty, tight turns with lots of roots, followed by a technical uphill with logs on one side or rocks on the other. No bailout here; just make it happen. Shortly after are stone steps set up like a spiral staircase on the edge of a steep bluff. A crash here sends you careening down the bluff, so ride smart. Fly through the bermed, downhill sweeper into the valley between ridges, then climb the other side on a short, steep grind over more stone steps. From here, twist through the woods and descend to the pirate bridge. The trail drops downhill to the bridge, abruptly climbs the other side of the bluff to a sharp left turn, and back down the hill and under the bridge. Cool. The path here is "armored" with cement pavers and stones and water bars to prevent erosion. Climb the other side of the valley on a significant climb with tight switchbacks on sandy, loose rock to a rest stop on top, and take a moment to stop hyperventilating. Then descend down a bumpy path from the ridge to a low area with an optional log pile obstacle, followed by rollers and longer switchbacks with rocks to climb over at the top of the next ridge. Trace the ridge to a severe downhill, bermed sweep, and climb again past the edge of a back lot to a long, gradual climb to the most challenging rock garden in park. The mature forest is beautiful here, verdant

Fat Tire Riding Unplugged

Hillside Park is home to legendarily fun winter riding and racing. Thirteen determined riders showed up at the first race roughly a decade ago, on a day with -15 temps and a cold north wind. The park is now a regular stop on the Minnesota Mountain Bike Series list of events, and hosts the challenging **SingleTrack Attack** event in July; mnmtbseries .com.

with more ferns and assorted green understory, and less brush. Don't forget to salute Tina on your way by. Perched on a stump trailside, Tina is like Hillside's siren of the forest, brought to "life" by local artist and Hillside upper management Sue Seeger, using discarded treasures found in the woods. Climb again for more ridgetop riding, then hit a big descent to the edge of the power lines, with a couple of skinnies to close out this section.

Section 4 is the longest, at about 3 miles, with the most elevation changes and biggest hills. It's not quite as technical as its predecessor but challenges rider with big climbs and descents. The entire section is either down or up. Follow the rim trail around a wooded depression with occasional dips to the bottom of the bowl. There's a cool section of rollers (little ones perfect for jumps) and curves to the bottom, then climb out along tight curves, tightly packed trees, and a rooty climb. A short plateau along the power lines rolls back to the interior with more big climbs, including a long S-curve with rock drop turns and a steep uphill, and the toughest, and steepest, climb of all with three water bars and a stone step at the top. From here the path meets a cool skinny made from boulders and logs, and sweeps downhill to the crest of the spine ridge of the park. There's a sweet roller-coaster stretch to a big ol' hill called The Shotgun that screams down the face of the bluff, on a big bermed curve back up the bluff to a steep crest, and another raging descent after that. The path climbs over root steps with steep fall lines and back to the interior and dense woods. Tight switchbacks lined with trees and logs lead to a descent to a sandy section, then a climb past handlebar-width trees to a series of curves and a steep drop to the edge of the road. The homestretch is fast and flowing with plenty of downhill reward for your efforts.

The mileages shown below are estimates and often in flux.

MILES AND DIRECTIONS

0.0 Start at the trailhead. Ride south into section 1, following either the more difficult or easiest trail options. The more difficult trail meets a teeter after just the third turn, and a rock garden about halfway through.

1.0 Expert jumpline.

2.0 Trail crosses power line corridor and into section 2. Two trail options here again (the easy path exits section 1 and stays to the west side of section 2, with a second option staying left and center).

2.2 Cross a rough-cut skinny.

2.3 Pass through the Fridge ravine.

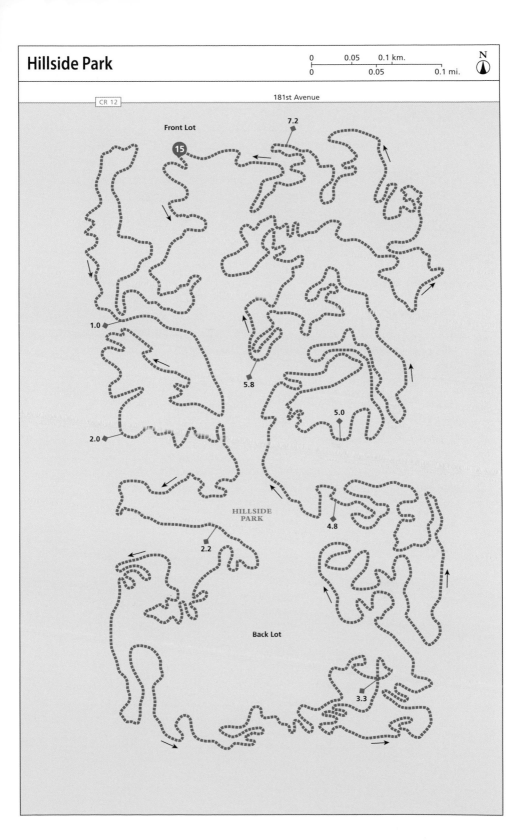

Hillside Park

181st Avenue

CR 12

Front Lot

7.2

15

1.0

5.8

5.0

2.0

HILLSIDE PARK

4.8

2.2

Back Lot

3.3

3.0 Blend into section 3, with an easy option following the outer edge and expert route through the interior.

3.2 Drop down a spiral berm.

3.3 Cross the pirate bridge.

4.8 Tina's perch.

5.0 Pass through power line corridor.

5.8 Challenge the Shotgun section.

7.5 Root Rodeo section.

RIDE INFORMATION

Restaurants
Prep for your morning ride with a banana waffle at **3 Squares Restaurant,** 12690 Arbor Lakes Pkwy., Maple Grove; (763) 425-3330; 3squaresrestaurant .com.

Erase the gains you just made on your ride, in grand fashion, with a giant burger at **5 Guys Burgers and Fries.** 7814 Main St. N, Maple Grove; (763) 425-5489.

Area events
A good ol' hometown celebration, with parades, car shows, fun runs, and tons of great food at **Maple Grove Days** in mid-July; maplegrovemn.gov.

Elm Creek Fat Tire Trails

New in 2011, Three Rivers Park District and MORC introduced 13 miles of sublime singletrack at Elm Creek, twisting around the northeast corner of the park through dense hardwood forest and open prairie, with a perfectly blended mix of beginner to expert terrain on fast-flowing path with only rare unintended obstacles. Decadent paved trails through the rest of the wildlife-packed park add bonus points.

Start: Main trailhead at northeast corner of park on West Hayden Lake Road. Southern trailhead at parking area across from dog park.

Distance: Roughly 13 miles for all loops (7.5 miles for the intermediate loop here)

Approximate riding time: 1–1.5 hours

Best bike: Mountain

Terrain and surface type: Flat to gently rolling on hardpacked singletrack

Highlights: Impeccable trail conditions, fast and flowing, gorgeous scenery, relatively crowd-free

Hazards: Hardly an exposed root or stray branch to be seen; very worry-free trail

Maps: *USGS Elk River*; Three Rivers Parks map

Getting there: From US 169 just south of Champlin, head west on West Hayden Lake Road 1.5 miles to a Y in the road. Go left, following the County Park signs. The trailhead is at the end of the road. GPS: N 45 10.113 W 93 25.324

THE RIDE

The two easier loops at Elm Creek, totaling a little over 2 miles, offer something you don't see every day on a mountain bike trail. The trails were designed to accommodate the wide wheelbase of three- and four-wheeled, adaptive mountain bikes and hand cycles. Grades are not typically more than 5 percent, although a 900-foot-long ascent will challenge riders on Loop A. The park and MORC volunteers have done a fantastic job of constructing this trail and providing access for yet another active group of cyclists. This trail and one at Murphy-Hanrehan in Savage are two of the very few hand cycle trails in the country, and Dan Fjell from the Three Rivers Park District is enthusiastic for future plans: "These types of accessible trails will always be in the mix for any new park trails, because of what we've done at Elm Creek." Indeed, the Twin Cities is already on its way to be the Midwest hub for adaptive mountain bike trails, with a regular and well-attended race series happening every summer.

On the trails, Loop A runs counterclockwise through a mix of open prairie and great views of surrounding wetlands and forests. Loop B is less than 1 mile with barely noticeable elevation gain, circling several ponds and tracing a squiggly, glacial ridge. Both are perfect warm-up loops prior to tackling more challenging trails to the south, with the intermediate trail next up and the expert loop at the far end.

I double-dipped on my Elm Creek day and rode both the paved and dirt trails, so this route starts from the dog park trailhead. Follow the road north to the junction with the paved trail and hop on the singletrack, cruising through an open, meadowy landscape to a short climb through a chunk of woods, then it squiggles around through the open again to meet the access Grizzland, the expert section dotted with technical features like log piles and rock gardens, and boasting the most elevation gain on the trail. It's a blast in there, but for now we'll focus on a broader, intermediate skill level (like mine) and ride to the east on the mid-level trail, curving through a splintered copse of trees, into the open again, and back into a large tract of woods near Lemans Lake. The path continues this trees-clearing-trees pattern northbound along a small rise, then drops gradually down to the northern trailhead. Curve around to the south and roll up and down through beautiful oak-maple-basswood forest on a fast and flowing stretch past a small pond and meadow. A "big" climb of about 70 feet takes you through more forest and around a huge meadow area to the final roller-coaster finishing straight.

Riding the stump bridge
NICK PETTIS

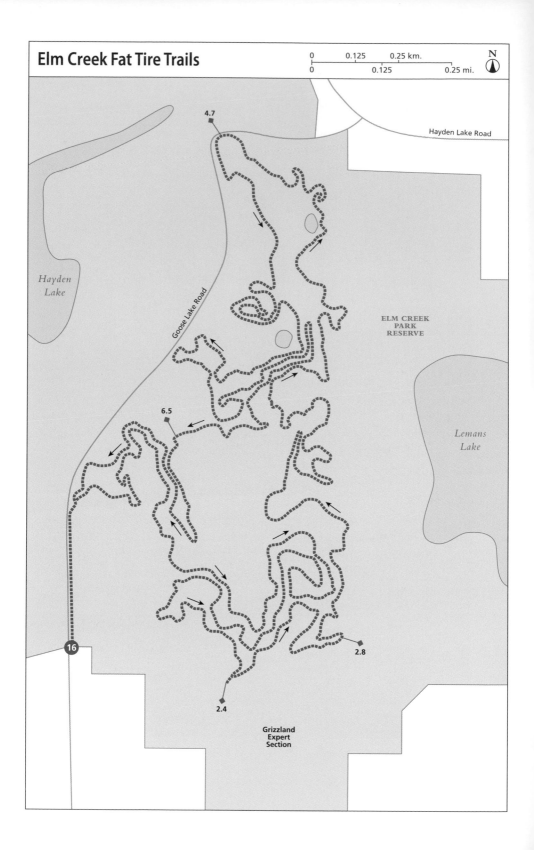

Elm Creek Fat Tire Trails

MILES AND DIRECTIONS

0.0   Start at the southern trailhead. Head north on the road to the paved trail.

0.2   Hop on the singletrack leading north from the bike path.

2.4   Junction with Grizzland. Turn left to follow the intermediate trail.

2.8   Enter the woods on east side of park.

4.7   Pass the northern trailhead.

5.4   Pass pond and meadow area.

6.5   Circle around west side of a huge, Wisconsin-shaped wetland.

7.3   Junction with bike path and road.

7.5   Arrive back at the trailhead.

RIDE INFORMATION

Restaurants
Pull up a bar stool and pillage a plate of French toast or burgers and fries at **Dehn's Country Manor,** an all-in-the-family tradition since 1958. Close to the trails at 11281 Fernbrook Lane, Maple Grove; (763) 420-6460.

Area events
Three Rivers Parks host a full calendar of activities throughout the year, like the canoe, kayak, and stand-up paddleboard programs. Newbies can learn different paddling techniques, roll a kayak, and see what the paddleboard craze is all about. Many different flavors of events available; threeriversparks .org.

Minnesota River Trail— Bloomington Segment

This longtime, local standby traces a sinuous, 5-mile line along the bluffs of the Minnesota River, darting through dense woods and climbing to overlooks of the valley. Distractingly scenic, the trail rolls past enormous cottonwoods and maples and aged cedar groves, complemented by easygoing creeks and quiet ravines teeming with wildlife.

Start: Parking area/boat landing at south end of Lyndale Avenue in Bloomington, in the shadow of the I-35 bridge

Distance: 6 miles out and back

Approximate riding time: 45–60 minutes

Best bike: Mountain

Terrain and surface type: Rolling, with some medium-steep hills, on hardpacked singletrack

Highlights: Entire length of ride in scenic, bluffside forest, original Gideon Pond house, river views

Hazards: Occasional downed tree limbs, sections of deep sand, voracious mosquitoes in summer, watch for hikers and gonzo riders on trail

Other considerations: Count on washed-out or closed sections in spring from regular flooding. Stay off the trail when wet to alleviate erosion and trail damage.

Maps: *USGS Bloomington*; MORC trail map at morcmtb.org

Getting there: For west trailhead, exit I-35 west at 106th Street and go east 0.1 mile to Lyndale Avenue (T intersection), then south down the hill to a large parking area at the river. N 44 80.249 / W 93 28.897. To reach east trailhead from I-35 west, follow East 98th Street 1.6 miles east to the transition to Old Shakopee Road. Continue due east to 11th Avenue,

West end singletrack

and head south 2 blocks to Indian Mounds Elementary School. Parking available in the lot. Ride to the end of the street and look for the gravel doubletrack dropping down the bluff. GPS: N 44 48.149 W 93 17.332

THE RIDE

The Lyndale Avenue trailhead often presents a quandary. Ride upstream or downstream? Both directions have distinct personalities—flats and dense, river bottom foliage heading upriver, and curvy with climbs and creek crossings heading downriver. You're in for a good ride either way, but let's focus on the hilly section here. From the parking area, the trail heads into the woods at the boat landing gate, curving away from the river almost immediately and growing from a singletrack path to a two-abreast boulevard (an old access road from long ago), crossing a river channel spur before turning north toward the bluff. As the elevation tips up, a singletrack spur forks right, and the fun starts here.

The trail generally follows the lower contours of the bluff on the early sections, rolling through a forest of gnarled oak and other hardwood giants. A

The Pond Mission

On a short, flat section of the ride, just about 1 mile in, a spur trail ramps steeply into the woods, ignoring the bluff's contour lines to reach a large clearing, in which sits a stately brick four-square house, with grand views of the river valley. This is the former home and mission site of Gideon Pond, one of the most influential people on the mid-1800s Minnesota frontier. Gideon and his brother Samuel were missionaries who mingled with the Dakota Indians and taught Christianity, farming, and construction, and were staunch advocates of fair treatment to Indian people. Following a move by the brothers' adopted Dakota tribe to the Minnesota River Valley around 1840, Gideon constructed a log home on this bluff to continue his teachings, and later built the larger house with material originating from the nearby river flats. Clay was dug, formed, and kiln-fired on-site to make the 60,000 bricks used in the home's construction. Today the Pond house is maintained by the City of Bloomington as a museum, and is listed on the National Register of Historic Places. See the City of Bloomington website for more. 401 E. 104th St., Bloomington; ci .bloomington.mn.us.

short stretch of platform provides solid surface above a formerly bike-stalling sand pit, and at close to 1 mile in to the ride, a spur trail ramps steeply up the bluff for an optional side trip. At the top is the Gideon Pond house, historical homestead of one of Minnesota's most influential settlers. See the sidebar for details on the great strides made with Indian relations right here on this bluff top, and the fascinating story of the construction of this elegant home. Past the spur, a gentle descent leads to a bridge crossing a skinny creek, running clear and lazily toward the river. After cruising through a cluster of towering, fragrant cedars, the path begins its first respectable climb. Don't worry too much about elevation gain, but halfway up the tread falls to the bottom of a pesky section that has eroded into a deep funnel, so be ready to navigate loose dirt, rocks, and other detritus. Around the corner at the top is Parkers Picnic Grounds, with great views of Long Meadow Lake below. (The Black Dog

Creek mirrors the frosty trail

> Bloomington's ample Minnesota River frontage and its wooded bluffs were home to many generations of American Indians. See the city's largest group of burial mounds at Mound Springs Park, 102nd Street and 12th Avenue, near the bluff's edge.

power plant detracts from the scene, but if you cover one eye, it goes away.) A fun descent ensues after the picnic grounds, with a couple of switchbacks on the way down to another creek. No bridge here, so ford the stream with as little impact as possible and follow the path's curve toward Long Meadow Lake and its continuing eastbound heading. After a few more fun turns, the trail ramps up again to just below the top of the bluff and the site of a long-abandoned city park. Forgotten picnic tables sit beside rusty, dilapidated barbecue grills, and resident foliage is inexorably reclaiming its own. The path heads downhill again from here, with yet another creek at the bottom. A well-used trail ascends from the creek, and another follows closer to the river. The upward path leads to Mound Springs Park (the optional eastern trailhead) while the riverside trail moves into federal wildlife refuge land. This final creek is the turnaround point. At last check there was no signage with a turn-back warning, but refuge officials are not fond of renegade riders. Retreat here, and enjoy the trail in reverse back to the Lyndale trailhead. Bonus: If you use the Indian Mounds trailhead, plan to use its proximity to the refuge to explore farther downstream on foot. The Minnesota Valley National Wildlife Refuge is a spectacular urban wilderness preserve, bursting with vibrant populations of hundreds of bird species and active, ground-based wildlife. Don't miss the chance to wander through.

Trail News: If you're a fan of this trail, you already know how special it is and its significance first to the natural state of things (wildlife habitat for dozens of species and nature's never-fail filtration system) and then to what it brings us: one-of-a-kind scenery and go-to destination for generations of hikers, birders, mountain bikers, hikers, and anyone else who appreciates the outdoors in its Sunday best. However, plans are in place to create a paved trail through this area to "improve" it. I can already see the Trail Closed signs after huge chunks of path are washed away or otherwise deemed unsafe.

Many grassroots organizations are working hard to put a stop to this madness. As I write this though, the trail remains wonderfully untouched… the way it should be.

MILES AND DIRECTIONS

0.0 Start at the Lyndale Avenue trailhead.

0.8 Trail approaches lower flanks of bluff and turns east.

1.0 Junction with spur trail up to Gideon Pond House.

1.0 Trail climbs to Parkers Picnic Grounds and descends almost immediately around a switchback and across a creek.

2.0 Trail ramps up to old city park.

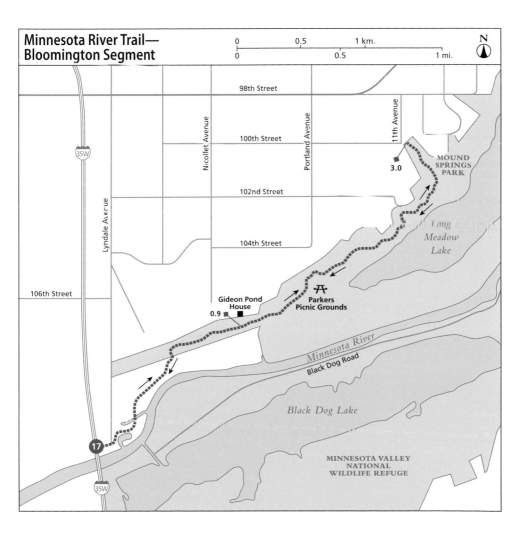

Minnesota River Trail—Bloomington Segment

3.0 Final creek crossing and climb up to Indian Mounds Park and east trailhead. This is the turnaround point.

6.0 Arrive back at trailhead.

RIDE INFORMATION

Restaurants

If only for sentimental reasons, head up to **David Fong's** to replenish your calories. One of the longest running, family-owned Twin Cities restaurants, Fong's still dishes up great food, just as it did on opening day in 1958. 9329 Lyndale Ave. S, Bloomington; (952) 888-9294; davidfongs.com.

Scandinavian cookies, pastries, and muffins do wonders for your climbing legs. Load up at **Taste of Scandinavia Bakery and Cafe** at 401 W. 98th St., Bloomington; (952) 358-7490; tasteofscandinavia.com.

Area events

Interpretive programs at the **Minnesota Valley National Wildlife Refuge** brings you up close to some of the best wildlife habitat in the river valley. Don't miss July's Minnesota Bat Festival and the summer-long Bird Language program at the Bloomington visitor center; 3815 American Blvd.; (952) 854-5900; fws.gov./Midwest.

Terrace Oaks Park

Short and fast, this entry- to intermediate-level trail winds through oak forest and wetland, with tight turns and a few punchy climbs. Ride a quick, shakedown cruise on the 2.5-mile loop, or scorch multiple racetrack laps to test your best times.

Start: Parking area and trailhead on Burnsville Parkway, 0.5 mile east of CR 11

Distance: 2.5-mile loop

Approximate riding time: 15 minutes

Best bike: Mountain

Terrain and surface type: Mostly rolling, with a few short, medium-steep hills on hardpacked singletrack

Highlights: Uncrowded; tight turns and sweeping descents; challenging, optional expert section

Hazards: Encroaching foliage, handlebar-grabbing branches, turtle crossings, ticks, mosquitoes

Maps: *USGS St. Paul SW*; MORC maps

Getting there: From I-35 west, exit at Burnsville Parkway and head east 2 miles, past CR 11, and down the hill 0.5 mile to the park entrance. Trailhead is adjacent to the hockey rink. GPS: N 44 46.464 W 93 14.345

Great Racers Born Here

Burnsville's little ski hill might elicit snickers from passersby familiar with the grand heights of the Rockies, but **Buck Hill's** pedigree as an incubator for superstars is undeniable. The hill's daunting 310 feet of vertical are lucky to see 50 inches of natural snow in a season, but that was enough to launch locals Kristina Koznick and Lindsey Vonn to the top echelons of the sport. Coached by Erich Sailer, Buck Hill's legendary Austrian ski trainer, Koznick tore up the slalom circuit for years and competed in three Olympics before retiring in 2006, and Vonn developed into one of the most decorated female racers in history, adding Olympic gold at the 2010 Games to her other 50 World Cup wins.

THE RIDE

Designed by the aforementioned trail building legend Gary Sjoquist, Terrace Oaks packs a lot of fat (tire) into a small package. The 230-acre city park is adorned with wonderfully gnarled old oaks and pocket wetlands, brim full of lush foliage and critters both winged and terrestrial-based. There is just enough technical flair, and a short expert section, to make it interesting for more accomplished riders, and an easygoing feel for beginners.

Start the ride adjacent to the hockey rink and roll into densely packed woods, moving quickly to a series of twisty turns past a pair of hidden ponds, navigating past the trees in a series of hairpins and tight squiggles. Long-armed shrubbery reaches out here and there and it's sometimes easy to scrape the bark off trailside trees, but this is a fun, keep-you-on-your-toes technical challenge. The trail is fast and flowy as it zigzags past two pond/wetland areas and climbs to higher ground on a short ridge. A nice descent drops down to the junction with the Hebel's Hollow expert section, which features a gravelly, hairpin switchback and log crossing, and a tightly wound, downhill switchback. The main trail continues on a lazy curve toward the initial copse of woods and the trailhead.

And just like that, you're done with a lap. Good news is, with the mountain biking hordes descending on the "money trails" like Lebanon Hills and Murphy-Hanrehan, Terrace is blissfully empty, and it often seems like your own private bike trail. Take a few laps and enjoy the peace and quiet.

MILES AND DIRECTIONS

0.0   Start at the trailhead. Ride twisty trail into the woods.

0.5   Pass the pair of ponds. Listen to the frogs.

0.6   Curve through the spaghetti stretch through the trees.

1.1   Climb up away from the ponds and loop back north.

Bike Shop

Lose a water bottle or air from your tires? **Penn Cycle's** Eagan superstore is only 2 miles away. The venerable shop hosts the long-running Buck Hill Mountain Bike Races on Thursday nights, with racing for kids to experts, door prizes, and all-around good times. Get the dirt on the event and weekly group rides at the Eagan store at 2290 Cliff Rd.; (651) 882-1241; penncycle.com.

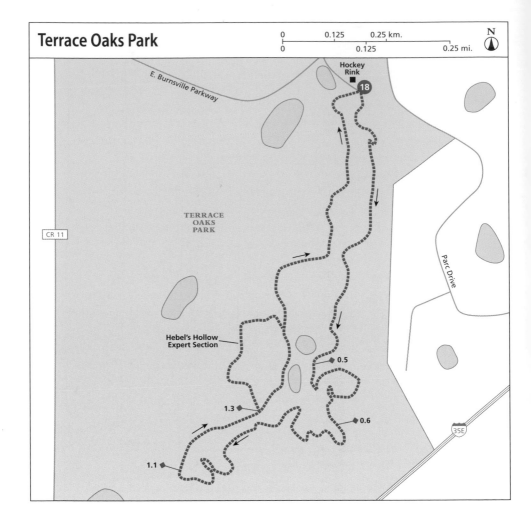

1.3 Junction with the Hebel's Hollow expert section. Check it out or continue down the hill to . . .

1.9 . . . the junction with the first copse of woods and back to trailhead.

2.5 Arrive back at trailhead.

RIDE INFORMATION

Restaurants
Family-owned for nearly fifty years, **J's Family Restaurant** still serves heaping omelettes and great pizza. Just 1.5 miles north of the trailhead. 2913 Cliff Rd. E, Burnsville; (952) 890-2669.

Similar to the naming of Black Dog Lake, the Dakota also inspired the name of another local landmark. When they gathered to fish at present-day Crystal Lake and watched white-tailed bucks drink from the lake, early settlers observing from the top of a nearby hill named their lookout Buck Hill.

Charge up with sustainable coffee at **Caribou Coffee** in Burnsville's downtown; 12601 Nicollet Ave.; (952) 895-1010; cariboucoffee.com.

Area events

Started in the late 1970s by a local resident and fire equipment collector, the **Burnsville Fire Muster** has evolved to a five-day community celebration, with carnival rides, parade, great food, and a rolling display of over one hundred fire trucks, including classic horse-drawn hand pumpers. Early September in downtown Burnsville; burnsvillefiremuster.com.

Murphy-Hanrehan Park Reserve

A local favorite for nearly thirty years, the trail system at Murphy has risen to the highest ranks of fat tire destinations, thanks to the dedication and cooperation of the Three Rivers Park District and MORC. Explore three expertly designed loops in this undeveloped, wildlife-packed park reserve.

Start: Trailhead is at 15501 Murphy Lake Blvd. in Savage.

Distance: Roughly 10 miles total for all loops (3.5 for intermediate loop shown here)

Approximate riding time: 45 minutes for intermediate loop

Best bike: Mountain

Terrain and surface type: Rolling, with a few punchy climbs, on sublime singletrack trail through open meadows and dense forest

Highlights: Vibrant avian life, and ground-based wildlife like beavers, deer, fox, and muskrats

Hazards: Minimal on easy loop, but look for exposed tree roots, rocks, and logs. Many potential hazards (challenges) on the expert loop. Watch for poison ivy, prickly ash (sharp thorns), and wild parsnip (a tall weed that will inflict ebola-like wounds upon exposed skin).

Other considerations: Trail will close if riding poses harm to conditions. Keep soft tread in top shape by postponing your ride after rains or spring snow.

Maps: *USGS Orchard Lake*; Three River Parks map; MORC maps

Getting there: From I-35 west in Burnsville, follow CR 42 west 2 miles to West Burnsville Parkway. Turn south past Cam Ram Park to Hanrehan Lake Boulevard and continue to Murphy Lake Boulevard, a left turn onto gravel. The trailhead is at the top of the hill. GPS: N 44 43.456 W 93 20.927

Riding in
NICK PETTIS

THE RIDE

One of the first metro area parks to ordain mountain bike–specific trails, Murphy-Hanrehan's early paths were created prior to the sensible trend of sustainable trail building. Often rutted or eroding, the trails charged up and down hills and shot through the woods with little regard to fall lines or harmonious relations with the natural terrain. While still a fun and challenging

Bike Shop

Erik's Bike Shop has a store conveniently located just a few miles away, loaded with their usual excellent inventory of gear and fuel for a full day on the trail. 501 CR 42, Burnsville; (952) 898-5111; eriksbikeshop.com.

Minnesota meadow
NICK PETTIS

The Billy Goat Bridge, an old wooden railroad bridge in the area of Judicial Road and Burnsville Parkway, was a main conduit for the comings and goings of residents in the townships south of Minneapolis, carrying horse-drawn sleighs and Model Ts to the post office, school, and church. The name was inspired by a group of billy goats from a neighboring farm that had a merry old time running back and forth across the bridge.

ride, clearer heads prevailed and relocated the entire mountain bike trail system to the park's southern meadows and oak forest. Murphy's 2,800 acres are generally split into steep, wooded hills and scattered wetlands in the northern section, and the aforementioned oak stands and prairie restoration in the southern sections. All that adds up to a remote wilderness vibe and close-in escape from surrounding frenetic life.

From the trailhead, the path cuts between two signs loaded with great park and riding info, and heads into open prairie to start the easy loop (Intermediate and advanced loops are only accessed via the easy loop, so more accomplished riders can use this as a warm-up). This entry loop was also (as of 2012) redesigned to accommodate adaptive mountain bikes and hand cycles. Keep your eyes peeled for soaring raptors like red-shouldered and Cooper's hawks scanning for a meal. Roll across the prairie and drop into the oak-laden woods on the intermediate loop, starting out over some rocks between the trees and a log crossing, then into some tight singletrack. The path follows a hairpin west, with an easy climb and a tour along the contours of the glacial ridge. Two more tight hairpin turns lead southeast to the junction with the advanced loop. Ride across the boardwalk to the edge of the wetland, take in sweet views of the beauteous landscape, and follow the rolling path along the wetland back to the easy loop junction and final stretch to the trailhead.

The advanced loop boasts some of the sweetest singletrack around, on a 7-mile carnival ride with high and narrow bridges, skinnier tread on steep sideslopes, bigger climbs and faster descents, and cool obstacles like the 45-foot-long ladder bridge and log ride. There are six total bridges and a few boardwalks peppered along the loop, making for great fun all the way through, and a few sections of open prairie, typically with wildlife all over the place, like deer, rabbits, fox, woodchucks, and raptors. Even just one lap provides a worthy challenge, but can you really resist doing another one?

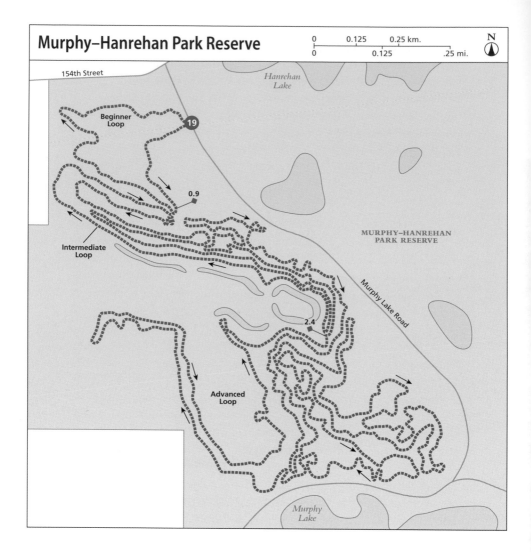

Murphy–Hanrehan Park Reserve

0   0.125   0.25 km.

0   0.125   .25 mi.

N

154th Street

Hanrehan Lake

Beginner Loop

19

0.9

Intermediate Loop

MURPHY–HANREHAN PARK RESERVE

Murphy Lake Road

2.4

Advanced Loop

Murphy Lake

MILES AND DIRECTIONS

0.0 Start at the trailhead. Start the easy loop to the left. The path mean-ders through the meadow on a back-and-forth route that generally forms a loop.

0.9 Junction with the intermediate loop. Follow the path directly into the woods on the skinnier trail with more steep sections and technical trail.

2.4 Junction with the advanced loop. Keep heading south here for the really good stuff; or to complete the intermediate loop, ride across the boardwalk and roll back through the woods, hit the easy loop again, and head back to the trailhead.

3.5 Arrive back at the trailhead.

Sunbeam turn on sweet singletrack
NICK PETTIS

RIDE INFORMATION

Restaurants

All manner of food stops are available just a few miles away on the Burnsville Center strip of CR 42, including the obligatory **Starbucks** and **Caribou** coffee shops, a plethora of fast-food joints, and plenty of "sit-down" restaurants.

Area events

Feel like **racing**? Murphy hosts weekly citizen races all summer long. Come on out and mix it up a little! Co-sponsored by Freewheel Bike and Maple Grove Cycling. The racing is always a blast, and there are prizes! Learn more at threeriversparks.org.

St. Paul Road and Pathways

Nearly every ride in the St. Paul section of this book is within sight of either the Mississippi or St. Croix Rivers, making for superlative riding with postcard backdrops. Minnesota's capital city fits snugly around a sweeping curve of the Mississippi, flanked to the south by a rounded snout of cave-riddled limestone bluffs. Wooded corridors provide purchase for ribbons of smooth, paved trails flowing upstream and down with the river's current for long miles of scenic cruising, like the River Tour ride from the downtown harbor to wildlife-packed Crosby Farm Park, or the Big Rivers Trail in Lilydale and Mendota. The trail along Mississippi River Boulevard treats cyclists to sweet river views

The Mississippi River and St. Paul harbor

on the Grand Round ride and a tour of Summit Avenue, the city's most elegant address. Like to climb? Short, punchy hills shoot to the bluff tops all around St. Paul; or for more elevation gain, head to the lumpy terrain around Newport and longer and steeper challenges near Afton. Make a day of it on the iconic Gateway Trail, with the new Brown's Creek segment leading to historic Stillwater, and go back in time with a double feature of Minnesota's annals in the diminutive hamlets of Marine on St. Croix and Scandia.

St. Paul Harbor River Tour

The Mississippi, as it does in Minneapolis, defines the personality of St. Paul. Much of the city's most celebrated views, architecture, history, and community are influenced by the river. This entire 13-mile ride hugs the Mississippi's shoreline from water level at the downtown harbor upstream to Crosby Farm Park, with a front-row view of towboats working around the harbor and restored paddleboats motoring along the wooded bluffs.

Start: Riverside parking and picnic area on Warner Road, 0.2 mile east of Jackson Street

Distance: 13 miles out and back, with many options to extend or shorten

Approximate riding time: 1 hour

Best bike: Road or hybrid

Terrain and surface type: Flat to gently climbing (with one steep hill), on mostly smooth, paved pathways

Highlights: Riverside view of towboats in the harbor, downtown St. Paul, Crosby Park, sinuous, water's edge trail and bluff views

Hazards: Watch for traffic at road junctions, prepare for downed limbs and sand on the trail through Crosby Park

Other considerations: Mosquitoes will devour you on a hot midsummer evening; some choppy sections of trail from past flood events

Maps: *USGS St. Paul East*

Getting there: From downtown St. Paul, follow Chestnut or Jackson Streets to the river at Shepard Road. Turn left (road becomes Warner Road) to first large parking area at river's edge. GPS: N 44 56.820 W 93 04.919

THE RIDE

The Mississippi River gets crowded in downtown St. Paul. From the trailhead parking area along Warner Road, visitors can get up close to the rumbling towboats moving barges to various staging or loading areas. On busy days, dozens of barges are docked along the riverbanks, awaiting their next tour of duty, and square framed towboats with crow's nest wheelhouses move about the harbor under the steely eyes of seasoned captains. It's fascinating to watch, and these workhorse skiffs are responsible for transporting upwards of five million tons of commodities, mostly grains, every year. A big number to grasp for us landlubbers, so let's take to the trail and see what else Ol' Miss has in store.

View west from trailhead

Bike Shop

A little north of downtown, but well worth a stop, the crew at the **Bicycle Chain** store has been doing bikes right since 1991. Check out their great shop, and join the Afton shop ride on Sunday, at 1712 Lexington Ave. N, Roseville; (651) 480-4513; bicyclechain.com.

Start riding upstream, following the paved path beneath the Lafayette Bridge and into the shadow of downtown's skyscrapers. Pass under Robert Street and Wabasha Street and look across to Raspberry Island, home to the Minnesota Boat Club since 1870, and host to present-day bandshell concerts and other events. The small atoll was known as Navy Island from 1948 to about the mid-1990s, named for the US Navy training facility once housed there, but the Raspberry moniker resurfaced with the departure of the Navy and planning of the fancy, new Wabasha Street Bridge. Just past the bridge are great views in all directions, most notably the downtown skyline, the Science Museum of Minnesota, and Harriet Island across the river. The buff-colored pavilion at river's edge dates back to 1941 and was a popular summer destination, with a public bathhouse, beach, and picnic areas. Today the building hosts wedding ceremonies and other festive events. At the east end of Upper Landing Park, split off to the left and roll past the fountains

Honeycomb Bluffs

The sandstone river bluffs in and around St. Paul contain a captivating labyrinth of caves and man-made mines, and the granddaddy of them all was **Fountain Cave,** a 1,150-foot-long passageway formed by the slowly eroding path of Fountain Creek, opening into the Mississippi about halfway between present-day I-35 and the old Schmidt's Brewery. Side tunnels led to many hidden antechambers, one of them a huge, circular room, and many more still unexplored. Some of the area's caves were used for storing goods, growing mushrooms, hiding gangsters, or as sites for speakeasies. After ne'er-do-well rogue Pierre "Pig's Eye" Parrant erected the first shack at the mouth of Fountain Cave, this place spawned the growth of the city, and early residents visited the cave for its cool air and water, and explored the cave's recesses. Increased human activity, as usual, led to the cave's eventual disappearance, at least from the surface. Its entrance might be buried, but below the streets are still a mysterious maze and legends in waiting.

Paddleboat passing under the High Bridge

and condo neighborhood, and be sure to look across the river again to see houseboats of all shapes and sizes, some of them year-round homes to hardy residents. While a few are ramshackle and appear barely able to float on the water, others are resplendent in lavish dress and complete with the very best in creature comforts. Very few of the floating abodes ever leave their moorings. Continue along the river, riding on what was once the old Shepard Road, passing beneath the soaring Smith Avenue High Bridge, 160 feet above. At the junction with Shepard Road proper, the route turns left and heads farther west on some gently rolling sections of the Samuel Morgan Regional Trail Corridor (this is also part of the 3,000-mile-long Mississippi River Trail), passing the site of the old Fountain Cave. The 1,100-foot, sandstone cave is St. Paul's birthplace, where Pierre Parrant ("Pig's Eye") staked a claim and the city grew up around his tough-guy saloon (see sidebar for more). The path climbs from

Best Bike Rides Minneapolis and St. Paul

> Bavarian-born Jacob Schmidt moved to St. Paul around 1884 and established the Schmidt beer brand from the landmark brewery on West 7th Street, producing family-made beer for 130 years.

the cave and descends to a flat stretch approaching I-35 east. Cross the freeway ramps with caution and in a few more pedal strokes arrive at the eastern entrance to Crosby Farm Regional Park. Roll down the hill and start the long and curvy tour of this heavily wooded park on the river flats. Named after English immigrant Thomas Crosby, who farmed the area in the late 1800s, the park today boasts nearly 7 miles of trails winding through a lush forest of immense cottonwoods and maples, Crosby Lake and wetland area, and, of course, the river. While plenty beautiful, the park's proximity to the river also means that spring floods carry tons of sand and other detritus onto the path, so be prepared for occasional obstacles. At the picnic shelters, follow the access road up the route's only steep climb, emerging at the top of the high river gorge. Pedal on to the overlook at MN 5 for great views of the river below and Ft. Snelling on the other side.

To extend mileage on this trip, keep right on riding on the path along Mississippi River Boulevard. It's a wonderful ride with postcard views of the river gorge and stately old homes, and traffic-free riding all the way to downtown Minneapolis. Today, though, turn around and head back to the top of the Crosby Park hill, and dart out onto the Shepard Road pathway, following this all the way along the road to the Randolph Avenue junction. This time, stay on the path along Shepard Road, enjoying stop-and-stare views of downtown St. Paul and a chance to race the trains on the adjacent tracks. Follow the path back past the bridges to the trailhead.

MILES AND DIRECTIONS

0.0 Start at the trailhead at Warner Road.

0.7 Pass Raspberry Island.

1.0 Upper Landing Park. Split left.

1.7 Smith Avenue High Bridge.

2.6 Randolph Avenue and Shepard Road junction. Turn left.

4.2 Junction with I-35 east. Continue straight ahead.

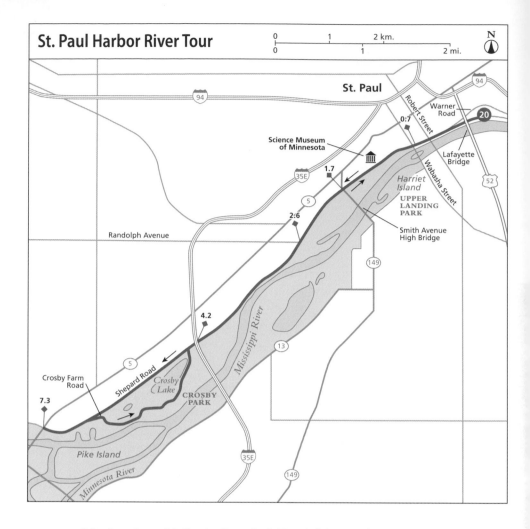

St. Paul Harbor River Tour

0   1   2 km.
0   1   2 mi.

N

St. Paul

Science Museum
of Minnesota

Randolph Avenue

Harriet
Island

UPPER
LANDING
PARK

Warner
Road

Lafayette
Bridge

Smith Avenue
High Bridge

Mississippi River

Crosby Farm
Road

Shepard Road

Crosby
Lake

CROSBY
PARK

Pike Island

Minnesota River

4.3   Junction with Crosby Farm Park. Turn left into park.

6.6   Turn left at the picnic shelters onto the park road and head uphill.

7.3   Ft. Snelling and river gorge overlook. Turn around here for return trip.

7.5   Turn left at top of the hill, onto the path paralleling Shepard Road.

9.3   Pass back under I-35E.

11.4   Randolph Avenue junction. Go straight ahead, following the path all the way back to the trailhead.

13.0   Arrive back at the trailhead.

RIDE INFORMATION

Restaurants

Load up on scrumptious buckwheat pancakes at **Day by Day Cafe,** a five-time award winner for best home cooking in the Twin Cities. 477 W. 7th St.; (651) 227-0654; daybyday.com.

Got the urge? Fix it at **Caribou Coffee's** trailside shop at Upper Landing. Do the right thing and enjoy their delicious Rainforest Alliance-certified coffee. 230 Spring St.; (651) 293-1612.

Area events

Get your outdoor groove on at the **Twin Cities Jazz Festival** at Mears Park. Late June at Mears Park, 221 E. 5th St., St. Paul; hotsummerjazz.com.

Riding the curves in Crosby Park

St. Paul Harbor River Tour

pickup was the plant's later pedigree, rolling off the line here from 1985 to the facility's closing day in 2011. From here, the route follows an S-curve past an overlook with great valley views to the northern entrance to Hidden Falls Regional Park and up a gradual climb, with a coast down the other side. Follow the road's curve to the southeast and Hidden Falls Park's southern gate and the junction with MN 5. Here the route joins part of the Harbor Tour ride, as it follows Shepard Road along the ridge above Crosby Farm Park to I-35E and on to the Samuel Morgan corridor into downtown St. Paul. Feeling like a shorter ride? Turn left onto Eagle Parkway, past the Science Museum, for the 15-mile route of the Classic. Wind past Irvine Park to Ramsey Street and either blast up the 18 percent grade of Ramsey, or a less painful approach up Grand Avenue to Summit Avenue, and roll past the elegant mansions on this famous street back to the trailhead.

Follow the path along the harbor and continue past the parking area on Warner Road for a great view of the rounded bluff of Indian Mounds Park and the barges working the river downstream. At Childs Road, the bike trail turns to keep pace with Warner Road, across the bridge over the railroad tracks heading in and out of the big cement plant and rail yards to the south. Roll along past the Minnesota DNR office and note the trail jettisoning off into the woods. This is a great ride through the woods out to US 61 and access to Battle Creek Regional Park's trails and more great riding in the Newport area. Continue the Grand Round riding along Warner Road to the bike/pedestrian bridge over the road and into Indian Mounds Park. The path shoots north to another that leads up a long climb to the top of the hill. Outstanding views await from a number of vantage points, and it's a great place to fill up some memory card space. This was a sacred place for ancient people of the area, and the site of nearly forty burial mounds at the top and flanks of the bluff. The original mounds date back over 2,000 years, but only six of the mounds

Bike Shops

For more than thirty years, **Grand Performance** owner Dan Casebeer has shared his passion for cycling with legions of area riders, from newbies to elite pros. Active club teams, rider development, and unparalleled commitment to the sport, be it fixing a flat or sizing up your dream bike. 1938 Grand Ave.; (651) 699-2640; gpbicycles.com.

County Cycles started selling bikes and gear in 1981 and remains one of the state's finest. Almost daily group rides from the shop, and sponsor of the Gopher Wheelmen cycling club, founded by local rider Ken Woods in 1934. 2700 Lexington Ave. N, Roseville; (651) 482-9609; countycycles.com.

Floral Arrangement

The grand glass dome and gardens inside at the **Marjorie McNeely Conservatory** were born of German inspiration in the early 1900s. Frederick Nussbaumer, a Baden, Germany, born lad, learned the landscape gardening trade at his father's greenhouse and later worked in London's Royal Botanic Gardens. Persuaded to come to St. Paul as a gardener by Horace Cleveland, Nussbaumer's skills rapidly gained him the position of superintendent of parks, where he crafted plans for a "propagating greenhouse" at Como Park. The original structure was opened in 1915 to rave reviews, and today is one of the country's few remaining Victorian-style domed gardens. Renamed in 2002 after Marjorie McNeely, former president of the St. Paul Garden Club, the conservatory boasts six indoor and three outdoor gardens with over 50,000 plants, including tropical palms and orchids, and the largest bonsai tree collection in the upper Midwest. The conservatory is a 1974 inductee to the National Register of Historic Places and is a don't-miss attraction on your tour of St. Paul.

remain. Set your sights on a perfect St. Paul skyline view and drop like a stone down the steep western slope of the bluff (control your speed) to Plum Street. Head back east on Plum and Pacific Streets to Hudson Road and hop onto Johnson Parkway, riding north through East Side neighborhoods to the south shore of Lake Phalen. The 3-mile path around the lake is packed with stellar views, and some short, punchy hills add some flavor, if you're up for a fun side trip.

From Lake Phalen, merge onto Wheelock Parkway for the trip west across the top of this loop. Watch yourself at busy intersections like Arcade Street, and follow the sometimes-there wide shoulder or sidewalk out to I-35 east. Wheelock is a tad choppy on this stretch, and more so west of the freeway, but traffic is generally light, especially on a well-timed early weekend ride. Past Rice Street, the parkway dips a bit and turns into a long, gradual climb to a hairpin curve, angling back south again and west to Lake Como. At the south side of the lake, shaped sort of like a big, wooden clog, follow the winding Como Lake Drive around to the northern shore, with a nice view of the elegant Como Lakeside Pavillion across the water. The huge building and grounds are home to all sorts of festive events like banquets, concerts, and plays. Looping around the north shore, the path blends into Como Park on rolling hills and past manicured gardens to the Como Zoo and Majorie McNeely Conservatory. The zoo is Minnesota's first and a magnet for kids squealing with glee.

Originally located on Harriet Island, the zoo was established in 1897 with a lineup of three deer, and moved to Como Park when more animals arrived and the island got crowded. Flanking the polar bears and giraffes and chimps, the McNeely Conservatory is a must-go Minnesota landmark, bursting at the seams with all manner of eye-popping flowers and unique foliage, under domes of glass. See the sidebar for more information.

The park's pathways lead away from the zoo to the west, taking Grand Round riders along Como Avenue and past the southern fringe of the state fairgrounds to Raymond Avenue. Head south past the bustling Energy Park and rail yard area to a busy crossing at University Avenue and, 2 blocks later, a jog to the right to meet up with Pelham Boulevard. The route passes the Pelham Triangle "mini park" to the junction with North Mississippi River Boulevard and the homestretch back to Summit Avenue. Local tip: A short ride east on Marshall Avenue leads to Izzy's Ice Cream, with handmade deliciousness all ready for post-ride indulgence.

MILES AND DIRECTIONS

0.0 Ride starts at Summit Avenue and South Mississippi River Boulevard.

1.7 Pass under Ford Parkway and past the former Ford assembly plant.

3.9 Junction with MN 5; continue straight ahead and onto the bike path paralleling Shepard Road.

6.0 Pass under I-35.

7.7 Junction with Randolph Avenue; keep on straight ahead.

10.0 Pass through downtown St. Paul's harbor.

12.0 Ride across Childs Road and continue on bike path.

12.7 At the bike bridge, cross over Warner Road into Indian Mounds Park.

12.9 Left turn onto the path heading uphill.

14.3 Right turn onto Plum Street, merging onto Pacific Street.

15.3 Left onto Hudson Road and quick left onto Johnson Parkway.

17.4 Meet the south shore of Lake Phalen. Veer left onto Wheelock Parkway.

20.0 Junction with I-35; keep riding west.

22.7 Arrive at east shore of Lake Como. Hop on the bike path and turn right, following East Como Lake Drive around the top of the lake to Lexington Parkway.

23.7 Ride across the Lexington Parkway bike/ped bridge. Path will merge into Kaufman Drive. Follow Kaufman to Estabrook Drive.

24.0 Right turn onto Estabrook Drive and a quick left onto the bike path down to Horton Avenue, where another right turn leads to Hamline Avenue.

24.6 Left onto Hamline Avenue and quick right onto Como Avenue.

26.2 Turn left onto Raymond Avenue.

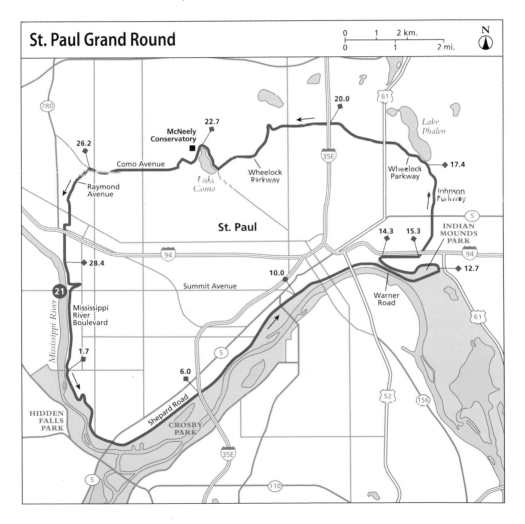

St. Paul Grand Round

Cruising along Mississippi River Boulevard

27.5 Turn right onto Wabash Avenue.

27.7 Left onto Pelham Boulevard.

28.4 Junction with North Mississippi River Boulevard. Turn left.

30.0 Arrive back at the Summit Avenue trailhead.

RIDE INFORMATION

Restaurants

Head to **Great Waters Brewing Company** on St. Paul's pedestrian mall for prime patio seating and a frosty mug. 426 St. Peter St.; (651) 224-BREW; great watersbc.com.

Since 1939, **Mickey's Dining Car** has served up thick-as-cement malts and juicy burgers, and it's on the National Register of Historic Places. 36 W. 7th St.; (651) 698-0259; mickeysdiningcar.com.

A Reuben and made-from-scratch soup from **Cecil's Deli.** Okay, and a root beer float, too. Mmmm. A proud Highland Park and Minnesota tradition for sixty-four years. 651 Cleveland Ave. S; (651) 698-6276; cecilsdeli.com.

Area events

Welcome summer at St. Paul's annual **Grand Old Day,** 30 blocks of arts, live music, and great food on the city's favorite destination street. First Sunday in June. Free bike parking on the Ayd Mill Bridge; www.visitsaintpaul.com/directory/grand-old-day-festivals-events/.

Don't miss live music outdoors from local bands and ensembles during **Music in the Parks** at the Como Lakeside Pavilion and the Phalen Amphitheater. Many shows are free of charge; ci.stpaul.mn.us.

The first Minnesota State Fair was held in 1859 near what became downtown Minneapolis, and it was not until1885, when Ramsey County donated a 210-acre parcel to the State Agricultural Society, that the fair found a permanent home at its current location, midway between the Twin Cities. The second largest fair in the United States, "The Great Minnesota Get-Together" has grown from a solely agricultural expo to include other exhibits, entertainment, and, of course, great food like hotdish on a stick. mnstatefair.org.

Gateway and Browns Creek State Trails

A perennial local favorite since its first days in 1993, the 18-mile Gateway Trail takes riders from the buzz of St. Paul's downtown area through dense wooded areas, parks, lakes, and wetlands, to open meadows and rural landscapes. The new Browns Creek segment adds another 6 fabulous miles to Stillwater's charming main street.

Start: Cayuga Park, 198 Cayuga St., St. Paul

Distance: 24.7 miles one way

Approximate riding time: 1.5–2 hours

Best bike: Road

Terrain and surface type: Primarily flat with occasional gentle hills on a smooth, two-lane paved path

Highlights: Brilliant variety of landscape including densely wooded urban areas, rolling farmland, and wildlife-packed wetlands

Hazards: Trail intersects roads with moderate traffic flow

Maps: *USGS St. Paul East*; printable map through the Minnesota Department of Natural Resources, at dnr.state.mn.us/maps/state_trails/gateway.pdf; more trail info at the Gateway Trail Association's website: gatewaytrailmn.org

Getting there: From downtown St. Paul, follow I-35 north to the Pennsylvania Avenue exit. Turn right onto Phalen Boulevard, a quick left onto North Mississippi Street, and another left onto East Cayuga Street. Parking available on neighborhood roads or at Cayuga Park. GPS: N 44 58.003 W 93 05.488

THE RIDE

In a leisurely 18 miles, the Gateway Trail captures the hybridization of Minnesota's urban and rural landscapes. Its humble St. Paul trailhead is enveloped by a quiet city neighborhood just a mile northeast of the state Capitol, and only a nondescript wooden sign marks the start of this revered trail. Built by the Minnesota Department of Natural Resources in 1993 along an abandoned Soo Line Railroad corridor, the path is one of the most accessible and popular rail-trails in the state. The 8-foot-wide path allows ample room for a smooth and stress-free Sunday afternoon spin to regular training rides, and the trail's proximity to downtown St. Paul makes it a perfect escape for city-dwellers in search of greener pastures. Traveling first through an urban residential and commercial jungle, the path soon meets large stands of hardwood forest with

Minnesota's state capitol in St. Paul
SHUTTERSTOCK.COM

dramatic views of adjoining farmland, passes rolling, open prairie, and curves through aromatic pine stands on the way into Stillwater.

The initial 1.5 miles of the Gateway Trail flirt with I-35 and weave through a largely commercial and industrial area of St. Paul, amidst the blur of freeway traffic. Just past the din, however, the trail passes the Gateway State Trail Community Garden and promptly recedes from the cityscape into a thickly wooded residential area. The Community Garden, cared for by residents under the guidance of the Gateway Trail Association and the Minnesota DNR, echoes the city-country vibe so characteristic of the Gateway. Seeing city folk carefully tilling soil and tending plants, with the highway behind and a verdant tunnel of trees ahead, lends a blurred sense of place—are we riding in a city or a developed wilderness?

The path travels through a woodsy wonderland for roughly 4 miles, ample buffers of foliage obscuring the residential sprawl just beyond, and slices through the center of Phalen-Keller Regional Park, a 750-acre oasis boasting a pair of lakes, swimming beach, fishing, paddling, and two golf courses (the links at the Keller section of the park were developed in the late 1920s, and the course was a regular stop on the pro golf tours). Spur trails branch into the park's extensive path circuits for noodling around the shoreline. Beyond the park, the trail intersects the Bruce Vento Regional Trail, a 7-mile rail-trail following a former Burlington Northern Railroad corridor. Named for the St. Paul native and US representative, the Vento trail is a tempting extension to a Gateway ride. Plan a side trip south to roll through historic Swede Hollow, site of downtrodden, 1800s-era immigrants, the Hamm's Brewery, and the city's early railroad days.

Approaching the 6-mile mark, the Gateway passes the North St. Paul Ecology Center, the trail's first of many serene wetland views. Farmland for decades, the City of North St. Paul, with the aid of the University of Minnesota Department of Landscape Architecture, restored the area to its original wetland landscape in the late 1990s, and the land now serves as a valuable environmental education tool for urban schools. The trail returns to an urban landscape for a few miles following the Ecology Center as the trail parallels MN 36. Stop for a photo op next to the world's largest stucco snowman at the Holiday gas station for one of the trail's only convenient places for food, water, and restrooms. (I wonder how Frosty looks in Lycra?) Bike break down?

Bike Shop

For two decades, **Gateway Cycle** has been the trailside go-to for on-the-spot repairs, gear restocking, and bike rentals. Across MN 36 at Century Avenue. 6028 MN 36 Blvd., Oakdale; (651) 777-0188; gatewaycycle.com.

The Munger Trail

Passionate Minnesota state legislator Willard Munger worked tirelessly for environmental protection and the establishment of long-distance recreation trails, and thanks to his efforts, cyclists have at their disposal one of the longest paved trails in the United States. The Willard **Munger State Trail** runs 70 miles between Hinckley and Duluth, following the former St. Paul and Duluth Railroad past spectacularly scenic countryside, especially the stretch from Carlton to Duluth, where the path crosses the St Louis River and glides through Jay Cooke State Park. The Munger Trail is part of a collection of three area trails, including the Alex Laveau Memorial Trail from Gary-New Duluth to Carlton, and the Matthew Lourey State Trail, a natural surface trail along Minnesota's east central border; dnr.state.mn.us, munger-trail.com.

The historic Stillwater lift bridge

Gateway and Browns Creek State Trails

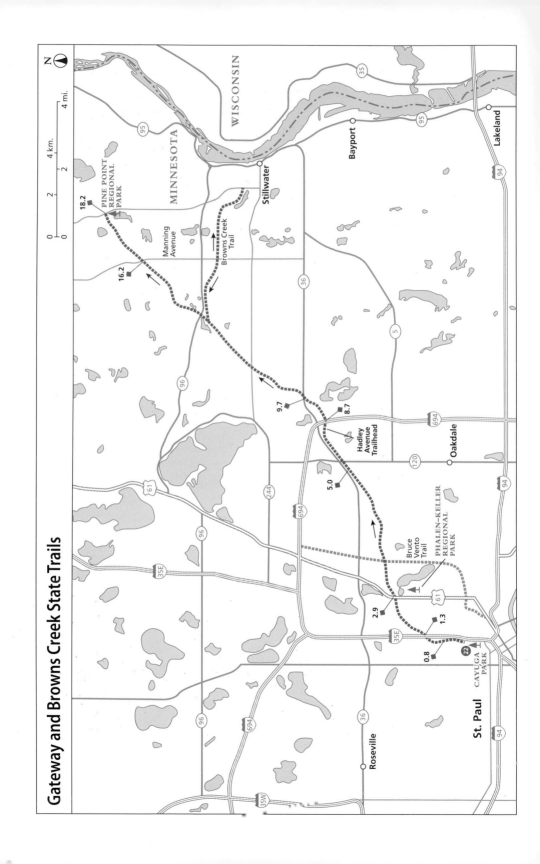

> One of Minnesota's only remaining wrought-iron bridge structures, Historic Bridge #5721 was moved from the state's far north to continue service as safe passage for trail users over CR 15 near Stillwater. The circa-1877 bridge boasts a unique camelback truss and is listed on the National Register of Historic Places.

Head across MN 36 at Century Avenue to Gateway Cycle for repairs and gear. Rentals available here, too, and at mile 8, at the junction with Hadley Avenue, is a parking lot, picnic tables, and restrooms; a great mid-ride rest stop or alternate trailhead for a shorter ride.

The ride takes on a completely new feel around mile 9, when the Gateway enters into rural Washington County. Likely to accompany cyclists and joggers on this trail segment are turtles crossing the pavement from one marshland to another (the Gateway passes an impressive fifty-eight individually protected wetland habitats) and wild turkeys rustling out from tall crops and grasses common to the area's farms. Glistening water, grazing livestock, and fields of baled hay replace views of highways and forested St. Paul backyards, and a separate, parallel trail for horses further transforms the cityscape into a pastoral paradise in a few short miles. In addition to transitioning from urban to rural, the landscape also takes on characteristics of northern Minnesota, with conifers and birch trees increasingly populating the trailside as the Gateway makes its way toward its northern terminus at Pine Point Regional Park, an area filled, naturally, with peaceful pines, as well as restrooms, water fountains, and parking.

By the time you read this, the Gateway will have sprouted an extension. The Browns Creek Trail curves along the former route of the Minnesota Zephyr tourist train for 6.5 miles from Duluth Junction through the woods into Stillwater, adding a dynamic dimension to the ride with Stillwater's stacked inventory of shops, restaurants, and riverside distractions. Stay tuned, as well, for future mileage to the Gateway heading south to the state capitol and north to Taylor's Falls.

MILES AND DIRECTIONS

0.0 Start at St. Paul trailhead at Cayuga Park.

0.8 Pass underneath Maryland Avenue.

1.3 Cross I-35.

2.9 Enter the Phalen-Keller park area.

4.0 Pass Bruce Vento Regional Trail.

5.0 Pass the giant snowman.

7.4 Junction with Century Avenue and access to Gateway Cycle.

8.1 Hadley Avenue trailhead, with restrooms, parking, picnic tables.

8.7 Pass under I-694.

9.7 Pass under MN 36.

13.7 Cross Dellwood Road.

16.2 Cross Historic Bridge 5721 over Manning Avenue.

18.2 Arrive at Pine Point Regional Park trailhead. The Browns Creek Trail continues 6.5 miles to downtown Stillwater.

RIDE INFORMATION

Restaurants
St. Paul's oldest family-owned Italian restaurant, **Yarusso-Bros.,** is a Twin Cities tradition, with delectable homemade pasta, sandwiches, and pizza. Ride in for free pasta on the first Saturday of the month in summer. 635 Payne Ave., St. Paul; (651) 776-4848; yarussos.com.

Area Events
The quaint town of **Stillwater** is a local hot spot for one-of-a-kind restaurants, antiques shopping, and boating on the St. Croix River. An enjoyable stop at any time of year, the self-proclaimed "best small town in Minnesota" is particularly worth the stop in fall with fiery colors reflecting on the rivers.

Washington County Tour

This 23-mile cruise is shaped like Santa's boot and treats you to the gift of rolling and open roads of Washington County, with a shoreline ride along Lake Elmo and a refreshing swim, and nearby eats, back at the trailhead.

Start: Lily Lake Park on Greeley Street in Stillwater

Distance: 23.2-mile loop

Approximate riding time: 1.5 hours

Best bike: Road

Terrain and surface type: Mix of flats and rolling on smooth paved roads

Highlights: Beauteous countryside, lake views, post-ride swim, and Stillwater distractions

Hazards: Use caution at busier road crossings like MN 36 and MN 5

Maps: *USGS Stillwater*

Getting there: From I-694, follow US 36 7 miles east to Greeley Street, and turn north 0.5 mile to Lily Lake Park. GPS: N 45 02.722 W 92 49.287

THE RIDE

This part of Washington County is a bastion of lots of open country, active farms, and some superb roads for riding. The route rolls gently past fields and woods and over a dozen lakes, including the eastern 1.5-mile Lake Elmo shoreline on a sublime tour southeast of Stillwater.

Head south from Lily Lake on Greeley Avenue, with a good shoulder after passing Carver Crest Boulevard, through light industrial and residential areas to MN 36. This is a busy road, but the controlled intersection allows a safe

Wooded and rolling on 30th Street

crossing. Still, stay alert and keep southbound on Oakgreen Avenue past a big, wooded area to your left and a narrow open space corridor with a bike path crossing leading through a residential neighborhood and a couple of tree farms. Resplendent, oversize homes are tucked in the woods along this stretch, right about where the road becomes Northbrook Avenue. Enjoy much of the same scenery to 40th Street and head east and south again past sprawling country estates, older farmsteads, and pothole lakes. Thirtieth Street rolls farther east into a heavily wooded area and down a fun descent to Stagecoach Trail, a favorite road of local riders that winds from Oak Park Heights all the way to the St. Croix River crossing near Prescott, Wisconsin. Ride southbound here, past a gigantic gravel pit and farm fields on your left and residential on the right. CR 10 leads westbound, paralleling I-94 about 1 mile to the south, on 4 miles of generally flat road. The route turns back north on Lake

Bike Shop

Fuel up with locally sourced and organic grub, and get a tune-up at the same time at **Chilkoot Cafe & Cyclery,** conveniently located near the base of the 23 percent ramp of Chilkoot Hill, for your riding pleasure. 826 4th St. S, Stillwater; (651) 342-1048; chilkootcc.com.

Elmo Avenue, beginning a gradual ascent and cruise past the entire eastern shore of Lake Elmo, with some good lake views through the trees. Originally named Bass Lake, this was a great fishing hole that attracted tourists from the Twin Cities and Stillwater, and the first town, Bass Lake Station (today's Lake Elmo) was home to a popular hotel and county fairgrounds. The main road to the action here in the late 1800s was the Stillwater Road (modern-day MN 5), used by stagecoaches shuttling passengers between St. Paul and Stillwater, and the little village enjoyed over a decade of success as a tourist destination, eventually giving way to a more agricultural-based town.

Take a quick jog west on MN 5 and back north on Lake Elmo Avenue, past a couple of farm fields and country homes to a second crossing of MN 36. Just about 1 mile up the road is the eastbound turn onto CR 12, past the last few crop fields before rolling into the outskirts of Stillwater's residential domain and a nice descent back to Greeley Avenue's homestretch (right past Nelson's Drive-Inn Dairy) to Lily Lake.

MILES AND DIRECTIONS

0.0 Start at the Lily Lake trailhead. Ride south on Greeley Street.

0.7 Cross MN 36, blending into Oakgreen Avenue.

1.0 Junction with North 58th Street; continue straight ahead. Oakgreen becomes Northbrook Avenue at about mile 1.5.

3.1 Left turn onto 40th Street.

3.4 Right turn to continue south onto Oakgreen Avenue.

4.5 Left turn onto 30th Street.

6.1 Right turn onto Stagecoach Trail (CR 21).

8.2 Right turn onto CR 10.

12.5 Turn right onto Lake Elmo Avenue (CR 17).

15.2 Turn left onto CR 5 (Stillwater Boulevard) and quick right to continue north on CR 17.

17.8 Pass MN 36.

19.3 Turn right onto CR 12, blending into Myrtle Street in Stillwater.

22.5 Turn right onto Greeley Street.

23.2 Arrive back at Lily Lake Park trailhead.

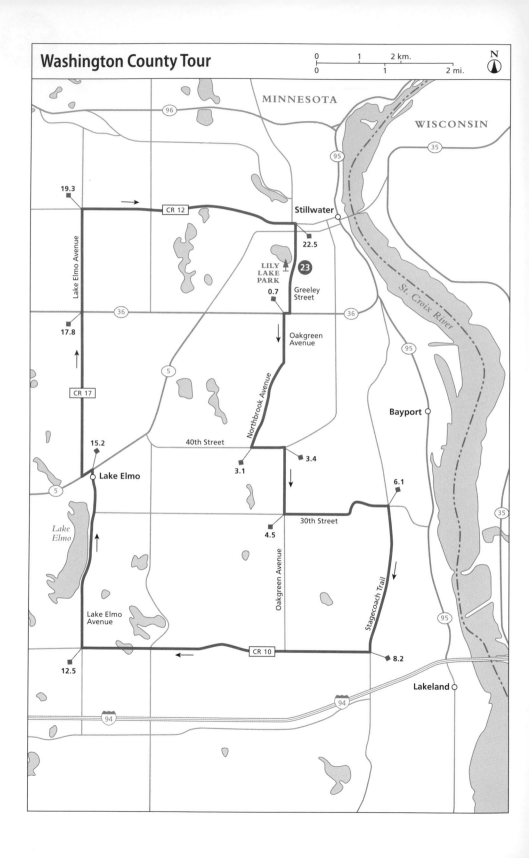

Washington County Tour

0   1   2 km.

0   1   2 mi.

N

MINNESOTA

WISCONSIN

96

95

35

19.3

CR 12

Stillwater

22.5

Lake Elmo Avenue

LILY
LAKE
PARK

23

0.7

Greeley
Street

36

36

St. Croix River

95

17.8

5

Bayport

CR 17

Oakgreen
Avenue

Northbrook Avenue

15.2

40th Street

3.1

3.4

6.1

5

Lake Elmo

Lake
Elmo

30th Street

35

95

4.5

Stagecoach Trail

Lake Elmo
Avenue

Oakgreen Avenue

12.5

CR 10

8.2

Lakeland

94

94

RIDE INFORMATION

Restaurants

Overindulge with giant scoops of bliss like Salt Carmel Nut at **Nelson's Drive-Inn Dairy** ice cream shop. 920 Olive St. W., Stillwater; (651) 439-3598.

Relax with a Triple Docker sandwich and glass of red on the deck overlooking the St. Croix at **Dock Cafe,** 425 E. Nelson St., Stillwater; (651) 430-3770.

Area events

Bring the family for the annual **Washington County Bluegrass Festival,** with great food, kids' activities, and camping. Early September at Lake Elmo Park Reserve, 1515 Keats Ave.; (651) 430-8370; co.washington.mn.us.

Big Rivers and Lilydale

This 14-mile out-and-back is one of the most scenic and relaxing cruises in the metro. The pan-flat path glides along long stretches of riverside frontage, curves around in river flats forest, and scores a halfway point rest stop with postcard skyline views of downtown St. Paul.

Start: Trailhead at Sibley Memorial Highway and MN 13

Distance: 14 miles out and back

Approximate riding time: 1–1.5 hours

Best bike: Road or hybrid

Terrain and surface type: Flat, paved trail, and short sections of road

Highlights: Great view of the Minnesota-Mississippi Rivers confluence, scenic river and St. Paul views, fun riding in wildlife-filled woods, nearby patio dining for post-ride cool-down

Hazards: Use caution at road crossings, especially at the Lilydale Road railroad bridge

Other considerations: Beware of water, sand, and other detritus on trail or roads after heavy rains or spring snowmelt

Maps: *USGS St. Paul SW*

Getting there: From MN 55, follow MN 12 0.8 mile to Sibley Memorial Highway. Turn right and a quick left into the trailhead parking and overlook. GPS: N 44 51.998 W 93 10.393

THE RIDE

I remember driving along MN 13 as a kid, before I-35 was completed to the south, to get over to the Mendota Bridge and I-494. The overlook obscured by shrubbery along the road intrigued me. There always seemed to be a tired, rusty Chevy parked there, or an old Triumph motorcycle holding up a road-weary hombre in a sun-faded leather vest. Questionable clientele and aging transportation aside, I wanted to stop for a closer look at what they saw over the crumbling stone wall, and that was a bird's-eye view of the treetops of the shallow Minnesota River Valley and a count-the-rivets close vantage of jets landing at the airport. It took awhile, but the freeway finally got finished and I eventually made it back to that same overlook, this time on my bike, and yep, the view is indeed a good one. The place is spick-and-span now, the stone wall is restored and handily holding up the earth around the parking lot, and a velvet-smooth bike path unfurls along the river. The Big Rivers Regional Trail is one of my favorites, with its elevated views of the confluence of its namesake rivers, twisty forest sections, and stellar city views.

Roll out from the trailhead and follow it across MN 13, riding along the old rail bed underneath the Mendota Bridge and through the tunnel into the bluffs of Mendota, one of Minnesota's oldest original settlements. Cruise past Lucky's 13 and Axel's (pick out a good spot on the patio for after the ride) and cross MN 13 again. Here the path is flanked by a limestone cliff on one side and a short way along passes the confluence of the Minnesota and Mississippi Rivers (good hiking trails over there for another day) on the way to Lilydale. When the path meets Lilydale Road, hang a left and ride past the yacht club (see sidebar), ditching the road in short order when the path darts into the trees. A bend in the trail at Pickerel Lake leads back across the road and into a fun stretch of curves adjacent to the river, under an old railroad bridge (short road section), and continues right along the riverbank. The trail briefly runs

Riverside Retreat

A ferocious flood in 1951 nearly carried away the Thompson home along the Mississippi in Lilydale, compelling the owners to sell and move on. A private organization purchased the property and built an exclusive club on the site, featuring obligatory, nautically themed decor to complement its famous river next door, including a large ship's wheel set in the ceiling and a ship's prow-shaped lounge. The Pool and Yacht Club opened to rave reviews in the spring of 1956, and loyal members still drop anchor at this under-the-radar retreat today.

Bluffside river overlook
WAYNE HOKLAS

out of space where the river squeezes in, and follows Water Street to the bottom side of Cherokee Park at Joy Avenue, resuming again through a corridor of dense foliage and intermittent river views to the shadow of the 160-foot Smith Avenue High Bridge. The original span was completed in 1895 and partially rebuilt nine years later after severe storm damage, and eventually deteriorated to the point of demolition. The highest in St. Paul, the landmark, arched bridge links St. Paul's Seventh Street and West Side neighborhoods. Past the bridge, a top-shelf panorama of the St. Paul skyline emerges around a gentle bend at Plato Boulevard, and this final section is a perfect place to just coast and take in the sights of Harriet Island, the harbor, and the rarified vibe of the city's river flats neighborhood. Hang out a bit and retrace your tracks back to patio dining in Mendota and the trailhead.

MILES AND DIRECTIONS

0.0   Start at the Sibley trailhead and overlook.

0.4   Cross Sibley Memorial Highway.

1.2   Pass under MN 55.

1.3   Ride through the tunnel under MN 13.

1.6   Pass the patio dining scene behind Lucky's 13 and Axel's.

1.9   Cross MN 13 again.

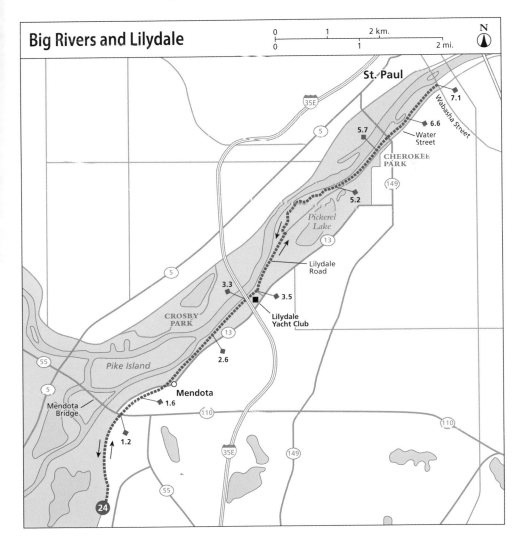

Big Rivers and Lilydale

Cruising along Lilydale Road
WAYNE HOKLAS

2.6 Pass the confluence of the Minnesota and Mississippi Rivers, just off your left shoulder.

3.3 Pass under I-35.

3.5 Turn left onto Lilydale Road. Follow the road a short distance to the continuation of the trail.

4.3 Meet Lilydale Road again and ride straight across.

5.2 Junction with Lilydale Road once again. Watch traffic, ride under the railroad bridge, and back on to the trail.

5.5 Short jog on the road and back to the trail.

5.7 Return to the trail, paralleling Water Street.

6.2 Pass under the High Bridge.

6.6 Junction with Plato Boulevard. Keep heading east past the Harriet Island bandshell.

7.1 Trail "ends" under the Wabasha Street bridge, but the riverside path continues for a bit along the river for great views of the towboats and barges. Retrace your tracks to the Sibley trailhead.

14.2 Arrive back at the trailhead.

RIDE INFORMATION

Restaurants
Carbo-load in style on the backyard patio at **Axel's River Grille,** 1318 Sibley Memorial Hwy., Mendota; (651) 686-4840; axelsrestaurants.com.

Area events
Head to Eagan's Central Park for the summer-long **Market Fest,** with a huge farmers' market, weekly concerts, and kids art tent. Wednesday, 4 to 8 p.m.; 1501 Central Pkwy; cityofeagan.com.

Lilydale's name was, not surprisingly, inspired by lily flowers, which grew in abundance and decorated nearby Pickerel Lake.

25

St. Croix—Scandia Tour

Allow plenty of time to soak in the scenery on this country ride. The entire route (16, 20, or 35 miles) follows quiet, rolling hills from the St. Croix River to Scandia's rural environs. Wide, smooth shoulders and only sporadic traffic make for a relaxing trip, and numerous spur roads inspire adventure. Be sure to stop in Scandia, the first Swedish settlement in Minnesota (1850), the old Hay Lake School, and the state's first commercial sawmill and other historic gems in Marine on St. Croix.

Start: Marine General Store, 101 Judd St., Marine on St. Croix, or anywhere in downtown Scandia

Distance: 16.5 miles on northern loop from Scandia, 20 miles on southern loop from Marine on St. Croix, or combine for a 35.6-miler

Approximate riding time: 1–1.5 hours southern or northern loops, 2-plus hours for both loops

Best bike: Road or hybrid

Terrain and surface type: Gently rolling (with one long climb) on smooth, paved roads and pathways

Highlights: Spectacular, rolling countryside; postcard-worthy rustic roads through the woods; great lakeside scenery; small-town charm; historical sites

Hazards: Traffic can get heavy on weekends in both towns; choppy pavement and narrow shoulder on CR 4

Other considerations: Check event calendars for town festivals and other celebrations, and plan your ride to avoid, or join, the crowds

Maps: *USGS Scandia*

Getting there: Marine on St. Croix is on MN 95, halfway between Stillwater and Taylors Falls. GPS: N 45 19.995 / W 92 76.786. Turn right onto Maple Street from MN 95 and park along Judd Street. Scandia is 11 miles east of I-35 on MN 97. GPS: N 45 11.906 W 92 46.171. Start anywhere in the vicinity of Olinda Trail and CR 52.

THE RIDE

Nestled in the folds of the western banks of the St. Croix River, Marine on St. Croix is an enchanting little hamlet with a firm grip on its proud history. Many town buildings still serve as originally intended and remain in impeccable condition along Judd Street. The 1-block "downtown" boasts the 1872 Stone House Museum, Village Hall, and the General Store. The Stone House is

Early spring at Gammelgarden Museum and historic site in Scandia

a beautifully rugged stone building constructed using techniques from Swedish pioneers. Inside are displays of articles from life in the village's young years. The Village Hall is the oldest building in the state still used for government purposes. Way back in '64, town residents had the vision to establish a Restoration Society to preserve buildings like these, and the community's character is as strong as ever, holding a proud position on the National Register of Historic Places.

This is also the site of the first commercial sawmill in Minnesota. Two lumbermen from Illinois traveled to the St. Croix River area and settled here, attracted by the majestic and plentiful pine forests. They built a sawmill, with three mill wheels powered by the little stream nearby, and enjoyed much success in the logging industry for nearly sixty years. When the logging era ended, however, many of the towns met the same demise as the trees, and fell into ruin or disappeared altogether. An interpretive trail and overlook in the woods adjacent to the stream's waterfall provides a look at the remains of the stone foundations of this mill and offers information on the village's history.

If you can extract yourself from this Norman Rockwell scene, roll out of town on a short climb on MN 95's wide shoulder (watch traffic here, especially on weekends) and ride 1 mile to the bike path on the west side of the road. The path parallels the highway through open meadow and mini pine stands to the entrance road to William O'Brien State Park. This sweeping valley's rich natural resources of wild game, plants, and ideal location for a village first attracted the Dakota and Ojibwe Indians, followed by European trappers filtering in to cash in on the fur-trade industry. In the early 1800s, the lumberjacks moved in and cut every stick of white pine in sight, and the collection of sawmills along the St. Croix River enjoyed great success until all the trees were gone. One lumber baron, William O'Brien, bought much of the land once owned by the lumber companies, and in 1947 his daughter donated 180 acres to be developed as a state park in memory of her father. Plan to stop back to explore the park as you continue north on MN 95 to the tiny town of Copas and head west on the curvy 199th Street. A long, steady climb through dense hardwood forest leads up to CR 52, which rolls along through a mix of

Bike Shop

A common sight in downtown Marine during the riding season is a couple of cyclists lounging outside the front door of Oliver Vrambout's **Bikery du Nord,** savoring a delicious European pastry. Vrambout's shop mixes his flair for baking and love of bikes into an irresistible blend, with vintage bicycle ads and jerseys on the walls, and regular club rides. 41 Judd St.; (651) 433-5801.

The author's kids at one of Marine on St. Croix's original homesteads.

open meadow and woods into Scandia, a small village of proud Scandinavian lineage and great place to whittle away some time. This is Minnesota's first Swedish immigrant settlement, established right here around 1850 by three strapping young men who traveled here and set up a farm near Hay Lake. The hamlet of Scandia grew up around the farm and today remains a tight-knit community of friends and neighbors, with lively celebrations and activities all year long. Central to the town's personality is the Gammelgarden Museum, a wonderfully restored collection of buildings displaying the history of early Swedish immigrants. Tour the site from May through October, and check their events calendar for programs and classes (gammelgardenmuseum.org). "Gammelgarden" means "old farm" in Swedish, and the 1868 log house on the Johannes Erickson farm near Hay Lake was also restored and moved to the historic corner of Scandia.

From Scandia, ride north on Olinda Trail to make the big northern loop. Impeccable homesteads with spick-and-span barns and idyllic pastures unravel from both sides of the road, and you're likely to see more tractors and cows than other people out here. The shoulder is wide and it is a fun, relaxing stretch of road. A jog west on CR 83 and south on CR 85 leads back south

> ## A River Runs Through It
>
> One of the eight original rivers designated by Congress at the 1968 establishment of the National Wild & Scenic Rivers Program, the **St. Croix National Scenic Riverway** is a 154-mile corridor of exceptional natural beauty, cultural history, and recreation. A vital trade and transportation route for American Indians, explorers, and traders from its headwaters at Upper St. Croix Lake in Solon Springs, Wisconsin, the St. Croix remains one of the last undisturbed floodplain rivers in the upper Mississippi River region. Traveling first through dense forest and around wooded islands, the river's lower reaches, from MN 70 to the confluence with the Mississippi near Prescott, are flanked with steep, rocky bluffs, winding side channels, and stellar views in all directions. Bald eagles are common sights along the river, best seen from the prow of a canoe or kayak en route to a riverside campsite.

through the wide-open countryside to the north side of Bone Lake. Wiggle down the shoreline road or arrow-straight Meadowbrook Road to return to Scandia on Oakhill Road.

The rest of the south loop starts with a long, barely rolling cruise on Olinda Trail, passing more old farms and decadent country estates to 195th Street, a smooth and blissfully quiet road passing the northern end of Long Lake. Start whistling the Andy Griffith tune in your head and turn north onto Mayberry Trail, winding up through the trees to Maxwill Avenue and dropping back south along the fringes of Big Marine Lake. Frolic along the zigs and zags of the southeast track past shoreline wetlands and great views of the lake's bays and resident critters like great blue herons, wood ducks, turtles sunbathing on slimy logs, and kingfishers hunting for a snack. Back at Olinda Trail, keep on southbound to CR 4 and ride east and south some more all the way to Oakland Cemetery, where the main road takes a hard left and descends into Marine on St. Croix. Watch the steep drop approaching MN 95; high speed and an abrupt stop sign don't go well together. Cruise back to the trailhead and plan on staying awhile.

Marine is a great place to lose track of time. Just moseying through town with ice cream from the Village Scoop is the perfect activity on a lazy summer day. Or sample hometown hospitality at the Brookside Bar and Grill, a 75-year-old town favorite, and the General Store. The town's charm is infectious, and it's common to see people wandering about with big grins on their faces for no apparent reason.

MILES AND DIRECTIONS

0.0 Start at Judd Street in Marine on St. Croix.

1.0 Dart left onto the bike path on west side of the highway.

1.8 Junction with William O'Brien State Park. Go right, back out to the highway.

2.9 Left turn onto 199th Street in village of Copas.

4.1 Left turn onto CR 52.

5.6 Junction with Olinda Trail in Scandia. Turn right for the big, 37-mile loop, or left to complete the southern 20-miler.

Option:

Northern loop mileages, heading north on Olinda Trail:

12.6 Turn left onto CR 83.

13.6 Turn left again onto CR 85.

17.6 Right turn onto 238th Street.

17.9 Left turn onto Meadowbrook Avenue (or ride a few pedal strokes farther west to wind along the shoreline of Bone Lake).

19.1 Go left onto Oakhill Road (CR 52), southeast back into Scandia.

22.0 Junction with Olinda Trail. Turn right and head south.

Continuation of long loop:

23.7 Turn right onto 195th Street.

24.0 Right turn onto Mayberry Trail.

26.1 Go left onto Maxwill Avenue.

27.2 Turn left again onto Lakagama Trail.

30.0 Turn right onto Olinda Trail.

31.5 Turn left onto CR 4.

35.4 Junction with MN 95. Cross carefully and roll back to the trailhead.

35.6 Arrive back at Judd Street trailhead.

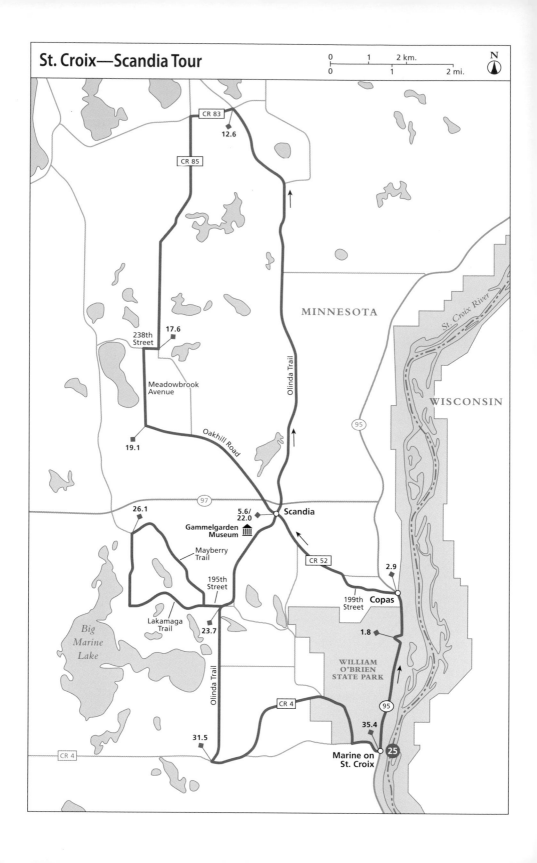

St. Croix—Scandia Tour

0   1   2 km.
0   1   2 mi.

N

CR 83
12.6

CR 85

MINNESOTA

St. Croix River

238th
Street   **17.6**

Meadowbrook
Avenue

WISCONSIN

Oakhill Road

19.1

95

97

26.1

**5.6/
22.0**   ◆   **Scandia**

**Gammelgarden
Museum** 🏛

Mayberry
Trail

CR 52

2.9

195th
Street

199th
Street   **Copas**

Lakamaga
Trail

23.7

1.8

*Big
Marine
Lake*

Olinda Trail

**WILLIAM
O'BRIEN
STATE PARK**

CR 4

95

31.5

35.4

CR 4   25

**Marine on
St. Croix**

25

RIDE INFORMATION

Restaurants

The eighty-years-strong **Brookside Bar and Grill** isn't actually at the side of the brook, but over it. Mill Stream runs right through the basement, where cans of milk were stored by the creamery originally housed here. Don't miss the great food and brews. 140 Judd St., Marine on St. Croix; (651) 433-1112; brooksidebar andgrill.com.

Formerly the General Store's chicken coop, the little building transformed to an ice cream shop in 1977. Renamed the **General Scoop** in 2012, new owners also added a patio overlooking the stream and yummy new flavors. Behind the General Store at 101 Judd St.; (651) 433-2445.

Head to **Meister's Bar and Grill** in Scandia to gobble their famous burgers and a frosty beverage. 14808 Oakhill Rd.; (651) 433-5230; meisters bar.com.

> Log jams were a frequent result of the overzealous and destructive practices of loggers in the 1800s. The granddaddy of them all happened in 1886 at a riverbend in a rocky gorge, when more than 150 million board feet of logs plugged up the river.

Area events

For one packed day of unadulterated fun, Scandia comes together for **Taco Daze,** with bucketloads of great food, a parade, kids' activities, and farmers' market. Early September; scandiamn.com.

Riding to William O'Brien State Park

West Side—Inver Grove Circuit

*Start at a scenic bluffside park above downtown St. Paul on this 25-mile ram-
bler, and roll a sinuous route through idyllic neighborhoods, with a couple of
big climbs thrown in to keep things lively. Great river and skyline views near the
Cherokee Park trailhead.*

Start: Cherokee Heights Regional Park; start at parking area at Cherokee
Heights Boulevard and Chippewa Avenue

Distance: 25 miles

Approximate riding time: 1.5–2 hours

Best bike: Road

Terrain and surface type: Rolling, with two big climbs, on paved roads

Highlights: Cherokee Heights Park and views of the Mississippi River,
Salem Church neighborhood, Dodge Nature Center

Hazards: Use caution crossing MN 110 and South Robert Street/I-494.
Moderate traffic along most of the northern section of the route, but
shoulders provide a cushion.

Maps: *USGS St. Paul East*

Getting there: From downtown St. Paul, follow the Smith Avenue High
Bridge south across the Mississippi. Turn right immediately across the
bridge onto Cherokee Avenue. Follow Cherokee Avenue to Baker Street,
and go right 2 blocks to the trailhead parking. GPS: N 44 55.592 W 93
06.430

THE RIDE

There is more than just pavement beneath your wheels on the start of this ride. Deep in the sandstone bluff below Cherokee Park are the remains of tunnels and caverns where Decorah shale was quarried and fired into bricks by the Twin Cities Brick Company, beginning in the late 1800s. Many of the original buildings of Minneapolis and St. Paul were built with bricks gleaned from this riverside bluff. A hike along the Bruce Vento's View/Brickyard Trail is a recommended side trip to get up close to this unique area (see sidebar).

The park road snakes south and merges with MN 13. Ride the smooth shoulder to the crest of the hill descending to "downtown" Lilydale, and turn left onto Sylvandale Road. This twisty road follows a long descent through quiet Mendota Heights neighborhoods to a crossing of a miniature streamlet

Babcock Trail

that falls into a wide half-moon bowl below, then to the Mississippi. Barely visible from the road, the huge ravine is well worth exploring on foot from the river. Climb back uphill and follow Clement Street (Sylvandale morphs into Clement, no turns) to a hard left at 1st Avenue, and out to Dodd Road at mile 2. A right turn here follows a smooth, wide shoulder southbound to Wentworth Avenue. Go left for a nearly 1-mile climb up past the manicured grounds of the Somerset Country Club, where golfers have tested their wits against a little white ball since 1920, to Charlton Avenue. Turn south and cruise past the Dodge Nature Center at mile number 4. This is one of St. Paul's don't-miss destinations, so stop to visit today, or plan to come back and stay awhile. One of the first nature centers in Minnesota, this 320-acre oasis has been a pioneer in environmental education and habitat restoration since its founding in 1967. Hiking trails wander through the center's three separate properties, and a working farm, bee apiary, sugar shack, and innovative pre-school are all based on the main grounds. (See sidebar for more information.)

Cross Marie Avenue and coast down the last section of Charlton to MN 110. This is a busy road, but regular breaks in traffic allow access to the other side. Cross carefully and continue southbound on a scenic stretch of gravel (Charlton Road) curving through hidden homesites in the Sunfish Lake neighborhood, to the junction with Delaware Avenue at 5.5 miles. Head south to Salem Church Road and veer left. This is a fun, windy road that climbs past sprawling acreages of palatial homes, most of which are hidden down long driveways concealed by 100-year-old oaks and maples and a phalanx of other foliage. Try to stop drooling over the real estate and roll for just over 1 mile to the top of the open ridge and the junction with South Robert Street. As expected, this is a busy road, but the ample shoulder provides a comfortable cushion. Head south across the overpass above I-494 to a careful left turn at Upper 55th Street. At the first gentle curve, on the south shore of Schmidt Lake, is the Old Salem Church, known by locals as the Little White Church. Impeccably maintained by dedicated area residents, the diminutive building, now over 120 years old, held a congregation of just thirty, and the scene inside looks just as it did at the last regular service in 1910. The original wooden pews, wood stove, and pump organ are perfectly preserved, and gentlemanly parishioners in top hats with lovely companions in long gowns and feathered

Bike Shop

Locally owned **Bike King** in Inver Grove Heights has a stacked inventory of road, mountain, and commuter rigs. Close to the route on 6489 Cahill Rd.; (651) 457-7766; bike-king.com.

Oasis in the City

Olivia Irvine Dodge grew up in St. Paul's Summit Avenue neighborhood and eventually settled on land in West St. Paul. Passionate about the environment, especially its influence on children, and way ahead of her time in sustainability-focused life choices and projects, she preserved the land around her home by starting one of the first nature centers in Minnesota. Today, **Dodge Nature Center** spreads across more than 300 acres, including a working farm and award-winning preschool. Hiking trails wind throughout the center's three different properties, and community programs provide opportunities to hone orienteering skills or enjoy a fall hayride. The center is an environmental education leader, introducing kids to nature and animals for over forty years. Kids get to see and feel what they learn right out the back door, learning about beekeeping and maple syruping and habitat restoration, and taking Olivia's message with them into the world—preserving our natural surroundings is the right thing to do. 365 Marie Ave.; (651) 455-4531; dodgenaturecenter.org.

hats would not be out of place. Directly south of the church is Salem Park, familiar to us from the mountain bike trails in Ride 35.

Continue east to a right turn at Babcock Trail, rolling and curving through a woodsy stretch to the 10 mile mark at 70th Street (Lone Oak Road). Keep pushing ahead for another low-traffic mile to 80th Street, where a left turn leads to the junction with Barnes Avenue and US 52. Go right here, paralleling the freeway to the overpass at MN 55. Just to the east, across US 52, a B-52 bomber on a 1958 training flight tragically crashed at the Kahl family farm, engulfing the house in flames. Only one of the flight crew survived, but the Kahls scrambled out to safety. A historical marker commemorates the location along Broderick Boulevard. Once across the highway, cruise a long downhill to 96th Street at mile 13, and turn left, dropping into a quiet neighborhood occupying the site of one of the area's original farmsteads. A long climb takes you back up to level ground alongside US 52, where the route blends into Courthouse Boulevard, heading back west to Barnes Avenue and the start of the return ride. Retrace your tracks to Babcock Trail, and at the junction with Upper 55th Street, continue straight ahead, following a gentle curve across I-494 to a controlled intersection at Mendota Road. Stay alert here, cross when safe, and continue north into West St. Paul on Oakdale Avenue, cruising past Southview Country Club's outer fairways. After only 0.5 mile, split from Oakdale on a left turn at Marie Avenue, and follow a lazy S curve up to

Pickerel Lake and the Mississippi from Cherokee Park

the junction with Robert Street. This is a busy intersection, but the wide lane provides safe passage, and in just a few dozen pedal strokes you're clear of the traffic bedlam, rolling back to the junction with Charlton Avenue. Head north here, riding again past Dodge Nature Center to a left turn at Wentworth Avenue and a northbound cruise on Smith and Delaware Avenues through a quiet neighborhood to Annapolis Street. Cool down on Chippewa Avenue for 7 blocks to Baker Street and hang a left to the trailhead.

MILES AND DIRECTIONS

0.0 Start at trailhead at parking area on Cherokee Heights Boulevard.

1.2 Left turn at Sylvandale Road.

1.9 Veer left at Chestnut Street.

2.1 Turn left onto 1st Avenue.

2.4 Turn right onto Dodd Road.

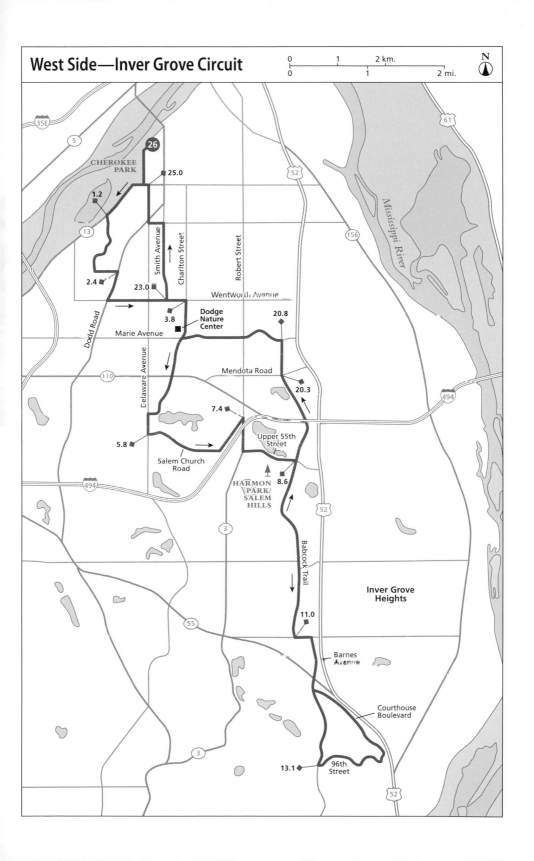

West Side—Inver Grove Circuit

0 1 2 km.

0 1 2 mi.

N

35E

5

CHEROKEE PARK

26

25.0

1.2

13

Smith Avenue

Charlton Street

52

Robert Street

156

Mississippi River

61

2.4

23.0

Wentworth Avenue

3.8

Dodge Nature Center

20.8

Dodd Road

Marie Avenue

Delaware Avenue

110

Mendota Road

20.3

494

7.4

5.8

Upper 55th Street

Salem Church Road

HARMON PARK/ SALEM HILLS

8.6

494

3

52

55

Babcock Trail

Inver Grove Heights

11.0

3

Barnes Avenue

Courthouse Boulevard

13.1

96th Street

52

2.8 Turn left onto Wentworth Avenue.

3.8 Turn right onto Charlton Street.

4.9 Junction with MN 110. Cross carefully to Charlton Road.

5.5 Left turn at Delaware Avenue.

5.8 Left turn at Salem Church Road.

7.4 Turn right onto South Robert Street. Use caution heading over I-494.

8.0 Turn left onto Upper 55th Street, passing the Little White Church and Schmidt Lake

8.6 Go right at Babcock Trail.

10.1 Junction with 70th Street (Lone Oak Road). Continue straight ahead.

11.0 Left turn at 80th Street.

11.3 Right turn at Barnes Avenue, heading south across MN 55.

13.1 Go left at 96th Street, dropping into a shallow valley and up the big climb, continuing on Courthouse Boulevard back to Barnes Avenue.

15.5 Right turn onto Barnes Avenue, retracing your tracks to Babcock Trail.

16.6 Right turn onto Babcock Trail.

20.3 Junction with Mendota Road. Continue straight ahead.

20.8 Left turn at Marie Avenue.

21.4 Junction with South Robert Street. Continue straight ahead.

22.2 Turn right onto Charlton Street.

22.6 Turn left onto Wentworth Avenue.

23.0 Right turn onto Smith Avenue.

24.0 Left turn onto Butler Avenue.

24.2 Right turn onto Delaware Avenue (use caution crossing Dodd Road).

25.0 Junction with Annapolis Street. Turn left and a quick right on Chippewa Avenue.

25.0 Arrive back at trailhead.

RIDE INFORMATION

Restaurants

Jump-start your trip with a specialty coffee and croissant at **Amore Coffee,** or an après-ride vanilla cap smoothie and sandwich. 879 Smith Ave.; (651) 330-0570; amorecoffee.com.

Head to the **Capital View Cafe** at the top of the High Bridge for heaping portions of homegrown goodness. A 20-year fixture on St. Paul's West Side, at 637 Smith Ave.; (651) 290-0218; capitalviewcafe.com.

Area events

With four days of events, the annual **Celebrate West St. Paul Days** celebration has enough distractions to keep the whole family busy, with a kiddie parade, car show, softball tournament, and live music. Third weekend in May, at various locations; celebrateweststpaul.org.

From the late 1800s through the 1970s, the Twin Cities Brick Company quarried Decorah shale from the bluffs below Cherokee Park, firing the stone into bricks in kilns near the river. Footpaths spider-web this fascinating area, passing remnants of quarries and ruins of the old kilns.

Afton Loop

Treat yourself to one of the metro's finest rides on this 31-mile loop with a warm-up on the wide boulevards and county roads of Woodbury and into the challeng-ing and distractingly gorgeous terrain through Afton and the St. Croix River's rolling bluff country.

Start: Ojibway Park in Woodbury

Distance: 31-mile loop

Approximate riding time: 2 hours

Terrain and surface type: Mostly rolling, with a few steep climbs around Afton, on smooth, paved roads

Best bike: Road or hybrid

Highlights: Spectacular scenery all the way through Afton; great views of the St. Croix River; super tough climb from the river; Selma's Ice Cream stop

Hazards: Traffic can be heavy on residential streets in Woodbury, some choppy sections of road south of Afton

Maps: *USGS Hudson*

Getting there: From I-494, exit Lake Road and head 0.3 mile east to Courtly Road. Turn left 0.8 mile to Ojibway Drive and south 1 block to the park. GPS: N 44 54.483 W 92 57.397

THE RIDE

This ride easily ranks near the top of my favorites list. It's a challenging one, with plenty of ups and downs, including one of the toughest climbs in the Twin Cities, and the rewards of a great workout match those of the stunning scenery along the bluffs of the St. Croix River. The route starts at Ojibway Park, in the midst of Woodbury's bustling sprawl. After an easy warm-up through a neighborhood to the south, head east on Lake Road, a main thoroughfare through the fray, but it comes with an ample shoulder and is a fun and curvy sorta rolling stretch of tarmac. Ride Lake Road 4 miles out to Settlers Ridge Parkway and follow it north on its serpentine path to Valley Creek Road and over to Manning Avenue (MN 95). Climb the hill north on the highway's wide shoulder, and bob up and down for a couple of miles on the highway's hills to Hudson Road, the east-west frontage road on I-94's south side. One mile of

Selma's in Afton

Old Town Days

When New England settler James Norris staked an 1842 claim in the area of present-day Lamar Avenue and CR 20, he called his farm "Cottage Grove." In just a few short years following, neighbors moved in and a small village grew up around a general store, and soon a wagon shop, dry goods store, blacksmith shops, and doctors' offices. The little town buzzed with activity for decades, aided in large part by its access to river towns on the Mississippi and St. Croix Rivers, and north to St. Paul, by wagon roads. Soon the development of tract homes and eventually a city center along US 61 transplanted the heart of Cottage Grove to its current location. Several of the original homes still stand in Old Cottage Grove and are listed on the National Register of Historic Places.

flat takes you to Neal Avenue, and onward up a gradual climb to Indian Trail. This is where the fun starts. Indian Trail is a life-list stretch of road not to be missed on your bike, rolling up and mostly down through pine and hardwood forest, on baby bottom–smooth tarmac, all the while passing sprawling properties punctuated with homes verily shouting with curb appeal. Drop down a couple of nice descents and past great views of Lake Edith to Stagecoach Trail. Round two of this elegant introduction to Afton starts here. Just try to keep your eyes on the road as you roll past bucolic countryside and impeccably preserved homes tucked into the woods and perched on meadow-fringed hillsides. Just before reaching the final turn into Afton, look for Afton Hills Drive ramping up into the heavens. This is a dead-end loop road with leg-busting grades for a little bonus workout. Cruise on to Afton's miniature main street and stop for a double scoop at Selma's, or refill your bottle with icy cold water for the big hills in your future.

Roll away from Selma's oasis and turn onto River Road, immediately south of town. This narrow corridor traces past the river, only feet from the water, with a few breaks in the trees for lovely views upstream and across to Wisconsin. Grand homes line the other side for a while, until the road leaves them behind and starts to climb. It's nothing you can't handle at first, but then the grade steepens, and rounds a curve and gets even steeper, and keeps going. A long and tough one, for sure, but great bragging rights. Follow 50th Street to and across St. Croix Trail into more postcard scenery to Trading Post Trail, a long ribbon of sweet road through quiet woods. As you merrily coast down a short hill, the road inexplicably turns to gravel (!) for just about 0.25 mile. One short-lived blemish on an otherwise perfect route, with no apparent reason for the lack of pavement. But you're back in business at the turn south onto Oakgreen Avenue, where silky tarmac leads up a nice hill to the junction with CR 20. There is more traffic on this road, but the shoulder is nearly as wide as another lane for much of the way. Cruise up a gradual hill and head west for about 2.5 miles, past the little village of Old Cottage Grove, and onward to Military Road. Glide along the flat to gently rising grade through wooded countryside to Woodlane Drive, another smooth and relatively quiet road heading back northbound. Pass Bailey Road and stay north to Lake Road, where a quick jog east leads to the homestretch back to Ojibway Park.

Tip: This 31-miler can turn into 10 miles or 100, with myriad options of intimate neighborhood or open county roads to adapt mileage to whatever your mood. Try the rolling hills south in and around Cottage Grove, or smooth and curvy routes north toward Lake Elmo.

St. Croix River

MILES AND DIRECTIONS

0.0 Start at the Ojibway Park trailhead. Ride south on the bike path and go left onto Ojibway Park Road.

0.6 Go left onto Lake Road.

4.5 Turn left onto Settlers Ridge Parkway (a bike path parallels the road for traffic-free comfort).

5.8 Turn right onto Valley Creek Road.

6.5 Left onto Manning Avenue (MN 95).

8.2 Turn right onto Hudson Road.

9.2 Junction with Neal Avenue. Keep on straight ahead.

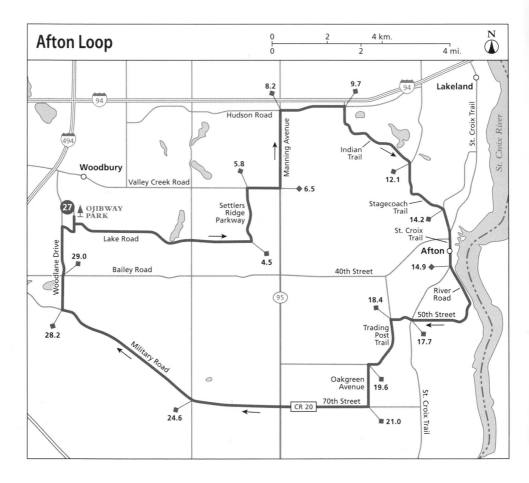

Afton Loop

9.7 Right turn onto Indian Trail.

12.1 Right turn onto Stagecoach Trail.

14.2 Junction with St. Croix Trail. Veer right, into downtown Afton.

14.9 Lean left onto River Road.

17.7 Junction with St. Croix Trail. Ride straight across on 50th Street.

18.4 Left turn at Trading Post Trail.

19.6 Left turn onto Oakgreen Avenue.

21.0 Go right onto CR 20.

23.4 Roll through Old Cottage Grove.

24.6 Junction with Keats Avenue. Head across to continue on Military Road.

28.2 Right turn onto Woodlane Drive.

29.0 Junction with Bailey Road. Head straight across.

30.0 Right turn onto Lake Road.

30.5 Turn left onto Wynham Way.

31.0 Arrive back at Ojibway Park trailhead.

RIDE INFORMATION

Restaurants
Afton lost some of its summer smile when **Selma's,** the oldest ice cream shop in Minnesota, closed down a few years back, leaving tourists and famished cyclists without their favorite treat stop. New owners saved the day, and the venerable ice cream shop is again serving up creamy goodness. Don't miss a giant waffle cone on the patio at 3419 St. Croix Trail; (651) 436-7003.

Area events
Spend a warm summer night with a slice of **Americana at Vali-Hi Drive in,** one of only a few drive-in theaters left in Minnesota. 11260 Hudson Blvd. N, Lake Elmo, (651) 431-7464; valihi.com

Start this 30-miler with a postcard St. Paul skyline backdrop, spinning a flat warm-up before tackling a huge climb to a roller-coaster midsection through the Newport hills and long coast to the Mississippi River. Great mix of flats and challenging climbs, with distracting scenery, legendary pit stops, and wildlife watching.

Start: Battle Creek Regional Park's lower trailhead, 0.5 mile north of Lower Afton Road on Point Douglas Road

Distance: 30 miles out-and-back

Approximate riding time: 2–2.5 hours

Best bike: Road

Terrain and surface type: Big hills at start and finish, flat in middle; mix of smooth and choppy pavement

Highlights: St. Paul skyline views; herons, ducks, and other water-based wildlife on Grey Cloud Island; rail yard activity near the trailhead

Hazards: Moderate to low traffic levels. Use caution at major road crossings like Bailey Road and Robert Street.

Maps: *USGS St. Paul East*

Getting there: From downtown St. Paul, follow Warner Road east to US 61, and head south to Lower Afton Road. Turn left and another left onto Point Douglas Road to the lower trail access of Battle Creek Regional Park. GPS: N 44 56.087 W 93 01.707

THE RIDE

In 30 miles, this ride covers a scenic and challenging course along the Mississippi River bluffs, through two proud, working-class communities, and across a historic Ol' Miss island. There are a few steep hills to test your climbing skills and enough recovery time between them to appreciate the views without hyperventilating.

Roll out from the lower Battle Creek trailhead, taking note of two more ride options: Follow the bike path upstream along the creek into the meat of the park, or dart through the tunnel beneath US 61 and head toward downtown St. Paul. On the short, initial spin, listen to the clanging, squealing, booming of railcars moving through the sprawling Canadian Pacific rail yard on the west side of the highway. After crossing Lower Afton Road, cruise a flat stretch to a left turn onto Springside Drive, leaving rail and road drone behind. The road immediately tilts steeply away from the river, winding up through a

View of St. Paul from Battle Creek trailhead

quiet residential neighborhood for over 0.5 mile. Catch your breath at Burlington Road and follow McKnight Road and Highwood Drive over another climb, this one long and gradual, to a speedy descent to Century Avenue. Ride south underneath I-494,where Century changes identities to Carver Avenue on the other side, at the base of a long, stairstep hill past Carver Lake and its namesake park. Let 'er rip from the park entrance, when the road turns west and drops in a hurry back toward the interstate. In the shadow of the highway's bridge, lean left onto Sterling Avenue, starting a mile-long roller coaster on smooth tarmac en route to Newport. This stretch will test your legs, but the corridor of oaks and maple and birch is distractingly scenic, with an occasional look down to the river valley. Sterling Avenue abruptly ends at Bailey Road, a major thoroughfare through Woodbury. Use caution here; turn left up the hill and a quick right onto Military Road (CR 20). On the left is the nerve center for the Bailey Nurseries empire, an industry powerhouse, family-run nursery with Minnesota roots dating to the 1800s. Large plots of the company's seedling and plant fields are scattered not far from here in southern Woodbury. A right turn onto Century Avenue leads to a long, windy descent through forested Wild Canyon Drive to Glen Road, and more coasting into downtown Newport. Follow 10th and 12th Avenues to the bike bridge at US 61, and continue on 12th Avenue on the other side, working your way to a southern heading through St. Paul Park, where CR 75 heads to a mix of open farm fields and woods. A fork in the road announces Grey Cloud Island Drive veering southeast toward the river, over a short bridge, and on to the island. Even with no grand, visual landmarks, there is a palpable feel of the history of this place; a subdued sense of pride of its original inhabitants pervades the island, way back to 100 BC and the time of the Woodland mound builders. Grey Cloud is also the site of the only known American Indian village in Washington County, settled by a group of the Mdewakanton band in the 1830s.

A flat stretch south and a hard left east brings riders to a second bridge crossing over a channel exiting Mooers Lake, and around the next bend across another bridge back to the "mainland." The bridge is a great spot to stop and check out the vibrant population of waterfowl and other wildlife, like herons, osprey, bald eagles, myriad songbirds, ducks, and geese. Curve past the Mississippi Dunes golf course and up the hill to Hadley Avenue, riding back north to St. Paul Park and across US 61. The eastern frontage road leads through Newport where Glen Road introduces the start of the route's closing hills. Spin a warm-up climb east on Glen Road, and exit on Woodbury Drive for nearly 2 miles of uphill to Bailey Road. Roll up and down along the ridgeline, backtracking on Sterling Avenue, and finally steeply down to US 61, where a bike path parallels the highway to Point Douglas Road and the home stretch to the trailhead.

Grey Cloud Island

Grey Cloud Island is part of the **Mississippi National River and Recreation Area,** a 72-mile corridor of parks, historical sites, natural areas, and a national wildlife refuge in and around the Twin Cities area. The only national park dedicated wholly to the Mississippi River, MNRRA is a "partnership park," managed by a group of like-minded businesses, regulatory agencies, nonprofits, and other landowners working to protect and preserve the Mississippi's unique natural and cultural resources. The park includes urban history of Minneapolis and St. Paul, like the old mill ruins and Stone Arch Bridge, migratory flyways for dozens of raptor species, and critical habitat for both waterfowl and terrestrial wildlife. The maze of coves, inlets, channels, and lakes of the park are best explored by boat, especially the island-dotted stretch between Newport and Hastings. Farther upstream, the Minnesota Valley National Wildlife Refuge is a gold mine for birders, hikers, and solace seekers.

MILES AND DIRECTIONS

0.0 Start at the trailhead at the Battle Creek parking area. Ride 0.5 mile south to Lower Afton Road and carefully cross to continue on Point Douglas Road.

1.6 Turn left onto Springside Drive. Prepare to suffer up the long, steep climb. (Bailout option: From the start, turn left at Lower Afton Road, ride 0.4 mile to the first right at Burlington Road, and follow this curvy route to the top of Springside.)

2.1 Right turn onto Burlington Road, and another quick right onto McKnight Road. Follow the wide shoulder southbound.

2.7 Left turn onto Highwood Drive.

3.7 Right turn onto Century Avenue, heading south underneath I-494 (morphs into Carver Avenue on the other side).

5.0 Left turn onto Sterling Street, a long roller-coaster road toward Newport.

6.0 Junction with Bailey Road. Watch traffic and turn left and a quick right onto Military Road (CR 20).

6.5 Turn right onto Century Avenue.

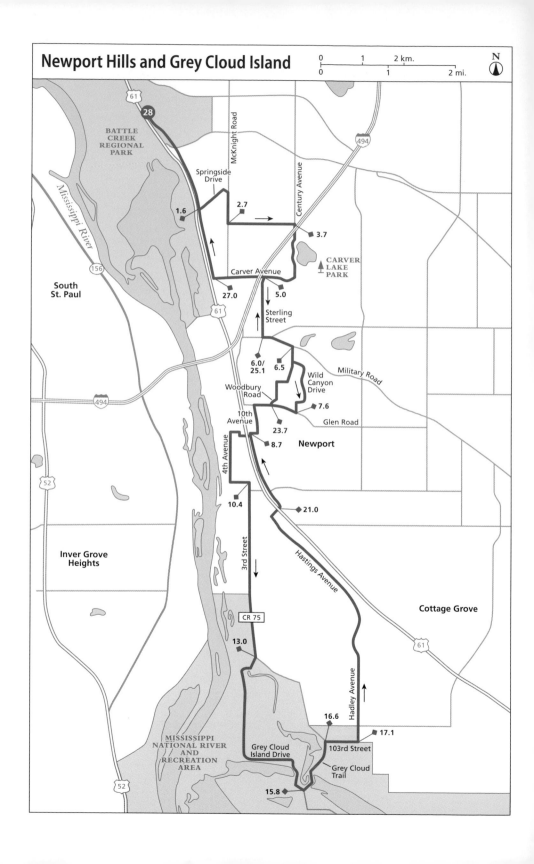

Newport Hills and Grey Cloud Island

BATTLE CREEK REGIONAL PARK

Mississippi River

South St. Paul

Springside Drive

1.6

2.7

McKnight Road

Century Avenue

3.7

CARVER LAKE PARK

Carver Avenue

27.0

5.0

Sterling Street

6.0/ 25.1

6.5

Military Road

Wild Canyon Drive

Woodbury Road

7.6

10th Avenue

Glen Road

23.7

8.7

Newport

4th Avenue

10.4

21.0

Inver Grove Heights

3rd Street

Hastings Avenue

CR 75

13.0

Cottage Grove

MISSISSIPPI NATIONAL RIVER AND RECREATION AREA

Hadley Avenue

16.6

17.1

Grey Cloud Island Drive

103rd Street

Grey Cloud Trail

15.8

6.7 Take the left fork onto Wild Canyon Drive and enjoy a long, windy descent.

7.6 Turn right onto Glen Road, coasting to downtown Newport.

8.3 Left turn onto 10th Avenue.

8.7 Right turn onto 12th Street. Follow 12th Street to the US 61 frontage road and turn left to access the bike bridge crossing US 61.

9.0 Follow 12th Street west to 4th Avenue.

9.3 Left turn onto 4th Avenue.

10.0 Left turn onto 2nd Street.

10.4 Veer right to 3rd Street, riding south all the way through St. Paul Park (3rd Street turns into CR 75 at the south end of town).

13.0 Take the right fork, following CR 75 (Grey Cloud Island Drive) southbound toward the Mississippi River.

14.5 The road takes a 90-degree turn east.

15.5 Cross a river channel flowing into Mooers Lake off your right shoulder.

15.8 Left turn onto Grey Cloud Trail, crossing another bridge over a river narrows, and a great place to spot herons, ducks, and other waterfowl.

16.6 Right turn onto 103rd Street, passing the Mississippi Dunes golf course to a steep climb to the ridgetop.

17.1 The road turns north here and becomes Hadley Avenue. Continue riding northbound back into the outer fringes of St. Paul Park, where Hadley Avenue becomes Hastings Avenue.

Grey Cloud Dunes Scientific and Natural Area, on Upper Grey Cloud Island, is punctuated by terraced sand dunes hosting a rare, river-influenced prairie ecosystem with the likes of little bluestem, penstemen, and sea-beach needlegrass growing in the wind-scoured crescents and blowouts. Take a hike and look for the elusive blue racer snake slithering over the dunes.

Mooers Lake

21.0 Right turn onto Summit Avenue, following increased traffic flow to the bridge over US 61. Cross the highway to the Hastings Avenue frontage road.

22.5 Junction with the bike bridge and 12th Street. Turn right onto 12th and left onto 10th Avenue, backtracking to Glen Road.

23.1 Turn right onto Glen Road, heading back uphill.

23.7 Turn left onto Woodbury Road, and another left onto Kolff Street, climbing steeply to Wild Ridge Trail.

24.0 Turn right onto Wild Ridge Trail and continue the long and steep hill to the Century Avenue junction and stay north to Military Road.

24.6 Turn left onto Military Road and head northwest back to Bailey Road. Use caution and turn left onto Bailey Road.

25.1 Right turn onto Sterling Street, rolling again northbound.

26.0   Left turn onto Carver Avenue, passing McKnight Road and flying down the steep descent to US 61. (Control your speed on the hill; the road ends abruptly at the busy intersection.)

27.0   Right turn at the stoplight, following Point Douglas Road along the highway. In 0.2 mile the road dead-ends. Look for the bike path and keep northbound next to the highway to the continuation of Point Douglas Road.

29.0   Junction with Lower Afton Road. Cross and ride the home stretch back to the trailhead.

30.0   Arrive back at the Battle Creek trailhead.

RIDE INFORMATION

Restaurants

Indulge with a half-pound burger or the Thursday night buffet at **Tinucci's,** over a half-century of family-owned Italian decadence. 396 21st St., Newport; (651) 459-3211; tinuccis.com.

Starting as a soda fountain sidekick of Village Drug in 1947, the **North Pole** restaurant is still a go-to favorite for gastro delights. Roll in for a BLT and big ol' root beer float. 1644 Hastings Ave., Newport; (651) 459-9053; north polerestaurant.com.

Area events

Mud volleyball, classic cars, and mini doughnuts at St. Paul Park's annual **Heritage Days Festival.** Third weekend in August.

smooth, county road steadily descends to the base of the valley, passing a handful of gravel lanes winding toward the bluffs and aged farms tucked into folds in the hills. After one mild climb, the route jumps a railroad track and meets US 61/63. Prepare for increased and faster-moving traffic on this road, but a 6-foot shoulder provides adequate cushion and room to maneuver past scattered, tire-puncturing debris. The scenery is no less spectacular along this 5-mile stretch of highway, and in early morning, fog from the river drifts inland to cloak the tops of the bluffs in shawls of soft gray. The junction with CR 2 arrives just shy of 10 miles, at Frontenac Station, an 1850s-era settlement that sprouted with the arrival of the railroad. The village of Frontenac proper, known as Old Frontenac, a few miles east on the shoreline of the Mississippi's Lake Pepin, grew from a frontier trading post to an attractive, lakeside setting for well-to-do residents, as well as a scenic, summer vacation destination.

Continue the ride westbound on CR 2, a mostly flat 5 miles past woods and fields to CR 5. Now it gets interesting, with a long, windy climb, ramping 300 steep feet to an open ridgetop. Trace the ridge along the cornfields, with one moderate ascent, to a fun flyer down to an immense, pastoral valley bordered by roller-coaster bluffs. Exiting the spectacular scenery, the county road morphs into a residential lane in Lake City, heading east to US 61/63 (North Lakeshore Drive in these parts) and the shores of Lake Pepin. With the lake in sight, ride south to Park Street and follow the shoreline through Chuta Park to a left turn at Chestnut Street and a final 0.25 mile to a rest stop on a pointy

Soaring High

It is difficult not to be inspired watching a bald eagle coast effortlessly on a summer updraft. The great birds moved Rachel Carson's spirit, too, and thanks to her efforts the regal bird thrives today. Carson's seminal book Silent Spring spurred the environmental movement in the 70s and was the catalyst for the banning of DDT and other nasty chemicals that pushed the eagle to extinction's brink. Our national bird came back strong and is now commonly seen nesting and hunting along the upper Mississippi River corridor. River towns like Red Wing, Lake City, and Wabasha are prime locales to spot the big birds, especially in nesting and migration seasons. Head to Colvill Park or Barn Bluff in Red Wing (superlative eagle watching from Barn Bluff's South and Prairie Trails), or the National Eagle Center in Wabasha for an up-close look at injured eagles living at the center, naturalist programs, and great views of fly-bys from the observation deck; redwing .org; nationaleaglecenter.org.

Bluffs near Lake City

peninsula with stellar views of Lake Pepin. Three miles wide and 28 miles long, this is the widest, naturally formed stretch of the entire Mississippi River. Eons of buildup of sediment from the delta of the mouth of Wisconsin's Chippewa River formed the lake, named for the brothers Pepin, two early French trappers. The lake has been a tourist favorite since the steamboat boomtown days and the settling of the village of Pepin, Wisconsin, in 1846 (birthplace of Laura Ingalls Wilder) and still attracts swarms of visitors, especially with the hot summer sun.

Like to waterski? This is the sport's birthplace. In the early 1920s, Ralph Samuelson spent countless hours attempting to ski across the lake on various platforms. First barrel staves, then snow skis, and finally pine boards with curved tips, Samuelson finally floated along the water just before his 19th birthday. He went on to perform the first ski jump on water, was the first speed skier in that fledgling sport, and showed his stuff at waterskiing exhibitions all over Minnesota.

Turn back west for the return ride, retracing your tracks back to Lakeshore Drive and CR 5. A few dozen pedal strokes past the railroad tracks, the route begins a steady rise in altitude through the scenic valley. Short, barely-there downhill grades rapidly give way to more noticeable uphill stretches, and around a corner flanking a distant farm, the challenge of the day comes into view. That giant hill back to the top of the ridge looms, silently taunting, and you fire mental salvos at the brute—I'll dance right up that thing. Thirty seconds faster today. Hills make you strong. Damn, that's a steep climb—throwing yourself closer to the battle. It's nearly 3 miles to the top, with the steepest pitch just before the crest. Once on the ridge, there are four consecutive uphill slopes to further test your resolve. Just about the time the hyperventilating ends, the road unrolls with a 2-plus-mile descent back to the CR 2 junction. Stay west here, passing a couple of quiet country farms toward a curve north, on to the ride's final climb. Point your bike uphill for over 2 miles to the junction with MN 58. A right turn merges into the homestretch on the highway's wide, smooth shoulder, back to Flower Valley Road and the finish.

MILES AND DIRECTIONS

0.0 Start at Red Wing High School. Turn left onto Flower Valley Road for a long downhill and great valley views.

4.6 Right turn onto US 61/63. Use caution with increased traffic, but a wide shoulder.

9.8 Turn right at CR 2. One gradual climb, then easy cruise beneath the bluffs.

14.6 Left turn onto CR 5. Climb the big hill, cross the ridge, and descend to Lake City.

24.1 Right onto US 61/63 (North Lakeshore Drive).

24.8 Turn left at Park Street, following the shoreline to the tip of an arrowhead point (and great views) on Lake Pepin.

24.9 U-turn at the point for the return.

25.7 Left at CR 5. Stunning bluff valley views prior to the steep, 450-foot climb back to the ridge.

35.2 Junction with CR 2; continue west on CR 5 through the valley. One final, long climb leads to higher ground at MN 58.

40.8 Right onto MN 58 for a fast homestretch on a wide, smooth shoulder.

42.3 Right onto Flower Valley Road.

43.0 Left at Eagle Ridge and arrive back at the trailhead.

River Towns and Hills Loop

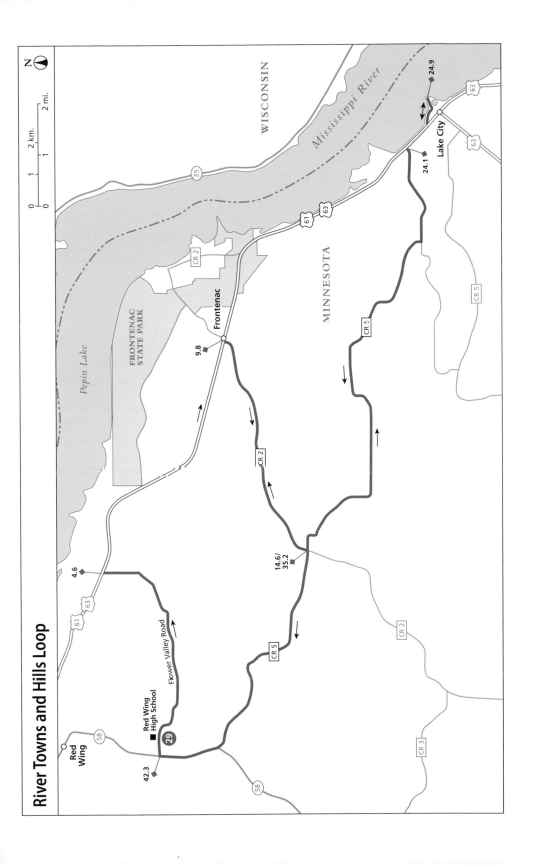

N

0 1 2 km.
0 1 2 mi.

WISCONSIN

Mississippi River

24.9

63

Lake City

63

24.1

MINNESOTA

CR 5

CR 5

35

63

61 63

CR 2

Pepin Lake

FRONTENAC
STATE PARK

Frontenac

9.8

CR 2

CR 2

61
63

4.6

Flower Valley Road

Red Wing
High School

29

42.3

Red Wing

58

14.6/
35.2

CR 5

CR 5

58

CR 3

RIDE INFORMATION

Restaurants

Homemade goodness at the **Chickadee Cottage Cafe.** Open mid-Apr–Oct. 317 N. Lakeshore Dr., Lake City; (651) 345-5155; chickadeecottagecafe.com.

Indulge post-ride with an ice cream float and fountain soda at **Bev's Cafe,** Red Wing's oldest restaurant. 221 Bush St.; (651) 388-5227.

Area events

Explore Red Wing the first weekend of August for **River City Days,** with live music, arts, parade, and Taste of Red Wing, all on the riverfront; rivercitydays .org.

Start in Lake City and pedal through historic bluff towns and beauteous scenery in early June's **Tour de Pepin;** lakecity.org/news-events/ tour-de-pepin.

Cannon Valley Trail

Spin past overhanging cliffs, lumpy bluffs, and wildlife-packed wetlands on this A-list rail-trail along the Cannon River. Enjoy a gradual descent through beauteous forest to a halfway-point ice cream stop, rub shoulders with limestone cliffs, and ogle great river views on a postcard-perfect 20-miler.

Start: Cannon Falls trailhead, at 500 W. Main St., across from EconoFoods. Alternate trailheads at Welch Station in Welch, and in Red Wing at Anderson Park on US 61 or Old West Main.

Distance: 20 miles one way

Approximate riding time: 1.5 hours (double that for round-trip and ice cream stop at Welch)

Best bike: Road or hybrid

Terrain and surface type: Flat, smooth, paved trail

Highlights: Great river views, forested bluffs, wildlife

Hazards: Trail gets crowded on summer weekends, occasional, sandy washouts on trail from heavy rains

Other considerations: For extra miles or another great destination, head for the Hay Creek Trail, just 2 blocks from Red Wing's Old West Main trailhead. The quiet, 6-mile path follows its namesake creek past wooded bluffs and idyllic countryside environs to the tiny village of Hay Creek.

Maps: *USGS Cannon Falls*

Getting there: From St. Paul, follow US 52 south to MN 19. Head east 0.75 mile to the trailhead. GPS: N 44 30.427 W 92 54.416

THE RIDE

It was an oft-occurring flub of the French language that earned the Cannon River its name. French fur traders called the river "Riviere aux Canots," after frequently spotting Native Americans and traders stashing their canoes near the mouth of the river, hidden from view from passing miscreants on the Mississippi. Oh-so-unrefined Eastern settlers thought the French were saying "cannon" and the Cannon River name stuck. A hard day's paddle upstream, the Little Cannon River, tributary to its larger sibling, also inspired the name of the town that grew up around the cascading waterfall discovered by a father-son explorer duo around 1853.

Three decades after the town of Cannon Falls was established, the Chicago Great Western Railroad began service on a new line from Cannon Falls to Red Wing, and transported grain and other varieties of produce and goods with great success until 1983, when the line was abandoned. Sharp-minded citizens saw a golden opportunity to boost tourism with a recreation path on the rail line, and with invaluable help from the Minnesota Parks Foundation (see sidebar), the Cannon Valley Trail came to life in 1986 and today treats nearly 100,000 self-propelled outdoor lovers to one of the prettiest rail-trails in the Midwest.

The trail requires a daily wheel pass (nominal fee), with funds going right back to maintaining this fantastic path. Fee stations are posted at all trailheads. Start the ride on a city trail with a coast past the multitiered Cannon Falls and small park area, underneath 4th Street and over to 3rd Street. The trail works its way along Water Street, past an old depot, and rolls out to the official start of the Cannon Valley Trail near the dead end of Hardwood Way. The trail slices through gorgeous forest on your right with intermittent river views through breaks in the trees to the left. Watch for ubiquitous rabbits darting in and out of the woods, plentiful white-tailed deer, and maybe a fox or two. A couple of miles in, limestone cliffs rise up and the trail curves gracefully around a bend in the river, out to a large open area of agricultural land and meadows. This is a great spot to see raptors riding overhead updrafts eyeing rodent-shaped snacks. Back in the woods, keep your eyes open for some of the rare plants thriving in the shady, moist recesses and mossy terraces near the cliffs, like the endangered kittentail, and dwarf trout lily, a plant found only within the borders of Minnesota.

Bike Shop

Rent a cruiser, and come back for a canoe trip, at **Cannon Falls Canoe and Bike Rental.** $15 for a half-day rental. 615 N. 5th St., Cannon Falls; (507) 263-4657; cannonfallscanoeandbike.com.

Fall colors on the Cannon Valley Trail
CANNON VALLEY TRAIL

Also of note is how you are drifting down the trail with hardly any effort. The path drops 115 feet in elevation by the time it reaches Red Wing, but spread out over 20 miles means a long coast for bikes, almost like riding the whole way with a tailwind. The 1 percent or less grade is barely noticeable— until the return trip. The path might look flat, but that 20 miles on a constant uphill grade, even one as tiny as this, gets your attention. It's not hard by any means; just be aware of what's in store on the westbound trip.

There are a few bridge crossings along the way, elevated over seasonal creeks or deep ravines, and distant views of barns and silos with high, rounded bluffs in the background. Cross a couple of gravel roads and pass a shooting range and campground, then lope around one final turn to the Welch Station trailhead, with restrooms, water, parking, and an info kiosk. Hop back on the trail and ride past Welch Village Ski Area, founded in 1965 and gradually expanded to include today's 60 runs on five separate ridges overlooking area valleys. If you're in the mood for some upward mobility, follow CR 7 up valley from the ski hill. It's a 5-mile climb to the postage-stamp "town" of Vasa, on a beautiful and winding road through the woods. Past the ski area, the trail soon skirts the edge of the Cannon River Turtle Preserve Scientific and Natural Area (SNA), a 900-acre preserve created to protect the endangered wood turtle, which nests in the river floodplain flanked by maple-oak forest. This is a sensitive area, and studies are still ongoing as to the health of the turtles' population, but, even so, refrain from tramping through here to keep the little shelled critters safe and sound.

At mile 15.5, the trail passes a rest area under US 61, and shortly after is a cool wetland observation deck and the Red Wing Archaeological Preserve. The latter is a unique site first discovered around 1885. The presence of 64 mounds and other evidence confirmed this was once a well-trodden village dating back to the 13th century. A final hook in the trail leads to the Anderson Park trailhead, and in 1 more mile the path ends at Old West Main and CR 1. Lots more great riding to be had from this point as well, including a leisurely spin along Levee Road and Bay Point Park, or the 6-mile Hay Creek Trail. Stay tuned to the latest trail news at cannonvalleytrail.com.

Trail Stewards

Many of the finest biking and hiking trails in Minnesota, like the Cannon Valley Trail, owe their very existence to the efforts of the **Parks and Trails Council of Minnesota.** The council's lineage can be linked all the way back to the 1954 formation of the Minnesota Council of State Parks, which thirteen years later sprouted a land acquisition division, the Minnesota Parks Foundation, as a means to direct donations and gifts of land, cash, and other endowments to help secure special places in Minnesota for parks and trails. Its first chore was a biggie, acquiring the land for Afton State Park, one of the state's gems, and it's been on a roll ever since. Ultimately settling on its current name, the Parks and Trails Council has worked for forty-six years to set aside over 10,000 acres of land that have evolved into some of our state's most recognized and popular destinations, like Gold Rock Point at Split Rock Lighthouse State Park, critical shoreline in Voyageurs National Park, Grand Portage State Park, and much more. Brett Feldman, the council's executive director, credits the focused efforts of his group's 3,400-strong members for these impressive results. "The only way to be successful," Feldman says, "is to build from the momentum we gained on the ground." Feldman's palpable enthusiasm is infectious, and that spills over to the council's invaluable work that we can see and feel and use in our own backyard. Hot on the latest agenda is acquiring land to help create the Mill Towns State Trail, linking the Sakatah Singing Hills and Cannon Valley Trails, preserving a key component of Minnesota's milling history. Check out more details, events, and how to get involved at parksandtrails.org.

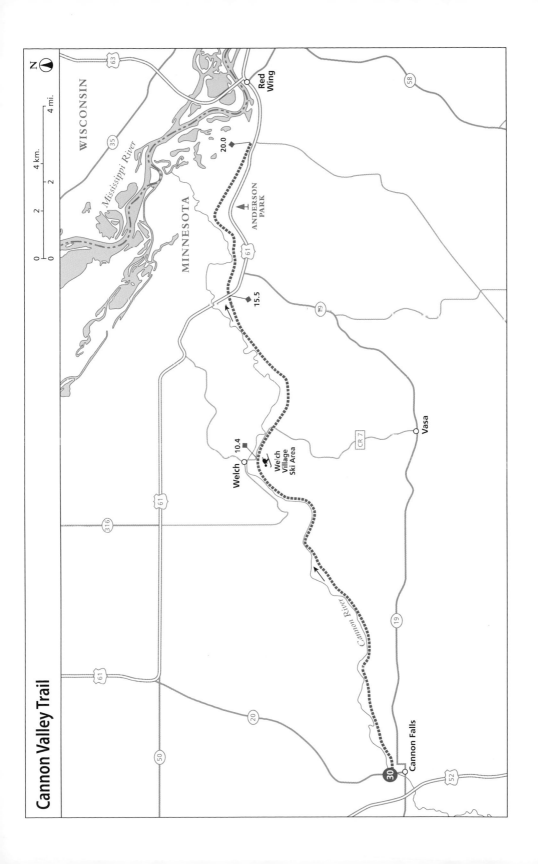

Cannon Valley Trail

N

WISCONSIN

Mississippi River

MINNESOTA

Red Wing

20.0

ANDERSON PARK

61

15.5

Welch 10.4

Welch Village Ski Area

Vasa

CR 7

Cannon River

Cannon Falls

30

0   2   4 km.

0   2   4 mi.

58

63

35

316

61

61

20

50

52

19

MILES AND DIRECTIONS

0.0   Start at Cannon Falls trailhead.

0.3   Junction with 3rd Street. Go left on the path.

0.4   Right turn onto Water Street. Follow the path past the old depot.

1.7   Official start of Cannon Valley Trail.

5.4   Cross Sunset Trail (gravel road).

9.7   Pass Hidden Valley Campground.

10.4   Welch Station.

10.9   Pass Welch Village Ski Area.

11.3   Cross CR 7.

15.5   Pass under US 61.

18.4   Anderson Park trailhead access.

20.0   Arrive at Old West Main trailhead.

> **A train reportedly carrying granite for tombstones derailed in 1912 near the Vasa Township road, and some of the scattered load is still visible on the slope of the adjacent bluff.**

RIDE INFORMATION

Restaurants

Food so good, presidents eat here. Score a made-from-scratch "Presidential" turkey sandwich at **Nick's Downtown Diner** in Cannon Falls, 2 blocks from the trailhead. President Obama dined here on a 2011 visit to Minnesota. (Maybe next time he'll bring his bike.) 331 Mill St. W; (507) 263-0003; nicksdowntowndiner.com.

Area events

Demolition derbies, fireworks, corn dogs, and cotton candy at a good old-fashioned small-town fair. The annual **Cannon Valley Fair** is held first week of July; cannonvalleyfair.org.

See the sweat fly in the final sprint and meet your favorite riders at the Cannon Falls stage of the **North Star Grand Prix** pro cycling race, mid-June; naturevalleybicyclefestival.com.

Schaar's Bluff Trail

Without hesitation, I'll say this is one of the best bike paths in the Twin Cities. This spic 'n' span trail nails it with calendar shot scenery, well-appointed park facilities, and varying terrain for a perfect day out. Bonus points for access to downtown Hastings attractions and the Mississippi River.

Start: Schaar's Bluff trailhead at Spring Lake Park Reserve

Distance: 8.6 miles out and back

Approximate riding time: 45 minutes

Best bike: Road or hybrid

Terrain and surface type: Smooth paved trail

Highlights: Veer-off-the-trail scenery with river views, velvety smooth trail, top-shelf park facilities, access to downtown Hastings

Hazards: Share the trail with other users

Other considerations: None

Maps: *USGS St. Paul Park*

Getting there: From US 52, follow MN 55 east 4.3 miles to CR 42 (Mississippi Trail) and turn left. Follow Mississippi Trail 1.8 miles to Idell Avenue. Signage indicates the park entrance. Turn left and follow the road 0.8 mile to the park. 8395 127th Street E, Hastings; (952) 891-7000; www.co.dakota,mn.us; GPS N 44 76.399 W 92 92.960

Schaars' Overlook

THE RIDE

Absolutely phenomenal. I tossed accolades like that around like so much confetti after finally, reluctantly, finishing my first ride on the Schaar's Bluff Trail. Dakota County Parks checked all the boxes on this one from start to finish. When I rode the trail, there were still bite-mark tracks in the dirt from equipment used to construct this gem. It's a superbly planned and crafted path that is just plain fun to ride. Keep in mind that when completed (only four miles to go!), this trail will run 27 miles in a ragged fishhook-shaped route from Hastings to Simon's Ravine in St. Paul.

From the trailhead, follow the signs leading west. After a couple of lazy turns, the trail reaches an overlook with killer views of the Mississippi and wooded shoreline far below. Have a look and keep rolling, enjoying a long, gradual coast across a deep ravine and into the woods. This is about a quarter-mile descent which is good fun but remember you have to go back up on the way back.

A short way along, the path cruises by a sprawling meadow packed with wildflowers and ground-nesting birds in the spring. Be sure to linger here a bit; it's a special place. From the meadow, the path lopes across a gravel access road and past outdoor group classroom sites and another bluff overlook on the home stretch to the west trailhead turnaround.

Schaar's Bluff Trail

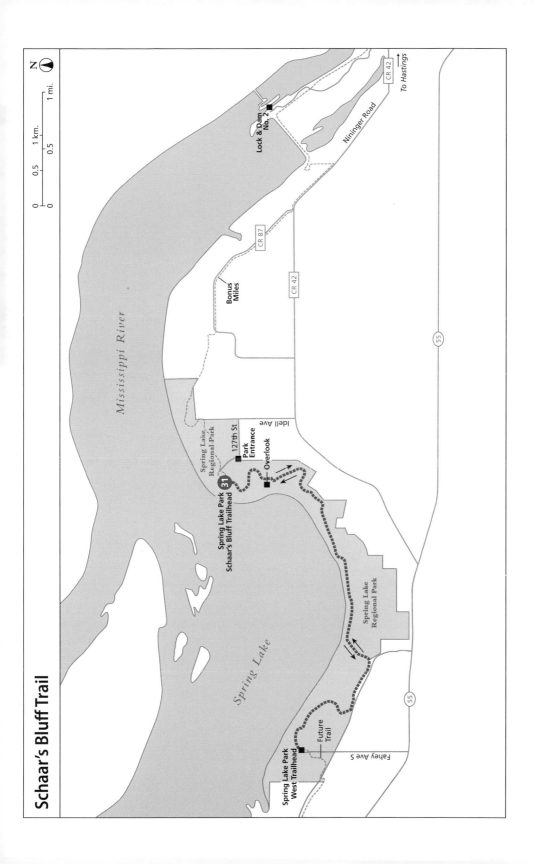

N

0   0.5   1 km.
0   0.5   1 mi.

Mississippi River

Lock & Dam No. 2

To Hastings

CR 42

Nininger Road

CR 87

CR 42

Bonus Miles

55

Spring Lake Regional Park

127th St

Park Entrance

Idell Ave

Overlook

31 Spring Lake Park
Schaar's Bluff Trailhead

Spring Lake

Spring Lake Regional Park

Future Trail

Fahey Ave S

Spring Lake Park
West Trailhead

55

Bridge crossing in the Salem Hills woods

Retrace the path back to the Schaar's Bluff trailhead and remember; that long hill is good for you. Take your time, listen to the birds singin', and you'll be at the top before you know it.

Hot tip: Don't miss another five miles of sublime trail eastbound to Lock and Dam No. 2 in Hastings.

MILES AND DIRECTIONS

0.0 Roll west from the trailhead along a few lazy turns.

0.6 Overlook stop with great river views.

0.8 Bridge crossing over a deep ravine.

4.3 West trailhead. Turn around for the return trip.

8.6 Arrive at Schaar's Bluff trailhead and parking.

Trailside bluff

RIDE INFORMATION

Restaurants

Head to **Lock and Dam Eatery** for juicy burgers and cold brew on one of the best river patios in Hastings. 101 2nd Street East; (651) 319-0906; lockand dameatery.com.

I don't know about you but I always seem to crave Mexican food when I'm out riding. **El Mexican** in historic downtown Hastings hits the spot every time. Stacked menu of eats and drinks at 119 2nd Street East; (651) 437-5002; elmexicanrestaurants.com.

Area Events

Don't miss **Rivertown Days,** a forty-year Hastings tradition with live entertainment, carnival, food trucks, and family activities at Levee Park. Third week in July; hastingmn.org/rivertown-days.

St. Paul Mountain Biking

Fat tire trails on the St. Paul side of the metro mix it up with a few cruiser paths, and others that spend lots of time traveling the elevation profile. Head to the Mendota Trail for a woodsy river flats spin, or to Battle Creek or Afton Alps for a grueling day in the hills. Check out the scoop on the full, Twin Cities mountain biking scene back on page 85.

Resident wildlife

Mendota Trail

The pan-flat companion to Ride 17's up-and-down affair, this 6-mile ride follows the Minnesota River's southern banks on a mix of single and double track on a mostly wooded heading through Fort Snelling State Park's wildlife-rich river flats.

Start: Trailhead parking area on MN 13 in Mendota, just east of St. Peter's Church

Distance: 12 miles out and back

Approximate riding time: 45-60 minutes

Best bike: Mountain

Terrain and surface type: Flat singletrack and doubletrack on hard-packed and sandy trail

Highlights: Close-up river views; herons, ducks, deer, raptors; Henry Sibley House

Hazards: Occasional downed tree limbs, sections of deep sand, waterlogged trail, watch for hikers

Other considerations: Steer clear of the trail when wet to avoid damage to the route

Maps: *USGS St. Paul West*

Getting there: From MN 55 at the Mendota Bridge, follow MN 110 on the south side of the river to the stoplight at MN 13. Go left and follow the curves past St. Peter's Church to the parking lot on the left side of the road, on the hill above downtown Mendota. GPS: N 44 53.241 W 93 09.907

THE RIDE

This ride starts in the shadow of Minnesota's oldest church, in one of the state's oldest towns, overlooking homesites of two of the most influential people in Minnesota's history. Longtime home of the Dakota Indians, the Mendota area also attracted the first white settlers to the young Minnesota Territory, jump-started by a bustling fur trade headquartered in this very spot. Roll through this time warp with a warm-up spin through Mendota's 2-block main street (MN 13), and drop down the hill on D Street past the historic Sibley and Faribault houses (see sidebar). The stone arch tunnel beneath the Canadian Pacific railroad line leads to Fort Snelling State Park land and the Mendota Trail. The Mississippi River is dead ahead, taking in water from the Minnesota River only a few hundred yards upstream. Ride west on wide hardpack, crossing a few intermittent, mini streams born of runoff from snow or rain, below the cement

Stone arch portal to the riverside trail

rainbow arches of the Mendota Bridge. Now paralleling the Minnesota River, a brief section of open grassland gives way to thick woods of elm, maple, and cottonwood, their dense canopy shading, in summer, an impenetrable green flood of assorted shrubbery and ground-level foliage. Heed not the call of nature in this section, lest the plethora of stinging nettles and poison ivy leave their mark on your . . . ride. And speaking of floods, this long ribbon of the river valley has been submerged many a wet spring, leaving dead fish hanging from tree branches and deep dunes of murky river sediment. The rising river will, of course, change the complexion of the trail, so plan accordingly and ride somewhere else when wet to keep trail damage at bay.

Riding along the riverbank, nearly at water level, the trail passes beneath the flight path for Minneapolis–St. Paul International Airport, and you have a good vantage for examining the underbellies of jets roaring over your head. At around the 3-mile mark the path S-curves under the dual span of I-494 and darts arrow-straight on a boulevard-like path shadowed by an awning of giant trees. At the end of the tree tunnel, the trail morphs into singletrack and shimmies between conveniently spaced riverbank trees, with a huge expanse of wetland meadow to the south. The natural environment and wildlife habitat here shares that of the Minnesota Valley National Wildlife Refuge land directly across the river. One of only four urban wildlife refuges in the country, we are fortunate to have this gem so close to home. Stretching along 99 miles of the Minnesota River in 14 linear units, the refuge provides critical habitat to over 200 bird species and other critters like white-tailed deer, red fox, and snapping turtles, thriving in marshland, lakes, remnant oak savanna, and floodplain forest.

Five bridge crossings provide safe passage over river tributaries and other soggy sections, and at time the trail is simply whatever path best travels among the changing tide of sand and river debris. Don't be surprised to be blocked altogether by high water at a few points along this stretch, but during summer and fall, it's mostly smooth sailing. The trees abruptly give way to tall shrubs, then just tall grasses on the last section of wide, fast trail to the Cedar Avenue bridge. Notes from here: The bike/ped bridge ramps up and parallels the buzz of the highway to the north side of the river and the new span of the Old Cedar Avenue Bridge into Bloomington. If you are aboard a mountain bike, eyeball the skinny singletrack right on the riverbank, adjacent to the bike ramp. This little number snakes through tall grasses and all manner

Bike Shop

Locals rave about the service at **OneTen Cycles** and their shop is located adjacent to miles of bike trails along the rivers. 1040 Dakota Dr., Mendota Heights; (651) 454-2066; onetencycles.com.

Henry Sibley

In the still-wild, northern frontier of a young country, the American Fur Company established a trading post near Ft. Snelling, across the confluence of the Minnesota and Mississippi Rivers. Known as the "Sioux Outfit," the post provided the impetus for the settlement and founding of Mendota, one of Minnesota's first towns. At the helm of the trading center was **Henry Sibley,** an ambitious young man pivotal in the fur company's success and in maintaining robust relations with the Dakota Indians. Named "Walker in the Pines" by the Dakota, Sibley lived on-site while pursuing political aspirations, thrice serving as Congressional delegate and affording key input in drafting Minnesota's constitution. He was a military commander during the Dakota War, accomplished businessman, president of both the Minnesota Historical Society and University of Minnesota Board of Regents, and published volumes of work on the state's history. During his tenure as Minnesota's first governor, Sibley kept an office in the 1835 stone house in Mendota, where he lived until 1862, when he moved with his family to St. Paul. Tour the house on weekends from late May–early Sept. $7 adult admission. 1357 Sibley Memorial Hwy., Mendota; (651) 452-1596; mnhs.org.

of encroaching foliage to eventually join the start of the Bloomington side of the river trails. A pretty cool, Huck Finn-on-a-bike kind of adventure.

MILES AND DIRECTIONS

0.0 Start at Mendota trailhead on MN 13.

0.3 Head under the railroad tunnel into Ft. Snelling State Park.

0.7 Pass under MN 55.

1.2 Trail meets and parallels Minnesota River.

3.0 Pass under I-494.

6.0 Arrive at junction with Cedar Avenue trailhead.

The Dakota named the joining of the Minnesota and Mississippi Rivers "mdo-te", or "meeting of the waters." It was a place of great spiritual and cultural significance for the Dakota and Ojibwe people for hundreds of years. Hike here on the Pike Island trail from the Ft. Snelling State Park Visitor Center.

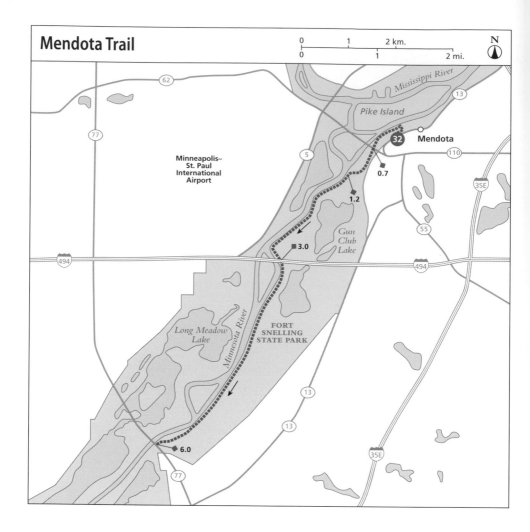

Mendota Trail

0   1   2 km.

0   1   2 mi.

N

Mississippi River

Pike Island

Mendota

Minneapolis–
St. Paul
International
Airport

0.7

1.2

3.0

Gun
Club
Lake

Long Meadow
Lake

Minnesota River

FORT
SNELLING
STATE PARK

6.0

RIDE INFORMATION

Restaurants

Lucky's 13 Pub in Mendota serves up good times and great food, with the Big Rivers Regional Trail right out the back door. 1352 Sibley Memorial Hwy., Mendota; (651) 452-0161; luckys13pub.com.

Area events

One of Minnesota's oldest cities gets its groove on in early July at **Mendota Days** with a parade, live music, and special attractions like the rolling heroics of the Twin Cities Unicycle Club. The action happens on Sibley Memorial Highway (MN 13) in Mendota. Check mendotaheights.patch.com for updated info.

Best Bike Rides Minneapolis and St. Paul

Memorial Park

"Let's do it again!" This familiar mantra is heard often from riders exiting the Memorial Park trails, and it is indeed difficult to resist heading back for another lap. A balanced mix of technical singletrack and beginner-friendly trails twist through dense woods and open meadow on a thrill-a-minute spaghetti-dish route on the crest of Sorin's Bluff, with stellar views of neighboring valleys and the Mississippi River. Challenge yourself on seesaw and log pile obstacles, or cruise easygoing ski trails at this must-ride area favorite.

Start: Memorial Park at the top of Sorin's Bluff. Follow Skyline Drive around the top of the bluff and all the way to the parking area at the road's end. The "official" trailhead for mountain biking is just past the last overlook on Skyline Drive. Either access gets you on the trails.

Distance: About 6 miles and growing for the entire trail system (just short of 4 miles for this intermediate loop)

Approximate riding time: 1–2 hours, depending on choice of loops

Best bike: Mountain

Terrain and surface type: Gently rolling and steep climbs on gravel and hardpack single and doubletrack

Highlights: Same as above, plus great bluff top views, bridges, jumps, obstacles, technical singletrack, mix of beginner to expert trails

Hazards: Tree roots, logs, handlebar-wide tree openings, steep, leaf-covered drops

Other considerations: Be aware of hikers, use caution on turns and steeps when wet

Maps: *USGS Red Wing*; excellent map resources at livehealthyredwing .com

Getting there: From US 61 in downtown Red Wing, turn onto Plum Street (follow sign for US 63) and head 5 blocks southeast to 7th Street. Turn left and follow 7th Street 0.5 mile to park entrance at Skyline Drive. GPS: N 44 33.315 W 92 30.436

THE RIDE

The views alone make this an unforgettable ride. All along the trail, natural clearings in resident flora reveal living postcards of Red Wing's bluff-ensconced neighborhoods to the south and vibrant downtown and Mississippi River valley to the north. The area attracted early Dakota, and later white settlers, with its prime spiritual and commercial location on the banks of the river. A frontier boom town, named for Dakota chiefs whose names were inspired by their symbol, a swan wing dyed red, was once the world's leading wheat market, and spawned household-name products like Red Wing Stoneware and Red Wing Shoes. The town retains its small-town charm and packs in tourists throughout the year.

Memorial Park sits atop 900-foot Sorin's Bluff, a massive, whale-shaped lump of limestone draped in heavy dress of a diverse hardwood forest. The long, paved entrance road switchbacks up to the top, where a handful of turnouts and overlooks provide opportunities to gape at the Norman Rockwell views. At the end of Skyline Drive, a 30-foot cliff wall topped with a fringe of birch trees flanks the trailhead, welcoming visitors to its realm. Ride into the woods on the stone and dirt path, following the cliff. A short, medium-steep

Luxury Lodging

Red Wing's stature as a world-leading wheat market rose in grand style with the addition of a top-shelf lodging establishment. The **St. James Hotel**'s elegant redbrick and white Italianate accents welcomed guests to a lavish interior on its Thanksgiving Day opening in 1875. Spawned from the vision of a group of area businessmen, the hotel spared no expense in presenting visitors with floor-to-ceiling decadence, like English velvet carpet, steam heat, parlors, and plenty of water closets. The railroad even adjusted its trips to coincide with the dinner hour demands of passengers to order up the legendary fare served by hotel chefs. The St. James was the talk of the town, and today's guests can savor that same experience, with river-view rooms and elegant patio dining. 406 Main St.; (800) 252-1875; st-james-hotel.com.

Stone memorial Soldiers Memorial Park

climb ramps away from the rocky walls for a quick warm-up, then the trail hairpins and swoops past stands of birch and aspen, with serrated views of the Mississippi through the trees, to a fork in the road, splitting hiking and biking traffic, with bikes generally rolling clockwise, and hikers the opposite. Follow the blue and red arrows onto a sweet stretch of singletrack, named US 61 Revisited, and brush shoulders with trees while practicing your bike handling skills in a series of tight turns. Spit out onto a wider path; it's time for a longer climb to another junction with a no-brainer decision to follow the arrows on more sublime singletrack. A few bridge and log crossings liven it up through beauteous aspen-hardwood forest, and the trail keeps you guessing with abrupt direction changes that seem to come around about every six pedal strokes. Ride past the Caution sign to descend through a steep ravine, or loop around All Along the Watchtower with great views of Ol' Miss far below. By now you've noticed the local avian population announcing itself in spirited song. Dozens of bird species live here, and it is a treat to be serenaded by melodious chickadees, cardinals, nuthatches, and orioles, with woodpeckers providing the percussion beat. It is well worth taking a break just to soak in the wilderness feel of the place.

The path leaves the woods briefly and parallels the sprawling meadow, the bluff's big bald spot. Well on its way to being restored to its native prairie self, the tall grasses are ideal habitat for little, ground-based morsels like mice and moles, delicacies on the menus of keen-eyed bald eagles and red-tailed hawks. Look to the sky to see the birds of prey riding the updrafts while planning a meal. Descend back through the woods on Radar Love to wide-open, four-way intersection. Decision time. The trails to the left follow more challenging terrain (think hills and logs) down toward Mississippi Links golf course, while a right turn heads up a long climb back to the top. Access to the most difficult sections of trail split off halfway up the hill, leading to Southern Cross and the steep and rocky Stairway to Heaven Trails. Stunning views open up off your left shoulder back at the meadow, where a trio of grassy ski trails split off in different directions. Head left here on a rollicking ride along the contour just below the crest of the bluff, then along grassy ski trail underneath the power line to another junction. Go left and left again (blue arrow) for more singletrack along dips and dives and curves back toward Skyline Drive. A pearl white birch tree at trailside seems to light up the whole area and is another great spot to ogle views. The arrow signs lead to the open field that marks the official start of the trail system, with a huge sign displaying a map of the different routes. Head for the Bike Trail sign back into the woods for yet more singletrack in Henke's Hollow, generally paralleling the road, and a chance to ride a couple of seesaw obstacles along the way. A few more turns lead to a short, steep drop, and a hard left takes you back along the cliff wall to the trailhead.

MILES AND DIRECTIONS

0.0   Start at the trailhead. Enter the woods at the cliff.

0.2   Turn left. Follow the blue and red arrows.

0.8   Lean left, paralleling the meadow.

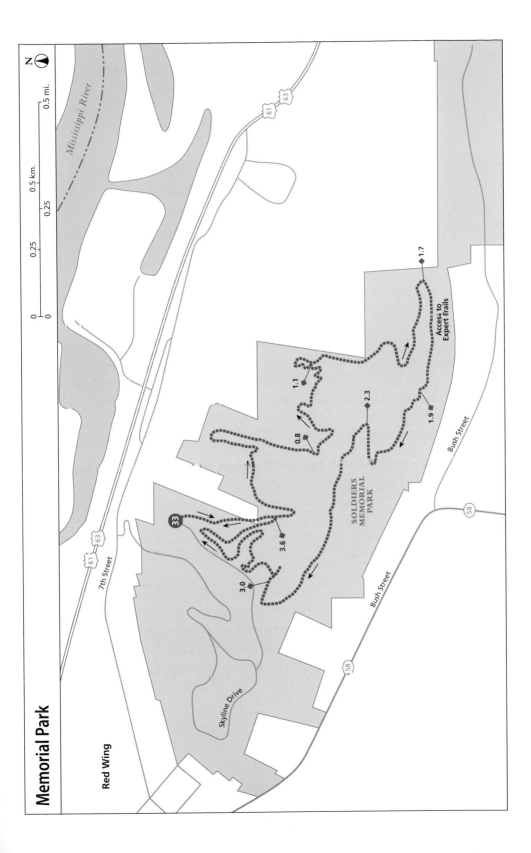

Memorial Park

Red Wing

SOLDIERS
MEMORIAL
PARK

Access to
Expert Trails

Mississippi River

Skyline Drive

7th Street

Bush Street

Bush Street

33

3.0

3.6

0.8

1.1

2.3

1.9

1.7

61
63

61
63

58

58

N

0   0.25   0.5 km.
0   0.25   0.5 mi.

1.1 Left turn into the woods on Radar Love.

1.7 Go left for more difficult trail, right for easier. This route turns right, climbing to the meadow.

1.9 Meadow junction. Turn left.

2.3 Powerline junction. Turn left and another left into the woods (blue arrow).

3.0 Main trailhead. Take the trail to the left of the map sign.

3.6 Hard left turn to return to trailhead.

3.8 Arrive back at trailhead.

RIDE INFORMATION

Restaurants

Grab a burger and cold brew on the **Harbor Bar**'s riverside patio, across the river from downtown Red Wing. Catch the Blues Fest in July. N673 825th St., Hager City, WI; (715) 792-2417; harborbar.net.

A house-brewed draft, pizzas, and calzones? Divine. Get it at **Red Wing Brewery,** 1411 Old West Main St.; (651) 327-2200; redwingbrewing.com.

Area events

Check out live music at **Concerts in the Park,** late June through early August, Central Park.

Eagle watch at Colvill Park from mid-February to mid-March. On US 61, 1 mile south of Red Wing.

Don't miss the world's largest boot at the **Red Wing Shoe Museum,** 315 Main St.; (651) 388-6233.

> The widely used Red Wing pottery and jugs were first manufactured at Red Wing Stoneware around 1877. Much of the impetus for the local industry began with the discovery of clay pit beds near the headwaters of Hay Creek, near present-day Goodhue.

Afton Alps

With 300 acres of skiable terrain, Afton Alps does not disappoint when the snow flies. The same continues in summer, when over 7 miles of singletrack open to challenge fat tire riders, with a full day's worth of loops for strong beginners to experts. Plenty of tough climbs and exhilarating descents on quiet and uncrowded trails.

Start: Highlands Chalet/golf clubhouse at top of the hill. Get a trail pass and shoot down the ski run directly below the clubhouse deck.

Distance: About 5 miles of trail to sample (3 miles for this modified loop)

Approximate riding time: Roughly 1 hour for a full lap

Best bike: Mountain

Terrain and surface type: Um, hilly. Either steep uphill or steep downhill, with a few "level" trails crossing ski runs, on singletrack with loose rocks and slippery gravel.

Highlights: Stellar views of the St. Croix River valley, fun downhills, winding singletrack through the woods, no crowds, lots of loop options

Hazards: Lots of steep drops, loose rocks, washouts, tough climbs

Other considerations: Daily use fee (nominal) that goes to trail maintenance

Maps: *USGS Prescott*; area maps at aftonalps.com

Getting there: From St. Paul, head east on I-94 to Manning Avenue (CR 15). Go south 7 miles to 70th Street, and left 3 miles to Afton State Park entrance. Follow the signs to Afton Alps. Trails start at the Highlands Chalet/golf clubhouse. GPS: N 44 5 1.259 W 92 47.450

34

THE RIDE

Keep your butt back. Words to live by when the ground ramps up or down. And there's plenty of that at Afton. Keeping your weight slightly back of center over the bike gives that rear tire the traction it needs to dig in and get you up a steep hill. Flying down a wall-steep descent? Keep your weight back even farther to let the bike roll safely along the path and over obstacles, without flipping you over the handlebars. As advertised, this is a ski hill, so expect climbing, and the trails granted "more challenging" status really are, while the "easier" trails stretch that moniker. This ride samples some of both on a short tour.

Afton's chalet placement is the reverse of what you normally see at a ski resort, with the main chalet at the top of the hill instead of the bottom. This is great fun for the start of the ride, but there is no escaping a long climb back up. Start from the deck of the chalet/clubhouse and drop straight down the grassy ski run, following the blue trail poles on the Deer Path Trail. In about

Chairlifts in repose

St. Croix Academy

One of the oldest high schools in Minnesota was established in Afton around 1867. A meeting was called with the village residents to discuss the education of the young men and women of the county and plans to build an academy in which they could learn. A site was chosen near the northern limits of the village on the main street, and construction began in the spring and continued until the **St. Croix Academy** was dedicated in the fall of 1868. The basement was used for storage and fuel, and also served as a gym "where the male students would practice the manly art of boxing." Eventually a steep drop in the number of students attending forced the academy trustees to sell the property, and the school was closed in 1884. The building served a short time as a seminary, then was abandoned.

ten seconds a red trail marker announces the first "more challenging" path, Deep Woods Express, darting off into the woods. Continue downhill, following the grassy slope to a short, steep hook to the north. Watch for loose rocks here that are very adept at slowing down inattentive riders (me). Deer Path rolls along the lower flanks of the hill to its meeting with River View Glade and The Plunge. Go ahead, take The Plunge, and it does just that, dropping elevation like a lead weight down two wall-steep hills, covered in loose rocks and laced with seasonal erosion channels. This is a great place to somersault over your bars and end up in a heap with a shovelful of gravel embedded into your hide, so take it easy. After the drop, the path crosses a ski run, makes a quick run through bordering woods, and climbs out onto another run above the Meadows Chalet at the bottom of the hill. Switchback down to and past the chalet to the junction with the Ho Chi Minh Trail. Cruise along the lower access road until you see the Bridge Loop Trail marker on the opposite side of the road. Head across the road and up the initial punchy, gravelly climb, recover on a short, almost level stretch, then hit a steep hill and over a hump, descending the other side to the trail's namesake bridge crossing a tributary creek. Across the bridge, the path continues to descend on moderately steep grade and rock tread to Ho Chi Minh. Ride on past frozen-in-time chairlifts to the Shady Lane Trail and a quick switchback to a short detour on the challenging Southern Switchbacks lower section, then back to Shady Lane, where the path goes long and steep enough to hurt up the south end of the hill. One last steep ramp skirts the edge of a fairway to Cedar Lane, cruising through the woods in a grove of said cedars to the final ski run crossing to the exit trail back to the clubhouse.

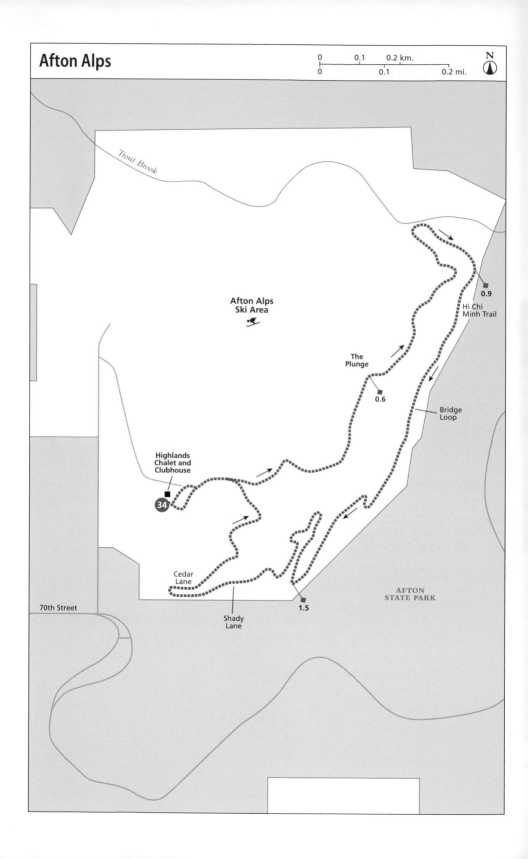

Afton Alps

Trout Brook

Afton Alps
Ski Area

Hi Chi
Minh Trail
0.9

The
Plunge
0.6

Bridge
Loop

Highlands
Chalet and
Clubhouse
34

Cedar
Lane

Shady
Lane
1.5

70th Street

AFTON
STATE PARK

0   0.1   0.2 km.
0   0.1   0.2 mi.

N

MILES AND DIRECTIONS

0.0 Start at the trailhead at chalet.

0.6 Junction with The Plunge trail. Follow it.

0.9 Junction with Ho Chi Minh trail, following lower access road and creek. Head across at the Bridge Loop trail for a fun detour.

1.5 Meet the Shady Lane trail. Continue around the switchback and make a quick loop on the bottom of the Southern Switchbacks trail, meeting back with Shady Lane and continuing up the hill.

3.0 Arrive back at the trailhead.

Racers navigating a twisty trail
JOHN REENTS

RIDE INFORMATION

Restaurants

Dine in style and stay the night at the historic **Afton House Inn.** 3291 St. Croix Trail S.; (651) 436-8883; aftonhouseinn.com.

Walleye fish and chips accompanied by a tall frosty brew. Need I say more? Get it at **The Lumberyard Pub**, 3121 St. Croix Trail S; (651) 337-2783; lumberyardpubafton.com.

Area events

Afton's **4th of July Parade** comes with all the traditional trimmings like great food, music in the park, and fireworks, along with relaxing cruises on the St. Croix; exploreminnesota.com.

Legend says the St. Croix River's name was created by Jesuit missionaries who likened the broad section of the river near Afton to the shape of a cross, granting it the name "Saint Croix," meaning "Holy Cross."

Battle Creek Regional Park

Battle Creek Regional Park's 750 acres of open meadows and dense oak forest is one of those wilderness-hidden-in-the-city places, packed with flora and fauna commonly found in much larger reserves far removed from urban centers. Explore 4 of the 10 total trail miles scribbled among the hilly woods, from easy-to-handle ski trails to technical singletrack.

Start: Battle Creek Community Center, at 75 S. Winthrop St. Trail starts on singletrack directly south of the building.

Distance: 4-mile loop, with 10 miles total on various loops

Approximate riding time: 45–60 minutes

Best bike: Mountain

Terrain and surface type: Hilly, with mix of short to medium climbs on wide, packed ski trail and singletrack

Highlights: Fun, twisty trail in dense woods, great views, lots of wildlife, nice mix of trail difficulty level

Hazards: A few sandy sections, occasional exposed tree roots, logs, potential crashes with other, opposite-direction riders

Other considerations: Signage is poor, no established trail direction

Maps: *USGS Lake Elmo*

Getting there: From downtown St. Paul, head east on I-94 about 5 miles to McKnight Road. Go right to Upper Afton Road and turn right again onto Winthrop Street. Go left and in just over 1 block, turn right into the Battle Creek Community Center. Trailhead is at the southwest end of the lot. GPS: N 44 56.315 W 93 00.766

Top side turn with Mississippi River in background

THE RIDE

Battle Creek boasts a trail network rivaling the best of them, and it is within sight of a major metro city. The rolling singletrack and variety of loops are whoop-it-up fun, and the dense woods, hills, meadows, and Mississippi River views are great bonus rewards. It's hilly here, being a former downhill ski area and all, so plan on a good workout, but there are easier trails at the west of the park, too, for a break from the climbs or a mellower riding day.

From the trailhead, follow the singletrack to the southwest on a sinuous rollout along the cross-country ski trail's lighted section of paths. This is a superb cross-country ski destination, running the gamut from easy glides to lung-busting climbs, and this front area is lighted for night skiing. At the far end of the ski trails, the singletrack enters a stand of tall pines and then into the thicker woods of the park at the first junction. Do a little zig and climb the access "road" (ski path) up to the top of the hill. From here you can pick your route. There is no standard direction of travel here (one drawback of the ride), but it also makes it cool for exploring what's out there. Just stay alert for other riders. No one wants a head-on collision as part of his or her day. Follow the ski sign to the left, rolling through gorgeous oak forest with good views here and there through trees of the Mississippi River. Pass a small meadow frequented by white-tailed deer, and at the meadow's far edge, shoot left on the partially hidden singletrack into the woods. This is a blast of a downhill with mini jumps and berms and rocks. Head up and watch your speed as you near the bottom; the steep drop is prime turf to go over the bars.

At the bottom, fork left over a short, steep hump and loop back east along Lower Afton Road. The trail climbs along the contour line through a mini pine and aspen forest, then back into the deeper woods. Follow the singletrack sign into a deep bowl carpeted with emerald green ferns and purple flower accents in spring. Here the trail loops around the bowl, up and down bumps with dense foliage all around. At the next junction, go straight up the hill and back to the original intersection near the ski trails. Go straight on, up to the ridge above the community center and descend the other side to a left turn into the woods again. Take that immediate right and descend gradually to a T junction. A right turn here heads along a fun, twisty course through sprig aspen and oak, eventually descending to another T at Battle Creek Road. Take a short jog right and back onto the dirt singletrack leading into the park's western section.

Pass several junctions from the right dropping down to Battle Creek, and to the left is a bowl of a former pond. Continue counterclockwise, listening for the train whistles from the Canadian Pacific yard at the river below. Check out the spur path leading to the crest of the hill for sweet views of the river valley. Head back toward the "lake" and take a right turn along a straight, old roadbed to Battle Creek Road, jog left, and ride back into the woods. An immediate right turn heads up a short but *steeeeep* climb to a T junction, and more

Flying High

The 60-meter ski jump at Battle Creek Park was one of the largest in the world when it saw its first jumper in the late 1930s. St. Paul's first jumping hill was built at nearby Mounds Park in 1924, but a violent wind storm destroyed the structure in 1939, prompting the larger replacement jump at Battle Creek, completed just in time for that year's St. Paul Winter Carnival and national ski jumping championships. The **Battle Creek jump** was used until the 1970s, when a new 40-meter hill was established at the south end of Maplewood, still used today by the St. Paul Ski Club. Check out the jumping program for beginners to experts, and don't let warm weather stop you. There's even summer jumping on the synthetic-surfaced hills; stpaulskiclub.com.

climbing to the right back up past the meadow. This time take a left into the oaks on smooth singletrack. Keep taking right turns and you climb steadily to the top of the hill and the exit back to the parking area.

MILES AND DIRECTIONS

0.0 Start at the Battle Creek Community Center trailhead.

0.4 Five-way junction. Head straight across.

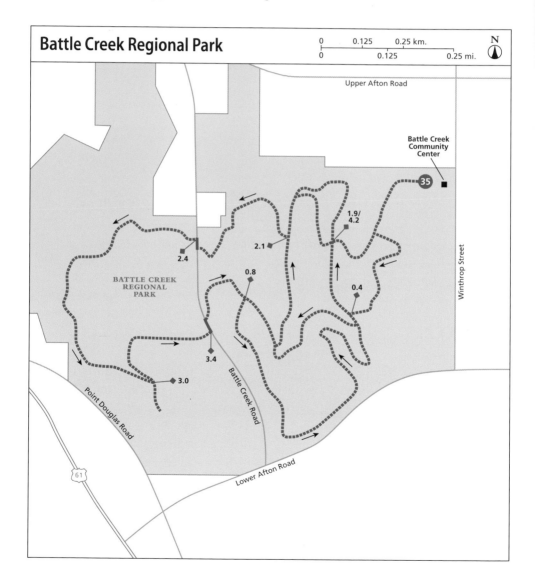

0.7 Junction with right-hand spur trail. Keep on straight ahead.

0.8 Left turn onto singletrack into the woods.

1.1 Round a turn heading back northeast, paralleling Lower Afton Road.

1.6 Back at the five-way intersection. Ride straight on through.

1.9 Hang a left into the woods.

2.1 Right turn at the T intersection.

2.4 Junction with Battle Creek Road. Go right and take a quick left back into the woods.

3.0 Take the little spur trail to the edge of the bluff to ogle great river views.

3.3 Lean right and follow the wide path back to Battle Creek Road.

3.4 Left turn onto Battle Creek Road, and quick right into the woods again.

3.5 Right turn at the top of the steep climb.

4.0 Turn left into dense oak forest. Follow the path uphill to a righthand fork to the junction with the ridge trail.

4.2 Junction with ridge trail. Head straight across and descend back to trailhead.

4.2 Arrive back at the trailhead.

RIDE INFORMATION

Area events

No dates, no start times, no competition. Just bring your sled and cross-country skis to the **Battle Creek hill** for one of the metro's best sledding hills and fantastic 1k and 5.5k partially lighted cross-country ski course.

Lebanon Hills

MORC's flagship trail and one of Minnesota's very best, Lebanon Hills is 100 percent singletrack bliss. The superbly designed trail system treats riders to 10 (and counting) miles of sinuous turns, rock gardens, log piles, bridges, open meadow, and dense woods. Beginners to experts can sample the wares on four connected loops, nested in a pattern of steadily increasing difficulty. The racing action here is always a blast, even deep into the winter.

Start: Trailhead parking on Johnny Cake Ridge Road

Distance: About 5 miles for intermediate loops (10 total miles on all four connected loops). Check out their website for updates, trail descriptions, and maps; lebanonhills.com.

Approximate riding time: Plan on around 1 hour, but stay for more

Best bike: Mountain

Terrain and surface type: Rolling, with short, punchy climbs and one long grind, all on hardpacked singletrack

Highlights: All of the above if you so desire, sublime singletrack throughout, excellent variety of trails, great scenery

Hazards: Stacked inventory of rock gardens, log crossings, jumps, narrow bridges, and other optional challenges

Other considerations: Trail gets crowded, especially on weekends

Maps: *USGS St. Paul SW*; excellent map resources at morcmtb.org

Getting there: From I-35, exit at Cliff Road and head east 0.7 mile to Johnny Cake Ridge Road and turn south. Parking and trailhead in 0.5 mile on west side of road. GPS: N 44 46.974 W 93 11.283

THE RIDE

This is where it all started. Minnesota's rise to a top mountain biking destination in the country first percolated in this little pocket of woods in a county park. Eroding trails, off-camber turns, and unstable tread were transformed, with an arsenal of earth-sculpting tools wielded by scores of dedicated volunteers, into a trail system so masterfully designed it is now a showcase, which many other trails are modeled after. Sustainably built trails weave seamlessly into the natural contours of the woods, flowing up and around hills and ponds and over strategically placed obstacles. The trails are flowing and fast, and arranged in a way that allows newer riders to hone their skills and advanced riders to challenge themselves on the more difficult inner courses. Many years in the making, the hard work put into these trails really shines. To accommodate Leb's overwhelming popularity, a recently completed trailhead complex

A challenging obstacle on the trail in the Lebanon Hills trails.

now offers ample parking, restrooms, changing rooms, picnic shelter, and posted trail maps. Adjacent to the trailhead is a new skills park.

The beginner loop wanders off from the northwest corner of the parking lot with a gentle climb through a small stand of pines. There are a few bypass sections where you can try your bike handling skills, or play it safe and stick to the main trail. A fast-paced downhill leads to an optional log jump, and a quick cross over the cross-country ski trail blends into open, flowy singletrack, with enough tight turns to keep it lively.

Start the intermediate and expert loops from the same spot, but ride west on Dream II, up through the pines on one of the longest climbs in the park (about 0.25 mile) and in some of the most handsome scenery. The trail moves along to some tricky rock gardens, a double jump, and then a fun descent to the Joey Trail. This is my personal favorite stretch of the loop, with a fast and winding path over just enough rocks and roots to elicit a few hoots and hollers. The path squiggles south, then turns east to the Stooges Run, a collection of tightly packed turns with a log pile and switchbacks leading to the Bypass climb, another long grind to some nice views on the Upper Bypass trail, looping around the top of the hill and through some tricky rock gardens to a descent to the big, spoked trail junction. The intermediate path continues east on more excellent singletrack, some manageable rock gardens, and even a cool rock jump as it winds back and forth in a bunch of finger loops to a pond, and the last section blasts around banked turns, more fast descents, and a challenging, three-tiered climb to the final descent. One of the newest sections (2011) is like a BMX track with rolling jumps and other technical features. Super fun to ride on a mountain bike, and it seems to bring other riders, like freestyle riders, out to give it a try and nail some airborne tricks.

The X and XX Loops are just that, for experts and even better experts. The X includes tons of log piles to shimmy over, and a handful of fun rock sections, with some that serve up a healthy technical challenge, like the bermed turn of Tedman's Curve. Some S turns lead up to a high point in the park, followed by a killer descent with a couple of log jumps to a bypass trail reconnection to the intermediate loop. Or hang a left and test your mettle on the XX Loop, featuring some of the most rugged terrain in the area, like rock-strewn hill climbs, narrow wooden bridges, a camelback feature, log stairstep climbs, and

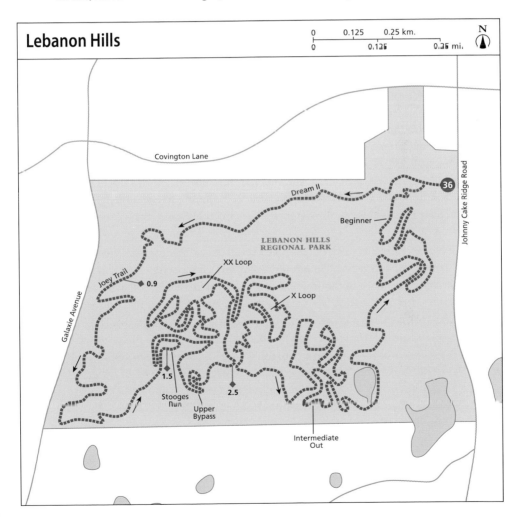

Lebanon Hills

0   0.125   0.25 km.

0   0.125   0.25 mi.

N

Covington Lane

Dream II

Beginner

LEBANON HILLS
REGIONAL PARK

Johnny Cake Ridge Road

XX Loop

Joey Trail   0.9

X Loop

Galaxie Avenue

1.5

2.5

Stooges
Run

Upper
Bypass

Intermediate
Out

screaming descents with bermed corners. And don't miss the log ladder leading to a fun rock obstacle. XX is a tough trail, but a genuine blast to ride.

MILES AND DIRECTIONS

0.0 Start at the trailhead.

0.9 Merge onto the Joey Trail.

1.5 Hit the twists and turns of Stooges Run.

2.0 Climb up Bypass, and curve around Upper Bypass.

2.5 Junction with expert loops. Hang a right to continue intermediate loop.

5.0 Arrive back at the trailhead.

Note: Trail names may be different or updated than what you see here.

RIDE INFORMATION

Restaurants
Pizza and brew is a tasty conclusion to your ride. Grab a table at **Green Mill,** 1940 Rahncliff Court; (651) 686-7166; greenmill.com.

How does a big ol' malt sound after a hot summer trail ride? **Dairy Queen** is only about a mile away and right next to Green Mill. How's that for a dual-purpose refueling stop?. 4630 Rahncliff Rd.; (651) 688-2725; dairyqueen.com.

Area events
Lebanon Hills Regional Park is packed with opportunities to get out there, like kayak lessons and rentals**,** and wilderness survival camps; co.dakota.mn.us.

Martin Diffley started a roadside vegetable stand in Eagan in 1973, ushering in a passionate commitment to organic farming on the family's farmland. The Diffley family continues to cultivate sustainable farming and growing practices through workshops, consulting, and public events.

Salem Hills Trails

This 4.5-mile linear trail at Harmon Park cruises a mellow course through wildflower-packed meadows and pine-hardwood forest on smooth, flowing, and gently rolling singletrack. It's the perfect place for new riders to get comfortable and gain confidence, and advanced riders can appreciate an easy trail day or speed workout.

Start: Harmon Park, 0.5 south of Upper 55th Street on Asher Avenue

Distance: 4.5 miles

Approximate riding time: 30 minutes

Best bike: Mountain

Terrain and surface type: Gently rolling on smooth, hardpacked singletrack

Highlights: Gorgeous scenery, low to moderate technical level and just-right distance for new riders, all on a stacked loop system, and great ski trails in winter

Hazards: None

Maps: *USGS Inver Grove Heights*; MORC maps at morcmtb.org

Getting there: From I-494, exit MN 3 (South Robert Trail) and head south 0.2 mile to Upper 55th Street. Turn left for 0.5 mile to Asher Avenue and turn south to the trailhead. GPS: N 44 51.925 W 93 04.403

Singletrack snaking through the meadows

THE RIDE

Don't let the short mileage at Salem Hills fool you. Every inch of the park's 4.5 miles is on sublime singletrack and is so addicting, plan on extra time to get your multiple lap fix. Salem's three linked loops offer a nice mix of scenery, with a woodsy start giving way to open prairie, a small pond, and a handful of bridge crossings. This is also a regular locale for the launch of the Minnesota Mountain Bike Series, and despite the absence of a lung-busting climb or white-knuckle downhill, many racers say it's their favorite event of the year.

Start the ride heading north into the woods on the Singletrack Sawmill, other aliases being the North Loop or North Forks Trail, with just under a mile of snaky singletrack as fine as any you'll find in the metro. Loop around and back to the south, rolling through prairie grasses and wildflowers (don't miss the in-season blackberries), past the entrance trail, to the Pond Loop, introduced

Inver Grove's Roots

German and Irish settlers filtered into the rolling hills and verdant countryside of present-day Inver Grove Heights around 1852, incorporating into a township six years later. Their young village was named after "Inver," an Irish fishing village, and "Grove," the German settlers' homeland.

by a high-speed banked corner that ejects you into rolling pine forest mixed with prairie grass. If rain has fallen within the past few days, this would be the most likely spot to encounter a puddle or two, as it is a sometimes soggy section. A short bridge crossing past the pond leads up a little hill to the junction with the Prairie Fire (South) Loop. Sweep across gorgeous Minnesota prairie planted with native grasses and wildflowers, and be on the lookout for bluebirds frolicking about. The trail leaves the prairie and moves into a hammerhead section in the woods, then a few more prairie-to-woods-to-prairie transitions leading to the far southern part of the park. Loop back north along the fringe of the woods and back into another fun stretch of meadow to the top of the loop, and turn left into the woods for the west side of the Pond Loop, a flat cruise to one more bridge and more open country riding. Salem's one obstacle, a big ol' boulder wedged in the path, appears near the top of the loop. Conquer the rock and ride around to the final turn back to the trailhead

Groovy trail rep: Salem Hills exists thanks to a team effort between MORC and the city of Inver Grove Heights, when the park won a place on IMBA's 2003 Hot Spots program, a nationwide effort focusing on building singletrack in urban areas across the country.

MILES AND DIRECTIONS

0.0 Start at the trailhead. Ride north on a counterclockwise loop.

0.7 Junction with the top end of the Pond Loop. Stay left, then right to start the loop.

1.0 Ride past the pond and over a bridge.

1.2 Turn left to start the Prairie Fire Loop.

3.4 Back to the top of Prairie Fire and continue west side of Pond Loop.

3.9 Junction with North Loop. Go right to finish the lap.

4.5 Arrive back at the trailhead.

RIDE INFORMATION

Restaurants

You can't beat a giant burrito and frosty beverage after a great trail day. Fill up at **Chipotle,** just up the road at 1857 S. Robert St., West St. Paul; (651) 552-2110; chipotle.com.

Area events

Trade your bike for running shoes and see Salem's trails at a slower pace at the **Harmon Farms Trail Runs,** mid-September at Harmon Park (aka Salem Hills); invergroveheights.org.

38

Carver Lake Park

A MORC-inspired gem, this 4-mile, zigzaggy trail system is a fast and fun metro escape. Cruise along the ridge above Carver Lake and deep into the park's wooded interior on shorter loops or the longer, main trail. Perfect for intermediate riders or a multi-lap training ground for experts. Hang around the park after the ride for a swim at the beach or a pick-up volleyball game.

Start: Carver Lake Park, at 3175 Century Ave. S in Woodbury. Trailhead is at west end of parking lot.

Distance: 4-mile loop

Approximate riding time: 30–45 minutes

Best bike: Mountain

Terrain and surface type: Rolling with short, flat sections on hardpack singletrack

Highlights: Great views of Carver Lake, impeccably maintained trail, wildlife, après-ride activities at the park

Hazards: A few exposed roots and logs

Maps: *USGS Lake Elmo*; MORC maps at morcmtb.org; City of Woodbury map at ci.woodbury.mn.us

Getting there: From I-494 and Lake Road, follow Lake Road east 0.3 mile to Courtly Road. Turn right and head west 0.5 mile to Century Avenue. Turn left to the park entrance on the south side of Carver Lake. GPS: N 44 54.237 W 92 58.789

THE RIDE

With 4 miles of trail already established and more on the way, this suburban trail system continues to notch higher on local riders' list of favorites. This is a superb work of trail-building craftsmanship and great example of how a well-planned, sustainably-built trail can seamlessly blend with the landscape. It's damn fun, too, with ideal distance and terrain for multiple laps. Follow the singletrack past the trailhead kiosk, with instant rewards of serrated lake views and swooping trail along the hill's contour lines, with a couple of mini

Winding through big trees

The Stockyards

You could smell them first, and then see their bobbing heads and swishing tails from the I-494 bridge. For 122 years, the **stockyards** in South St. Paul were once among the largest in the world, a bargaining place for millions of cattle, hogs, goats, and sheep, and workplace of thousands. Central Livestock operated the maze of wood slat pens until urban sprawl and a changing industry marched forth, closing another of history's doors when the last cow was sold in the spring of 2008. An unimaginative bulldozing of the yards followed, replacing the auction barn and pens with 100 acres of industrial park, corralling corporate workers, and relocating the livestock and their future offspring to outstate yards and auction houses.

rock gardens, a short balance beam obstacle, and boardwalk bridge. The path hairpins back to the east, through stately mixed hardwood forest, and past a junction to the expert section, looping around like a plate of spaghetti, over a ravine crossing, and underneath power line towers to a series of berm turns and the park entrance road. Cross carefully here to the next section of path, cruising past the archery range to the back edge of one of Bailey Nurseries' huge shrub plots. The trail rolls through a tight stand of birch, maple, and scattered pine and down a long, gradual descent into dense woods with a thick understory of scrub foliage. Dropped here like a *Survivor* castoff, you'd have no idea you're in the middle of a sprawling suburban area, what with all the deer, bird life, and quiet forest. At the junction with the paved bike/hike path, head straight across for a fun, descending stretch with whoop-de-do jumps and past a secluded lake loud with chirping frogs. A short climb takes you back to and across the paved path again, noodling next through a thick and pungent stand of white pine and along a sinuous rolling section to the archery range. Here the path hooks back away from the road for one more descent to a hairpin curve before exiting to the parking area.

Recently constructed skinnies and fast camber turns ramp up the adrenaline. Don't miss it.

Bike Shops

Venerable powerhouses and Twin Cities mainstays **Penn Cycle** and **Erik's Bikes and Boards** both have Woodbury shops close to the trails.
Penn Cycle, Lake Road Terrace; (651) 731-9458; penncycle.com
Erik's Bikes and Boards, 1825 Radio Dr.; (651) 259-4600

Carver Lake Park

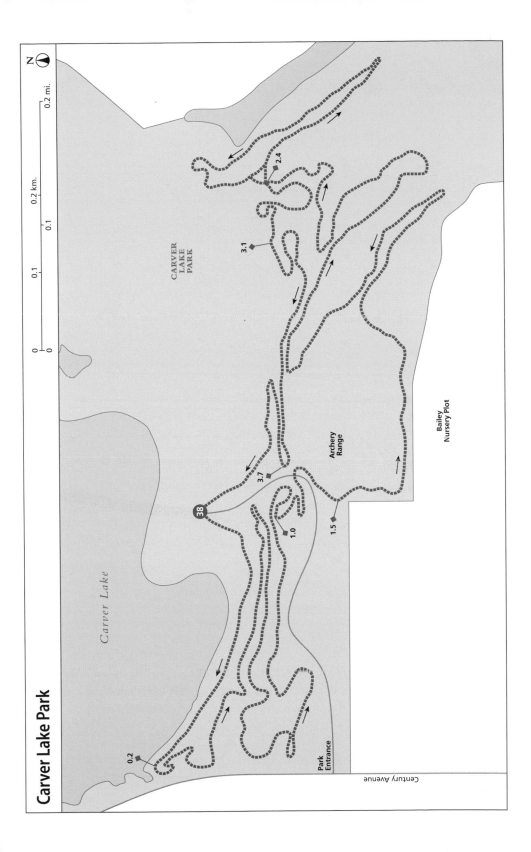

Carver Lake

CARVER LAKE PARK

Archery Range

Bailey Nursery Plot

Park Entrance

Century Avenue

N

0   0.1   0.1   0.2 km.
0   0.1   0.2 mi.

38

0.2

2.4

3.1

3.7

1.0

1.5

MILES AND DIRECTIONS

0.0 Start at the trailhead.

0.2 Balance beam and bridge to first turn.

0.3 Big, swooping turn heads back to the east.

1.0 Boardwalk bridge crossing over ravine.

1.3 Power line berm turns and road crossing.

1.5 Pass archery range.

2.4 Junction with paved path. Ride straight across.

2.9 Second crossing of paved path.

3.1 Pine stand tour.

3.7 Final hairpin to exit.

4.0 Arrive back at the trailhead.

RIDE INFORMATION

Restaurants
Refill your tank with a giant enchilada and icy beverage at **Acapulco,** 1795 Radio Dr., Woodbury; (651) 739-6360; acapulcomn.com.

O'Malley's Irish Pub opened on St. Paddy's Day in 2005, built almost entirely by hand by the O'Malley family. Relax on the patio with a pint o' Guinness and toast another great day of riding. 1775 Radio Dr., Woodbury; (651) 578-7007; omalleys-pub.com.

Area events
Ojibway Park hosts the annual **Woodbury Days,** a two-day town festival with sporting events, carnival, and live music. Late August; woodburydays.com.

The St. Paul Ski Club improvised their summer training in 1958 with a wood-frame ramp along the banks of the St. Croix River, allowing jumpers to practice their form and timing, with a cool and refreshing water landing.

Wisconsin Rides

Because the Twin Cities metro is so close to the magic kingdom of southwest Wisconsin, I would be remiss not to include a few of my favorites. This area of the Badger State is packed with so many life-list rides, it deserves an entire book of its own. Hundreds of miles of sublime tarmac wind across open ridges and into deep, wooded coulees, with hardly a car to be seen. Feel like climbing? Hang-a-picture-on-it steep hills are everywhere, with some brutes tilting up to the 20–25 percent range. Charming small towns and idyllic farmsteads dot the countryside, with frame-worthy views around every corner. This has been a go-to training ground for me for two decades, and when you're looking for a day out of the city, get over here.

Pastoral Wisconsin charm
LORAN STILES

Wisconsin Hill and Dale

On this ride you can challenge yourself on a former queen stage course of the race formerly known as the Nature Valley Grand Prix through some of Wisconsin's most elegant scenery. (The race now goes by North Star Grand Prix.) Pass quaint, small towns to Menomonie's halfway-point rest stop near the Red Cedar River, and tackle wall-steep hills on the southern return to a high-speed descent into Elmwood.

Start: Elmwood, in the vicinity of CR P and Race Avenue

Distance: 80-mile loop, with shorter options

Approximate riding time: 5–6 hours

Best bike: Road

Terrain and surface type: Mix of flats, rolling, and several monster-size climbs, all on smooth paved roads

Highlights: Life-list scenery in all directions from practically any given point on the route, Lake Eau Galle, Red Cedar Trail, downtown Menomonie

Hazards: Traffic is wonderfully light throughout the loop, with a slight increase in Menomonie. Use caution at country road crossings, control your speed on steep descents.

Other considerations: Beware sand and other debris on steep downhills after heavy rains

Maps: *USGS Spring Valley*

Getting there: From Prescott, Wisconsin, follow US 10 east 21 miles through Ellsworth and merge onto WI 72, continuing eastbound another 16 miles into Elmwood. GPS: N 44 46.840 W 92 08.820

THE RIDE

Starting as a modest, two-day race in the Twin Cities in 1999, the Nature Valley Bicycle Festival evolved into a highlight on the summer calendar for racers and fans alike. The ten-day, two-wheel-inspired event is part bicycle gala, part warp-speed professional racing. Fearless track riders kick off the action at the National Sports Center velodrome (subject to change), followed by the five-day North Star Grand Prix, the most prestigious road race on the domestic pro circuit, with criteriums and road stages in and around Minneapolis-St. Paul and surrounding areas. The festival includes a packed lineup of family and fan-friendly activities, like stunt riders, bike and fitness expo, kids' races, live music, and unbeatable citizen rides.

The queen stage starts in Menomonie and sends riders into the drop-dead gorgeous Wisconsin countryside, where they face grueling climbs. This version of the course moves the start to Elmwood, for multiple options up the many back roads and coulees to suit your tastes, and to take in one of my favorite climbs in all the land.

Ride north on CR P to 50th Street and turn up the valley. (Note for adrenaline junkies: Riders have hit speeds over 60 mph on the CR P descent into Elmwood.) The ride continues as 50th Street follows a winding stream through a narrow valley punctuated with wooded bluffs and narrow corridors of verdant farmland, like a Kincaid painting come to life. The breathtaking scenery does so literally as the road turns north and ascends a steep climb to the top of the ridge and back to CR P. Roll along about 9 miles of wide-open country to a northbound crossing of I-94, and watch your speed and road condition down the ensuing steep descent (potholes and tire-eating cracks have been known to appear). Cruise through this tiny town and head north on a long,

Crescent Cove

Crescent Cove (formerly Children's Lighthouse of Minnesota and past benefitting charity of the North Star Bicycle Festival) is a nonprofit organization dedicated to building an independent home to provide short respite breaks for children with life-limiting conditions and their families, and an option beyond the hospital or home environment for compassionate hospice care. The first of its kind in the Midwest, Children's Lighthouse offers a family-focused environment, along with therapy rooms, recreational space, and family suites designed for families to stay together while enjoying a temporary vacation from the constant demands of caregiving; crescentove.org.

Rolling through the countryside

gradual ascent to higher ground, with a couple of big climbs on the way to a nice coast into Boyceville, another little town surrounded by sprawling crop fields and forested bluffs. Head south from here, riding through a mix of fields and woods back under I-94, where a huge hill lurks around the base of a bluff, ready to wallop your quads with its punishing grade. Recover for another dozen miles to a final beast of a hill leading to the roll into Menomonie. Load up on grub, taking in the lovely Red Cedar River at Riverside Park, then head back down Rustic Road 89 for arguably the prettiest stretch of the course. The road gently climbs up above the river, serving up sweet views through the trees, and passes the Devils Punch Bowl natural area before hitting the steep ramp of Calvary Hill. Now it's time to roller coaster through the hills to the long, narrow smudge of Lake Eau Galle, a roughly 300-acre reservoir in its namesake river. Loop around the lake and shoot straight north on CR D, veering off the official race course on CR C. (To continue the pro course, stay north on CR D to 350th Avenue and go west, where you will encounter the 17 percent grade of Star Hill, what many consider the toughest climb in the entire county. If you make it up, the reward is a meteoric descent into Elmwood.) A jog from CR C on to 150th Street lopes up a short power climb to reveal an iconic Wisconsin farm country view so beautiful it's mandatory to stop and ogle the scene. A couple of stairstep turns takes you to the base of a mile-long ascent through absolutely stunning forest and a deep ravine alive with senses-tingling smells and sounds to completely take your mind off the screams of pain howling from your legs. Recover on the flats over to CR P, speeding on a downhill conclusion into Elmwood.

MILES AND DIRECTIONS

0.0 Start location in Elmwood (pick anywhere that suits you). Ride north on CR P.

0.9 Left turn onto 50th Street, one of the prettiest roads you'll ever ride.

5.5 Right turn onto 850th Avenue.

6.6 Left turn onto CR P.

7.8 Follow CR P (890th Street) to the right.

9.3 Turn left onto CR Q.

10.6 Junction with WI 29. Turn right and next left to stay on CR Q northbound.

13.5 Turn right onto 640th Avenue.

14.5 Turn left onto 160th Street, crossing I-94.

16.0 Turn left onto 155th Street, which merges into 171st Street, descending into Knapp.

17.8 Turn left onto Miller Street, and ride east to Main Street through town.

18.6 Junction with US 12. Turn left, and first right onto CR Q.

20.1 Stay north on 150th Street, when CR Q turns west.

24.6 Turn right onto 150th Street.

26.5 Turn left onto 180th Street, and quick right onto WI 170.

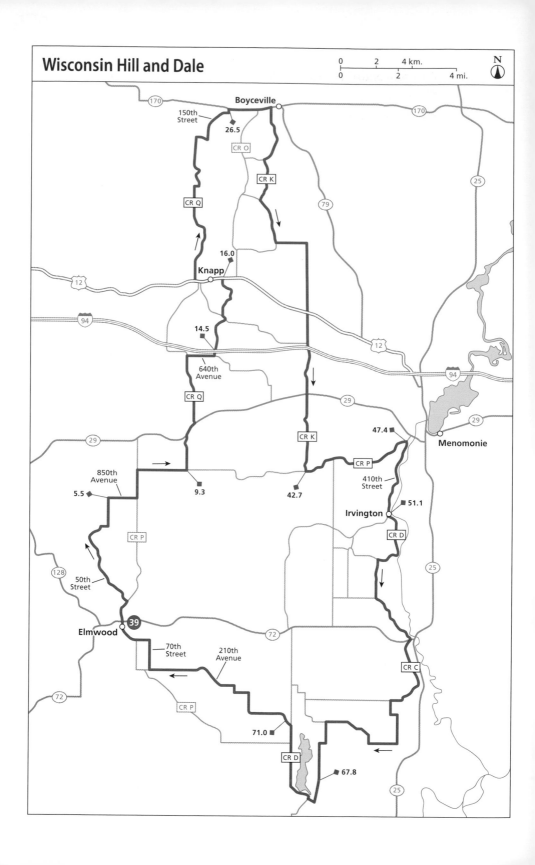

28.1 Turn right onto CR K in Boyceville. Ride south all way past I-94 and WI 29.

42.7 Turn left onto CR P.

46.8 Turn right onto WI 29.

47.4 Menomonie rest stop, then ride back to CR P.

48.2 Turn left onto 410th Street (Rustic Road 89).

51.1 Turn right onto CR D, and quick left onto 420th Street.

54.0 Turn left onto 380th Street.

55.0 Curve left at 440th Street.

57.1 Cross WI 72 and continue south on CR Z/C.

57.4 Stay left on CR C.

61.0 Turn left onto 420th Street.

61.8 Turn right onto 130th Avenue.

64.0 Turn left onto CR Z.

67.8 Junction with CR D. Turn right, looping around south end of Lake Eau Galle.

71.0 Turn left onto CR C.

71.7 Turn left onto 170th Avenue.

73.4 Road morphs into 210th Avenue.

77.4 Turn right onto 70th Street. Road curves west on 250th Avenue to CR P.

79.0 Turn right onto CR P.

79.8 Turn left onto Race Avenue in Elmwood.

80.0 Arrive back at the trailhead.

Starting with one small mill on the Red Cedar River, the Knapp, Stout, & Co., grew into the world's largest lumber company, with annual timber cuts approaching 90 million board feet.

RIDE INFORMATION

Restaurants

Quick and easy refueling at the **Cenex** convenience store at WI 29 and 25 in Menomonie; (714) 232-6262.

Area events

Catch the semi-pro **Menomonie Thunderhawks** football team at a summer game at UW-Stout's Williams Stadium; menomoniethunderhawks.com.

Don't miss a hike into **Devils Punch Bowl,** a delicate and fascinating sandstone canyon packed with rainforest-thick foliage and shadowy recesses. Right on the course, on Paradise Valley Road; menomoniechamber.org.

UFO Loop

Treat yourself to a long escape in the fairy tale environs, and challenging terrain, of southwestern Wisconsin's Coulee Country. River views give way to ridgetop riding past orchards and idyllic dairy farms, all on traffic-free, velvety tarmac. Tough climbs and high-speed descents highlight the 74-mile day, and the Elmwood rest stop has aliens and spaceships.

Start: Downtown Maiden Rock, along WI 35 and CR S

Distance: 74.3-mile loop

Approximate riding time: 5.5 hours

Best bike: Road

Terrain and surface type: Mostly rolling, with short, flat stretches and long, steep climbs on sublime paved roads

Highlights: Lake Pepin, postcard views in every direction, Elmwood's resident aliens

Hazards: Practically devoid of traffic, but watch for loose sand and other debris on the fast descents, especially after heavy rain

Maps: *USGS Maiden Rock*

Getting there: From Red Wing, Minnesota, follow US 63 3 miles to WI 35. Head south on WI 35 12 miles to Maiden Rock. The ride starts at the junction with CR S. GPS: N 44 33.650 W 92 18.567

THE RIDE

Raise a glass (of milk) to Wisconsin's dairy farmers! Their neat-as-a-pin farm-steads are linked to market by a web of silky back roads through the state's most dramatic landscapes. This is destination-travel country for cyclists, with hundreds of miles of blissfully traffic-free routes through deep, wooded valleys and along scenic ridgetops. Thanks to William Dempster Hoard's decades-long efforts of promoting the dairy industry, and responding zeal from enterprising farmers, by 1899 nearly every farm in Wisconsin raised dairy cows (at about the same time as tentacles of engineered asphalt roads spread across the country). Keeping the roads in perfect condition keeps the milk flowing to where it needs to go, and Wisconsin's tarmac is like a red carpet and equally velvety. This 74-mile loop starts in Maiden Rock, on the shores of Lake Pepin, the postcard bulge in the Mississippi River. At first glance, the little village appears to be a sleepy river town, but streams of travelers drift through here all summer long for events like the June Summerfest at Village Park or homegrown goodies at the Smiling Pelican Bake Shop.

The high, rounded bluffs bordering this stretch of the Mississippi are a perfect backdrop for all things outdoors, and a siren song for cyclists seeking challenging climbs and drop-dead scenery at every turn, both of which come early on this ride. Roll out southbound on the Great River Road (WI 35), with magnificent views of Lake Pepin to start the day. A left turn at CR AA drops into a shady glen along Pine Creek, and the road rapidly tips up a long, steep ramp away from the river. Power up to the ridgetop past Maiden Rock Winery and Cidery, and head east along a curvy course inland to the tiny burg of Lund. Gentle rollers give way to a long, fast descent on CR SS through bluff-lined farmland across Plum Creek and Gates Hill to CR D, where the route diverts northwest on Sunnybrook Road for no other reason than to add even more glorious scenery to the day. The road passes an idyllic farmstead and tilts steeply away from Porcupine Creek, stairstepping back to CR D and on to CR N. From here it's a fairly flat cruise through Arkansaw and picture-perfect farms to Gap Hill, with decadent views on the way up and a nearly 50-mph descent to the Eau Galle River and its namesake town. (No kidding on this one. Riding down this hill is

Dakota Indian legend recalls a young woman named We-no-nah, who opposed her father's choice of a brave for her husband. To ensure the union would not take place, she leaped to her death from the high bluffs above Maiden Rock. The tiny town was named in tribute to the tragic event.

Little Green Men

The accounts are similar to hundreds of others of this ilk. A squad car radio goes dead in mid-broadcast; a bright saucer shoots a blue light beam; a blinking object blasts into the sky like a meteor in reverse. Hazy tales of scatterbrained townsfolk, say the skeptics, but if alien life is out there, they were frequent visitors to the small village of Elmwood in the mid-70s. More than thirty residents claim they spotted mysterious sights, and the town quickly became the go-to destination for extraterrestrial enthusiasts. **UFO Days** was launched in 1978, and fans still line the streets for a parade, treasure hunt, and UFO burgers. Last week of July; elmwoodwi.org.

like falling off of a building. Have fun but stay alert and in control.) The river leads the way north along CR D, past Smith's Honey and Maple Syrup Farm, to CR C, where silky pavement diverts through the resplendent Weber Valley, dotted with tidy farmsteads hugged by high, forested hills. The road darts toward the base of a hill and tilts rapidly skyward through dense woods on one of the prettiest climbs around, the same one from the North Star ride. (Keep thinking that when the grade creeps toward 12 percent.) A short run across the ridge leads to 70th Street and a fast descent into Elmwood for a rest at the 50-mile mark. Check out the sidebar for more on Elmwood's claim to fame as a favorite landing zone for aliens.

WI 72 heads south out of town, and in 2 miles a skinny, hidden road darts up through the woods on a long climb to rolling farmland. A southwest bearing points to the miniature neighborhood of Rock Elm and over hill and dale to one last flyer down a steep coulee road to the Rush River. (Stay alert for loose sand in the turns and control your speed on this one.) A relaxing, 6-mile cool-down on CR A on one side of the river, and 385th Street on the other, heads downstream to WI 35 and back to Maiden Rock.

MILES AND DIRECTIONS

0.0 Start in Maiden Rock, at WI 35 and CR S. Head south on WI 35.

1.0 Left turn at CR AA.

2.0 Left at CR K.

9.3 Merge onto CR J, and to CR SS past the town of Lund.

16.8 Turn left onto CR D, and left again at Sunnybrook Road. Climb to Vosker Road.

20.8 Right turn onto Vosker Road, stairstepping through farm fields back to CR D.

24.2 Turn left onto CR D (turns east in 1 mile).

26.8 Turn left onto CR Y (turns east in just over 1 mile).

28.8 Turn left onto CR N. Flat cruise to Arkansaw and US 10.

30.0 Turn left onto US 10 for 0.5 mile to CR X.

30.2 Right turn onto CR X (curves into CR Z in 1 mile).

31.3 Turn right to continue north on CR X and up the big climb to Gap Hill.

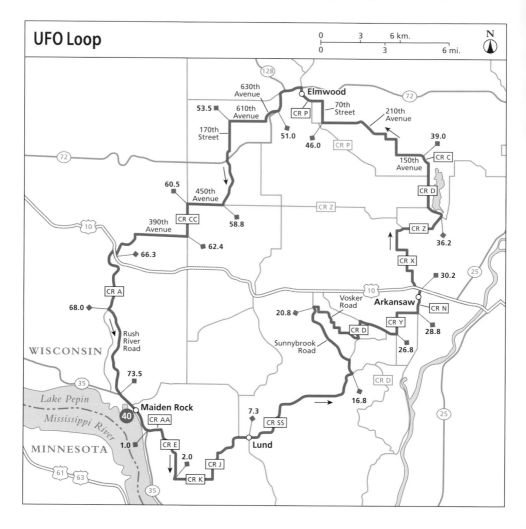

36.2 Turn left onto CR D, heading into Eau Galle. Follow CR D through town.

39.0 Turn left onto CR C, west 0.75 mile, and straight ahead on 150th Avenue (on the curve where CR C turns back north).

46.0 Right turn at 70th Street.

47.6 Turn left onto 250th Avenue.

48.0 Turn right onto CR P, descending into Elmwood.

49.5 Turn left onto WI 72 to a well-deserved rest stop at the Cenex convenience store. Fuel up and follow WI 72 south out of town.

51.0 Lean right at 630th Avenue.

53.5 Left turn at 170th Street (Rock Elm Road). Use caution crossing WI 72, and stay south on 170th Street.

58.8 Turn right onto CR HH.

60.5 Left turn at CR CC. Slight increase in traffic.

62.4 Turn right at 390th Avenue.

66.3 Right turn onto US 10. Watch traffic.

66.7 Turn left onto CR A.

68.0 Dart left across the river at 385th Street (East Rush River Road).

73.5 Turn left onto WI 35.

74.3 Arrive back at Maiden Rock trailhead.

RIDE INFORMATION

Restaurants
Do not miss the chance for post-ride refueling at the **Smiling Pelican Bakeshop,** with decadent home-baked goodness at this riverside bakery. Indulge on their front porch with lavender cookies or white cake with butter cream frosting. 3556 WI 35, Maiden Rock; (715) 448-3807

Area events
Maiden Rock Winery and Cidery, at the top of the hill on CR E, hosts fun events all year and tastings and tours during warmer months; maidenrockwinerycidery.com.

Prescott Loop

This 50-mile ride from the mouth of the St. Croix River rolls through River Falls's college town and out into open farm land before looping back through bluff country and up two sinister climbs to close the day.

Start: Anywhere near the river in downtown Prescott

Distance: 50 miles, with lots of options to go shorter or longer

Approximate riding time: 3 hours

Best bike: Road

Terrain and surface type: Rolling with a few steep climbs on smooth, paved roads

Highlights: Fun cruise through River Falls, stellar views from bluffs and ridges, remote back roads, challenging hills

Hazards: Use caution at road crossings

Other considerations: Watch for heavier traffic in River Falls on weekends and when school is in session; no convenience stores or other refueling stops after River Falls

Maps: *USGS Hastings*

Getting there: From downtown St. Paul, follow US 61 south 20 miles to US 10 and head east 4 miles to Prescott. GPS: N 44 44.947 W 92 48.240

A serene corner of 640th Street

THE RIDE

With its easy access from the metro, Prescott is the ideal launch pad for epic Wisconsin rides of any distance that fits your mood. Best thing is, you can turn down nearly any road out here and follow it to a cozy hollow or rolling field or big hill, for a 10-mile afternoon jaunt or all-day suffer fest, and like the two rides before this, do it all with nary a car in sight.

Start this oak-leaf-shaped loop with a short climb away from downtown Prescott, and in just over 1 mile, head on to a long and tough warm-up climb to scattered residential properties giving way rapidly to farmland. Work north and across WI 29/35 to a handsome section of rolling hills and quiet farms, with round-topped, wooded bluffs bubbling up here and there. Traffic picks up a bit on the highway into River Falls, but the shoulder is adequate and a bike path parallels the road most of the way if you'd like more of a buffer.

Prescott's Ferry

Philander Prescott had an eye for location when he built a cabin at the confluence of the St. Croix and Mississippi Rivers in the early 1800s. Situated on the site of the present-day town that honored his name, Prescott worked with officers from Ft. Snelling to establish a post, and the first county board bestowed a license for him to start a ferry across the St. Croix River. Prescott's ferry and pivotal river transportation hub led to the settlement and growth of a permanent village.

Cruise through downtown River Falls and shoot out of town on CR M, passing under WI 35/65 and up a long climb to farm country. From here, it's a 6-mile spin on mostly flat tarmac to CR W, where you can make a call to keep on heading east for a long and challenging, 90-mile day to Spring Valley and Elmwood, or stick with this more manageable route.

Roll south on CR W into a gorgeous, shallow valley, cross WI 29, and drop through a stunning corridor of bluffs and woods and small ribbons of farmland to WI 65. Ride the highway's wide shoulder south to CR J, with smooth tarmac delivering you to another dreamy back road, introduced with a postcard Wisconsin barn and neighboring stream. Enjoy the comfy scene, because just around the corner a big ol' climb ramps up out of the valley, with a few miles of recovery time before a final, sinister hill soars skyward for a closing battle with your tired legs. Catch your breath and spin over the last miles of rolling hills to the downhill coast to Prescott, then promptly dust yourself off and head to Muddy Waters for a cold one.

MILES AND DIRECTIONS

0.0   Start in downtown Prescott. Ride south on WI 35.

1.3   Left turn onto Hollister Avenue (570th Avenue) and up the big climb.

4.3   Turn left onto 1170th Street.

5.8   Turn right onto 620th Avenue.

6.8   Turn left onto CR QQ.

8.0   Turn right onto WI 29/35 and left to continue on CR QQ.

9.1   Turn right onto CR MM.

10.1   Go left onto WI 29/35, and quick left on 1090th Street.

Prescott Loop

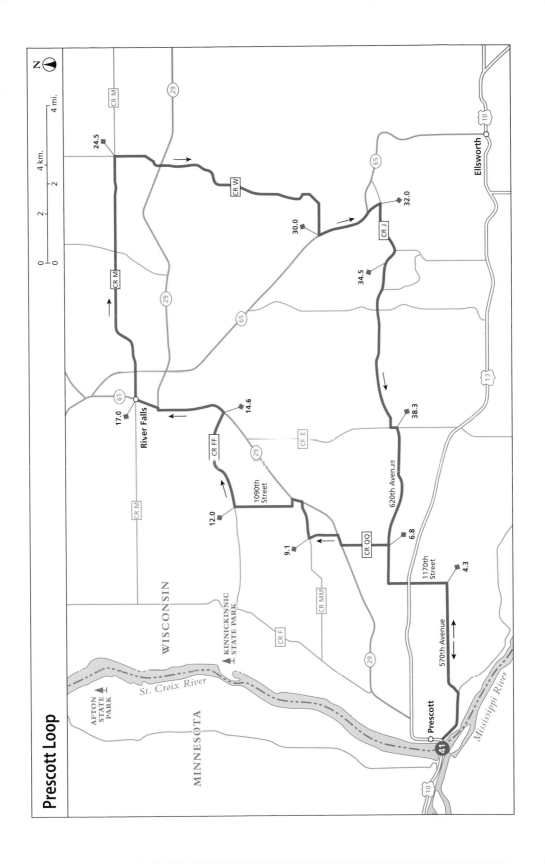

12.0   Right turn onto CR FF.

14.6   Watch traffic and turn left onto WI 29/35.

17.0   Turn right onto CR M (Division Street).

24.5   Turn right onto CR W.

30.0   Junction with WI 65. Turn left and ride the wide shoulder south.

32.0   Veer right onto 780th Avenue, and right again on CR J.

34.5   Right turn onto 640th Avenue.

38.3   Left turn onto CR E, and quick right onto 620th Avenue.

42.2   Turn left onto 1170th Street.

44.1   Turn right onto 570th Avenue.

47.0   Right turn onto WI 35.

50.0   Arrive back in downtown Prescott.

RIDE INFORMATION

Restaurants

Built by hand and cooked from scratch, the blend of warm architecture and delicious food at **Muddy Waters** is the perfect post-ride cool down. Score a top-side table overlooking the rivers and jam to live blues. 231 N. Broad St., Prescott; (715) 262-5999; muddywatersbarandgrill.biz.

Area events

Time your ride for early September and join the party at **Prescott Daze,** with a parade, fun run, kids' events, fishing contest, and more; prescottdaze.com.

> **The Point Douglas Drawbridge in Prescott, the only drawbridge in the Twin Cities metro area, uses a moving gear-hydraulics system, rather than a counterweight, to raise the road deck. The drawbridge was used until 1990, when a new bridge was built to accommodate increasing growth.**

Whitetail Ridge

Only a short drive from the Twin Cities' eastern fringe, Whitetail Ridge offers some of the best fat tire riding in the Midwest. Masterfully constructed trails mix flowing singletrack in dense woods with wide-open meadows, rock and log crossings, some steep climbs and fast descents. The 6-mile trail system is perfect for intermediate riders, and experts can test their skills on technical features like teeters and balance beam skinnies.

Start: Trailhead is at end of Whitetail Boulevard. Look for the sign at the edge of the woods.

Distance: 6 miles total, with various loop options

Approximate riding time: 1 hour

Best bike: Mountain

Terrain and surface type: Rolling sections, with plenty of steep climbs and descents on hardpacked singletrack

Highlights: All of the above, plus fast-flowing tread, vibrant, dense forest mixed with open meadows, no crowds

Hazards: Lots of exposed roots, log crossings, rock gardens, steep drops

Other considerations: Beware the mosquito swarms in summer

Maps: *USGS River Falls East*

Getting there: From I-94 in Wisconsin, follow WI 35 south 6 miles to Whitetail Boulevard (in the Whitetail Ridge corporate park). Turn right and head to the end of the road, next to the Little Adventures daycare center. Start riding at the trail sign at the edge of the woods, following the loop clockwise. GPS: N 44 53.247 W 92 38.112

THE RIDE

Laced through a heavily wooded ridge adjacent to bucolic farmsteads in western Wisconsin's rolling hill country, Whitetail originated from the minds and muscles of local runners and riders Rick Cleary and Fred Johnson. With the formation of Kinni Off-Road Cyclists (KORC) in 2007, the trails received lots of attention from an enthusiastic and dedicated group of riders who continue to foster the fun of a great bicycle club and are out on the trails all season, tools in hand, keeping Whitetail in top form.

From the trailhead, hang a quick left onto Hooked, cruising on speedy, sinuous singletrack along the edge of the forest. After some fun turns and easygoing rollers, the path moves into the Chunnel Trail at a stand of tall white pines. The path pinballs between the trees and loops back to meet Roller Derby, paralleling the initial trail on a gradually ascending route farther into the woods. A couple of handlebar-grazing tree passages keep it interesting as the path drops back down level with the field near the corporate park, with more squiggly turns through beauteous mixed hardwood forest with emerald green ferns and other lush foliage. At the junction with the Jeep Trail, you can head uphill or keep on to the BFH Trail, a manageable expert-level path. This section starts with a short, flat intro before a hairpin switchback rapidly gains elevation to the Tower Trail at the top of the ridge. Turn left for a fun cruise through a wide-open meadow packed with wildflowers, butterflies darting about, and good southern views. The skinny path, barely tire-width wide, heads toward the treeline on the far side and hangs a 90-degree turn to follow the trees to the Catwalk Trail. A short dip crosses a rock garden and skinny bridge to a fun stretch along tight curves and past a cool fern grove at the top of a deep ravine to the start of the Three Bridges Trail, the first of which is introduced by a collection of small boulders acting as a ramp onto the wooden bridge. Two more follow in quick succession, followed by three more, so more fun than the advertised trail name promises. Lots of exposed roots and rocks as the path winds into a nice mix of cedar and aspen to the Wild Turkey Trail, which continues to curve around to the edge of a cornfield and the Sundown Trail. Great views ensue once again from this vantage point as the path hugs the treeline northbound to Ape

Bike Shop

Versatile staff at **CrankWorx** dials in top-shelf cycling gear in summer, and keeps you out there in winter with a full line of snowshoes. 122 S. Main St, River Falls.; (715) 629-7246; crankworxbikeshop.com.

Through the wildflowers on the Tower Trail

The Kinni

The Kinnickinnic River starts from springs in St. Croix County and meanders 25 miles southwest, where it pours into the St. Croix River in a wide, sandy delta. In the sights of the encroaching 1960s Twin Cities metro sprawl, the area was a likely development target, but several determined landowners worked selflessly to save it. Several citizen groups proposed a new state park to preserve the pristine trout stream and unique natural beauty of the confluence of the two rivers, and three families donated parts of their land to the Wisconsin DNR to reach that goal. Other property owners added their support, and the overwhelming drive and concern won over the DNR, and **Kinnickinnic State Park** was established in 1972. Today the park is a stunning mix of restored upland prairie atop a deep limestone gorge, with a legendary trout population and vibrant wildlife activity. Nearly 7 miles of trails wind through the park, with a great swimming beach on the St. Croix.

Hanger, a long and fast descent back down the ridge, followed again by more tight turns to a decision-time junction with the Jeep Trail North, Dakine, and Hurt Locker. Lots of expert terrain downhill to the right, and more meadow cruises straight ahead. Today's version checks out Hurt Locker, a short expert stretch leading back to the start of Ape Hanger. I lost my bearings for a minute at this point and rode back against the grain on Three Bridges back to Jeep Trail, and exited that path to the corporate park field. It worked, but try to stay clockwise to avoid run-ins with other riders. If exiting at the bottom of Jeep Trail, simply follow the road back to the trailhead.

MILES AND DIRECTIONS

0.0 Start at the trailhead with a left turn onto Hooked.

0.4 Ride through stand of white pine on the Chunnel Trail.

1.1 Junction with Jeep Trail. Head straight across on the BFH Trail. (BFH is deemed expert level, but is plenty rideable for solid intermediates, too.)

1.5 Left turn at Tower junction.

1.8 Catwalk Trail bridge.

2.3 Meet the Wild Turkey Trail. Veer left to the forest edge.

2.7 Trail emerges at edge of a cornfield, underneath a big power line, then dives into the Ape Hanger Trail.

4.0 Left turn onto Hurt Locker. Return along Three Bridges and exit down Jeep Trail.

4.8 Meet the field and hop onto the road back to the trailhead.

6.0 Arrive back at the trailhead.

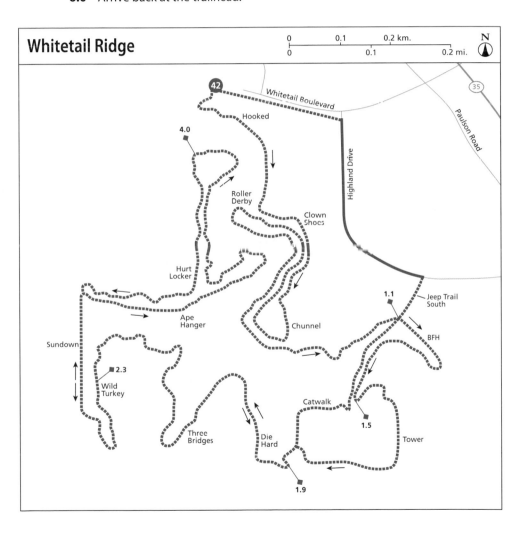

Whitetail Ridge

RIDE INFORMATION

Restaurants

Thinking about a big ol' burger and beer? Beeline to **Bo's N' Mine** at 110 S. Main St.; (715) 425-9064; bosnmine.net.

Area events

Get your speed on at the weekly **Thursday night races** at Whitetail Ridge, beginning at 6 p.m. all summer long, with beginner to expert classes. Check the KORC website for the latest; kinnioffroad.com.

The **River Falls Roots and Bluegrass Festival** brings in spring with great live music at downtown venues in mid-March; riverfallsbluegrass.com.

> The first pioneer settler to this area nearly single-handedly spurred the growth of River Falls. Joel Foster, who had a striking resemblance to Abe Lincoln, built the first house near the two junctions of the Kinnickinnic River, established the first crops, and served as a judge of St. Croix County.

Rides at a Glance

1–10 MILES

11–20 MILES

21–30 MILES

31–40 MILES

41 MILES AND UP

Area Clubs and Advocacy Groups

Here is a short list of the many organizations that make Minnesota a great place to ride a bike.

NICE RIDE MINNESOTA

Modeled after similar bike-sharing systems throughout the world, Nice Ride started with 65 bike stations in Minneapolis, and has since expanded to 145, in both downtowns and neighboring communities, with roughly a half million rentals. In 2010, Nice Ride was the largest bike-share system in the United States, and the program's initial fleet of 700 bikes has grown to over 1,300. The solar-powered stations communicate with a central server and report the number of available bikes and docking points at each location in real time to users through online maps and phone apps.

Users buy access to the bikes by the day, month, or year, during which time they can take one bike at a time from any of the 145 locations, and return it to any other location. A $65 annual subscription allows access to the bikes, with no charge for the first 30 minutes, and usage fees for additional time. The clock starts over after returning to a station, so you could do those short, in-town trips all day long for free, with so many convenient station locations. The program has been wildly successful and is another feather in the cap of the metro's rise to the bike-friendly top of the heap. Nice Ride operates the stations from April to November. Get all the dirt at niceridemn.org.

Bicycle Alliance of Minnesota
bikemn.org
Working to make Minnesota even more bicycle friendly

Minnesota Off-Road Cyclists
Minnesota's mountain biking scene would not be what it is today without this dedicated group.
morcmtb.org

Bolder Options
bolderoptions.org
Teaching and promoting healthy youth development

Full Cycle
fullcyclebikeshop.com
Local shop that employs and trains homeless youth

Open Streets Minneapolis
openstreetsmpls.org
Advocating to make Minneapolis a better place to ride

Minnesota Cycling Federation
mcf.net
Minnesota's bike racing headquarters

Explore Minnesota/Pedal Minnesota
exploreminnesota.com/pedal-mn
An invaluable route-finding tool, with area tours and events

For much more information and links to other groups, bike clubs and teams, and gear companies, check out the Twin Cities Bicycling Club page, at bike tcbc.org

Index

About the Author

Steve Johnson is a self-propelled recreation junkie and fan of all things outdoors. He grew up roaming the northern lakes and forest regions of Minnesota and Wisconsin and spent his nascent college years exploring up high in the Colorado Rockies. An avid hiker and huge fan of road and mountain biking, Steve can usually be found on a hiking trail in the woods somewhere, or with his bike and a wide open road. With a spare hour or five, he is outdoors and in tune with nature's finest.

A regular contributor to *Backpacker* and other regional magazines across the country, some of Steve's other work includes *Loop Hikes Colorado*, *Bicycling Wisconsin*, *Mountain Biking Minnesota*, and spinoff sporting events projects. And don't miss his first children's book, *Jack & Lauren in The Big Bog*. Steve lives and writes in southeastern Minnesota and far north Wisconsin.

A portion of the proceeds from sales of this book will be donated to The Nature Conservancy.